Journey to Freedom

Uncovering the Grayson Sisters'
Escape from Nebraska Territory

GAIL SHAFFER BLANKENAU

University of Nebraska Press
LINCOLN

© 2024 by Gail Shaffer Blankenau

Parts of this book were previously published in *Nebraska History Magazine*, Summer 2022.

All rights reserved
Manufactured in the United States of America

The University of Nebraska Press is part of a land-grant institution with campuses and programs on the past, present, and future homelands of the Pawnee, Ponca, Otoe-Missouria, Omaha, Dakota, Lakota, Kaw, Cheyenne, and Arapaho Peoples, as well as those of the relocated Ho-Chunk, Sac and Fox, and Iowa Peoples.

Library of Congress Cataloging-in-Publication Data
Names: Blankenau, Gail Shaffer, author.
Title: Journey to freedom : uncovering the Grayson sisters' escape from Nebraska Territory / Gail Shaffer Blankenau.
Other titles: Uncovering the Grayson sisters' escape from Nebraska Territory
Description: Lincoln : University of Nebraska Press, 2024. | Includes bibliographical references and index.
Identifiers: LCCN 2023039394
ISBN 9781496231529 (hardback)
ISBN 9781496238603 (epub)
ISBN 9781496238610 (pdf)
Subjects: LCSH: Fugitive slaves—Nebraska—Biography. | Slavery—Nebraska—History. | African American women—Nebraska—Biography. | Grayson, Celia, 1836– | Grayson, Eliza, 1838– | Escapes—Nebraska—History—19th century. | Antislavery movements—Iowa—History—19th century. | African American women—Nebraska—Biography. | Sisters—Nebraska—Biography. | Nebraska City (Neb.)—Biography. | Grayson County (Va.)—Biography. | BISAC: HISTORY / United States / State & Local / Midwest (IA, IL, IN, KS, MI, MN, MO, ND, NE, OH, SD, WI) | SOCIAL SCIENCE / Slavery
Classification: LCC E445.N2 B536 2024 | DDC 306.3/6208209782092 [B]—dc23/eng/20230913
LC record available at https://lccn.loc.gov/2023039394

Set in Garamond Premier Pro by A. Shahan.

Contents

List of Illustrations	vii
Prologue	ix
Acknowledgments	xiii
Introduction	1
1. Growing Up in Appalachian Mountain Slavery	11
2. Adjusting to New Lives in Missouri	31
3. The Opening of Kansas and Nebraska Territories	47
4. Life in Nebraska City, a Missouri River Town	59
5. Politics Running High	79
6. Fugitive Slave Excitement in Nebraska	91
7. The Consequences of "Villainy and Meanness"	107
8. Slave Hunting and Eliza's Chicago Rescue	127
Epilogue	149
APPENDIX A. Transcription of the Enslaved Listed in Nuckolls Account Book	173
APPENDIX B. Grayson Family Tree	174
APPENDIX C. Nuckolls–Bourne–Hail Relationship Chart	176
Notes	177
Bibliography	229
Index	249

Illustrations

1. Historical Nebraska City mural — viii
2. Map of Four Corners geographic area — 5
3. Grayson County, Virginia — 12
4. Old kitchen built by Lewis Hale — 17
5. Nuckolls homestead — 18
6. Steamboat — 30
7. Stephen Friel Nuckolls — 34
8. Lucinda Bourne Nuckolls — 35
9. Nebraska Territory map — 48
10. Nebraska City mural — 60
11. Close-up of map showing Nuckolls residence — 61
12. Nebraska City old blockhouse — 63
13. 1854 map by Rev. John Todd — 94
14. Celia and Eliza's escape route — 105
15. Fake bank note mocking Nebraska as a "Land of Liberty" — 128
16. Harding Hampton — 159

1. Nebraska City mural by Kent Schwartz, ca. 2013. Photo by the author. Used with permission from Nebraska City Chamber of Commerce.

Prologue

Situated on a bluff above the Missouri River, Nebraska City is a beautiful small town in the southeastern corner of the state. The downtown area features brick buildings with tin ceilings, a lively café that serves good sandwiches and coffee, boutiques, and businesses of various kinds. Residential areas are a mix of old and new houses, and in the summer the trees lining the streets become a verdant canopy, with dappled light and shade below.

But what permeates the atmosphere is the open celebration of Nebraska City's history and heritage. The town stands on the site of what was "old" Fort Kearny. This military installation, with a blockhouse, barracks, and a small hospital, was located here from May 1846 until the fall of 1848, when the army decided to move the fort (which never had walls) inland and closer to the Oregon Trail so the soldiers could better protect the stream of settlers following the trail along the Platte River. When the army moved, the site was not completely abandoned. People were left in charge of the buildings, and ferryman John Boulware of Iowa continued to operate the service that had begun when the fort was established. It is no surprise that when Nebraska Territory opened for settlement, the site's advantages beckoned. First called Table Creek after the rivulet that flowed into the Missouri below the blockhouse, the town became Nebraska City, an aspirational name for those who settled there, hoping it would indeed become a major city—a transportation hub on the Missouri River.

Incorporated in March 1855, Nebraska City is home to the Civil War Veterans Museum and GAR Memorial Hall, Kregel Windmill Factory Museum, Missouri River Basin Lewis and Clark Visitor Center, Museum of Firefighting, 1857 Nelson House, Old Freighters Museum (also in a historic house), Otoe County Museum of Memories, River Country Nature Center, Wildwood Historic Center (house), historic and unusual Wyuka

Cemetery, and most famous of all, Arbor Day Farm, along with the Mayhew Cabin and John Brown's Cave of Underground Railroad fame.

Little did I know when I first saw Nebraska City at age twenty that someday I would write a book of history centered on this scenic place. Nor did I fathom the town's legacy of enslavement. Alfred Andreas's *History of the State of Nebraska* includes a brief section under the heading "Slavery in Nebraska" but also dismisses enslavement in the state as a peculiarity of short duration. After all, the early censuses never listed more than thirteen enslaved people, so Nebraska was not really slave territory, and the state did fight for the Union.

In the 1990s my husband and I took our children to Nebraska City almost yearly. We enjoyed the Apple Jack Festival, toured Arbor Day Farm, rode in horse-drawn carriages, and marveled at the beauty of the J. Sterling Morton mansion, which resembles a Southern plantation house. Regarding Nebraska City's legacy of enslavement, the emphasis was on John Brown's Cave, where guides told stories of intrepid abolitionists who hid fugitive slaves on their way to Iowa and beyond on the Underground Railroad.

Today Nebraska City is adapting to the times. A lovely public space, a courtyard dotted with benches, has been added downtown between two brick buildings. Small trees have been planted so that someday it will be a shady and cool place in summer. To enhance the park setting, the city hired an artist to paint murals that depict the town's history on the brick walls—part of a long-term project that started in 2011, with the majority of them completed in 2013. J. Sterling Morton, his wife, and their home, Arbor Lodge, feature prominently in the work and are large and central. As visitors face this visual summary, off to the left is a small nod to freedom seekers. The artist used the old standard newspaper figure for a freedom seeker: a dark man with the requisite bindlestick, a long stick with a bundle of possessions slung over his shoulder.

Missing from the picture are Celia and Eliza Grayson, the first documented freedom seekers from Nebraska Territory. Prior historians had related their flight to freedom in short sections on slavery in Nebraska. But these bare facts did not begin to acknowledge all the turmoil and tension their actions revealed to a nation that was teetering on the brink of a civil war.

I began my own journey to find out more about the legacy of slavery in my home state in a class that focused on territorial history. When choosing a topic for my final paper, I decided to write about Celia and Eliza. Previous histories of the women's story included them in larger accounts because their story fits into more than one kind of narrative, such as works on freedom seekers and the Underground Railroad.[1]

The more I researched, the more I realized their part in the troubled history of enslavement in Nebraska Territory was much larger than previously supposed. Their journey to freedom was splashed across newspaper pages nationwide. Far from being a footnote of history, the women were famous—at least as freedom seekers—in their own time. I was fascinated and dove into primary sources. Indeed, their 1858 flight from Nebraska merited extraordinary attention at the time and is worthy of more detailed analysis now. Their flight prompted commentary on the political turmoil of the 1850s and challenged the nation to consider slavery's potential acceptance into new territories and in diverse climates.

In researching the Graysons' story, I also heard puzzlement. Historians and nonhistorians often reminded me that Nebraska was never a "slave state." They accepted early historians' contention that the territorial government did not support slavery or pointed to the small number of slaves in census counts to emphasize that the tenure of humans as property was too brief to merit much attention.

Of course, Nebraska was not a state until 1867, so technically it was not a slave "state." However, under the provisions of the Kansas-Nebraska Act, the slavery issue was left to the territorial legislature to decide. Antislavery bills were introduced three times. The territorial council postponed the first antislavery bill "indefinitely." The second time, the legislature passed the bill by a slim margin, only to have it vetoed. The third time it was introduced was after Abraham Lincoln's election and while Southern secession was already underway. The territorial governor also vetoed this effort, but in 1861 the balance of the territorial legislature had tipped to the Republican side, and the veto was overridden.

In the meantime, enslaved people lived and worked in Nebraska Territory. When Celia and Eliza escaped, their actions highlighted the ambiguous question of slavery's legality in the territories until they became states, one of the many reasons their case drew national coverage. Nebraska's Territorial Court of the Second District (based in Nebraska City) allowed their enslaver, Stephen F. Nuckolls, to sue sixteen Iowans under the 1850 Fugitive Slave Law, establishing a legal precedent that slavery was recognized in Nebraska Territory. Nuckolls also instituted a lawsuit under the Fugitive Slave Law in Chicago because of Eliza's rescue from reenslavement in 1860, and again many Northern newspapers asked how a woman from Nebraska Territory could be considered a slave. It was widely believed that these two lawsuits prompted by Celia and Eliza's actions would go to the U.S. Supreme Court. And the makeup of the court at that time was proslavery.[2]

Was Nebraska Territory slave or free? Could enslavement exist in a Northern climate? Was popular sovereignty working in Nebraska? Celia and Eliza's flight to freedom accentuated these questions and affected the political debate over the future of slavery as well as the future of the country.

Acknowledgments

In the production, research, and writing of such a large project, there are people who contribute to it in ways both large and small. I extend special thanks to my thesis adviser, Dr. Christopher Steinke, as well as to Dr. David Vail, Dr. Nathan Tye, and Dr. Vernon Volpe, at the University of Nebraska–Kearney for their comments and encouragement when this book was a thesis. They encouraged me to pursue the project as a full-fledged book, for which I am very grateful. Many thanks go to Bridget Barry at the University of Nebraska Press, who ushered the manuscript through its development. In addition, I would like to thank copyeditor par excellence Joyce Bond.

I also thank the staff at the History Nebraska Archives (formerly the Nebraska State Historical Society) in Lincoln, especially the incomparable Martha "Marty" Miller (now retired).

The history's main location, Nebraska City, is a special place, and many residents there helped me along the way. Katie Rudy at the Otoe County Register of Deeds office welcomed me multiple times, patiently answering questions and helping me locate places, with unparalleled knowledge of her hometown. Janet Riege, clerk of the Otoe County District Court, also lent a huge hand in finding early court records. Donna Kruse at the Morton Library helped me go through the library's photo collection and brought out its rich collection of local lore for my perusal. Tracking down other details about Nebraska City as the manuscript neared completion were Amy Allgood, Tammy Partsch, and Dean Shissler.

Sandra Bengston of the Fremont County Historical Society in Iowa deserves special mention. When I could not go to Sidney, Iowa, during courthouse hours, she did the legwork to locate the dockets and check for case files, taking a genuine interest in my work. She also introduced me to

Harry Wilkins of the Tabor County Historical Society, who graciously sent images of primary documents from its collections and provided an early map of the area.

I owe a huge debt of gratitude to Brett Conover, a Bourne descendant who generously scanned and shared letters and photographs from his personal collection. Also deserving thanks are Dave Holmgren of the Iowa Freedom Trail Project, Des Moines; the staff at the Atchison County Courthouse in Rock Port, Missouri; Trish Okamoto of the Page County (Iowa) Historical Society; and volunteers at the Grayson County Historical Society and Louisa County Historical Society, both in Virginia. Robert Beebe, archivist at the National Archives–Kansas City, also deserves mention.

In addition to research and archival help, I could not have completed this book without the generosity of people who read the manuscript during its development. Dr. Lauret Savoy's close and sensitive reading of the story both encouraged me and challenged me to consider important questions about the story. Her encouragement and insights were invaluable in the writing of this narrative. Other readers were Cheryl Stubbendieck, Susan Meckel, and Anna Meckel, whose observations and comments improved the manuscript and identified areas where nonhistorians might need more explanation. I am touched by their kindness and friendship in taking on this task in the midst of all their other projects.

David Bristow, the editor of *Nebraska History* magazine, read my thesis and my manuscript and saw the narrative grow and evolve over a long period of time. He provided important feedback and suggestions for improvement. In addition, he and graphic artist Ben Kruse also helped me develop the maps for Celia and Eliza's route, as well as the four corners of Nebraska, Iowa, Missouri, and Kansas. Ben, who "loves a mystery," not only discussed the project but also examined the conflicting evidence I had amassed about where Celia and Eliza lived in 1858. His input was invaluable.

I would be remiss if I did not mention the support of my husband, Don, who cheerfully cooked dinner almost every evening during the writing and editing phases and put up with papers, articles, books and more books strewn about the house.

Last but not least, I thank Celia and Eliza Grayson, whose courage and determination inspired this book.

Journey to Freedom

Introduction

> Worshipping heroism, as typically defined, works against the idea that the lives of more common people count and hold lessons for us as well.
> —Annette Gordon-Reed, *On Juneteenth*

On the cold, wintry night of November 25, 1858, two enslaved women, Celia Grayson, age twenty-two, and her sister Eliza Grayson, age twenty, slipped out of a house in the frontier river town of Nebraska City, Nebraska Territory. Twenty-three-year-old Black Cherokee freeman John Williamson, described as "a mulatto of considerable shrewdness and deal of experience in the world for one of his years," had arranged to meet them. Williamson was a familiar figure in the towns that dotted both sides of the Missouri River, engaged in small trading back and forth between Iowa and Nebraska. He was well positioned to help enslaved people cross the river. The women traveled about eight miles north to a small Missouri River ferry landing called Wyoming Station. Once the trio reached the landing, they boarded a skiff (flat-bottomed rowboat) to cross frigid waters running with ice. The young women were headed for their first stop on the Underground Railroad at Civil Bend, Iowa.[1]

The next morning Celia and Eliza's enslaver, Stephen Friel Nuckolls, whom friends and family called by his middle name, discovered the women's absence and sprang into action. He sent word to his two brothers in Glenwood, Iowa, and a brother-in-law in Sidney, Iowa, telling them to post lookouts at strategic river crossings. He then gathered a search party. The next issue of the local *Nebraska City News* declared that Nuckolls's female "servants" had been "enticed" away by "some vile, white-livered Abolitionist" and would "doubtless be found in some Abolition hole." Nuckolls offered a $200 reward for their return.[2]

The announcement did not contain any descriptions of the women. In other newspaper accounts, Eliza was described as "stout and sharp," meaning she was strong and intelligent. Another writer, given to flowery language, called her a "ginger-hued damsel." There are no descriptions of Celia.[3]

While history has not been silent on the existence of slavery in Nebraska Territory, historians have taken a small view of it. Early historians framed slavery in Nebraska as little more than an interesting item of curiosity because the numbers of enslaved people in antebellum Nebraska were always small. But how small? Federal territorial census counts of enslaved and free Black people ranged between eleven and eighty-two from 1854 to 1860. The earliest censuses were certainly undercounts. One newspaper asserted in 1855 that there were "no less than forty slaves in Richardson County alone," which could have been an exaggeration, but it is almost certain that enslaved people were there without being counted. The number of enslaved people in Nebraska Territory was in constant flux.[4]

According to researcher James Bish, most of the Blacks in Nebraska in 1860 were free, and just ten enslaved people lived in Otoe and Kearny Counties, as well as at Fort Randall. Bish stated that "Commander Charles May of Fort Kearny owned two slaves and junior officers owned five more."[5] Yet the digitized census pages online reveal no enslaved people in Charles May's household. They count six Blacks at Fort Kearny with no designation of whether they were enslaved or free. Questions remain as to whether some of these Blacks counted as free were actually working under conditions of enslavement.

The 1858 Nebraska City tax census counted twenty Black people total, some enslaved and some free, out of a population of 1,483—a little over 1 percent of Nebraska City's population. Other evidence reveals that federal appointees to government positions brought enslaved people into the territory who never made it into any census count.[6]

Moreover, for those people enslaved in the territory, the issue was important regardless of the numbers. They came from places where the numbers of enslaved people had been small and the landscape challenging. Indeed, the terrain had not prevented the institution from taking hold with steady growth. No matter what the numbers were, slavery in Nebraska was their everyday reality.

Between fifteen thousand and twenty thousand people sought their freedom during the 1850s in the United States, yet only a fraction of these incidents merited wide publicity.[7] Why did Celia and Eliza's story capture national headlines? At least part of the reason was their location in Nebraska Territory, established with Kansas Territory in the 1854 Kansas-Nebraska Act. The legislation included provisions for new territories to choose whether to become free or slave states. Both abolitionists and proslavery settlers turned their focus to Kansas, lying south of Nebraska, as having the most potential to become the country's next slave state. Anti- and proslavery factions poured in to settle in Kansas and attempt to tip the population balance their way. The factions clashed and violence broke out, leading to the period known as "Bleeding Kansas," highlighting the contentious and ongoing national dispute over the expansion of slavery into the West.

While the battle lines were clearly drawn in Kansas, some consciously sought to downplay enslavement and its prospects in Nebraska Territory. J. Sterling Morton, an early Nebraska City settler and later a prominent political figure in the territory, used the Nebraska City newspaper to denounce "Black Republicans," "Radicals," and their antislavery rhetoric on a regular basis.[8] Newspapers swung between "nothing to see here" dismissals of the issue as a waste of time and editorials claiming there was no reason slavery should not exist in Nebraska, where the institution could be a positive good.

In this context, Celia and Eliza's flight to freedom became, as Richard J. M. Blackett has noted in other cases, "politically charged with national implications."[9] The women's actions took center stage in the fractious national debate over slavery. Were Celia and Eliza enslaved or free? This question was entangled in the larger question whether the territories were slave or free until they voted on the issue. Would the doctrine of popular sovereignty—a government subject to the will of the people—settle the argument once and for all?

No Magic of Geography

Many antebellum leaders and editors felt that Northern territories were not suited to slavery and therefore the worries about the extension of slavery into territories were misplaced. They seemed to believe in a magic of geography that would contain enslavement to Southern climes. Daniel Webster, the Whig senator from Massachusetts, evinced no concern over slavery's expansion, believing that the law of nature would prevent its spread. Kentucky senator Henry Clay also felt that slavery could not exist in the West, assuring Northerners that they had nature on their side. These arguments were echoed in the debates over Kansas and Nebraska Territories.[10]

Yet what historians call "small-scale" domestic enslavement worked in Nebraska, as it had in other parts of the country, such as the Upper South areas of Kentucky and Tennessee and the Appalachian plateaus of Virginia and North Carolina, and could be found as far north as Minnesota. What led to its eventual downfall was the ongoing controversy surrounding human bondage—and ultimately the Civil War.[11]

Nebraska City, in the southeastern corner of Nebraska Territory, was part of a "four corners" geography. Although not as tidy as the later four corners of New Mexico, Arizona, Colorado, and Utah, Nuckolls's corner of southeastern Nebraska shared a border to the south with Kansas, where the tensions between proslavery and abolition forces often resulted in outright violence. To the south and east was the slaveholding state of Missouri, while east across the Missouri River lay Iowa, a free state with a strong minority abolitionist movement.

Proximity to free territory was one of the factors in enslaved people's decisions to make the break for freedom.[12] The free state of Iowa, just across the Missouri River, may have beckoned to Nebraska's enslaved people in this way.

Kansas Territory's James Henry Lane, an abolitionist originally from Indiana and later a U.S. senator, is credited with establishing an Underground Railroad route to transport freedom seekers from Kansas, Missouri, Arkansas, and other points south into the free state of Iowa. The route led north out of Kansas, crossing Nebraska's southeastern corner and going through Nebraska City, before turning east to cross the Missouri River. This was the route traveled by famous abolitionist John Brown and his men in early 1859.[13] Thus Nebraska's southeastern corner was a strategic location where the worlds of popular sovereignty, slavery, and abolition intersected and clashed between territorial and state systems.

One of Nebraska City's most popular tourist attractions has been John

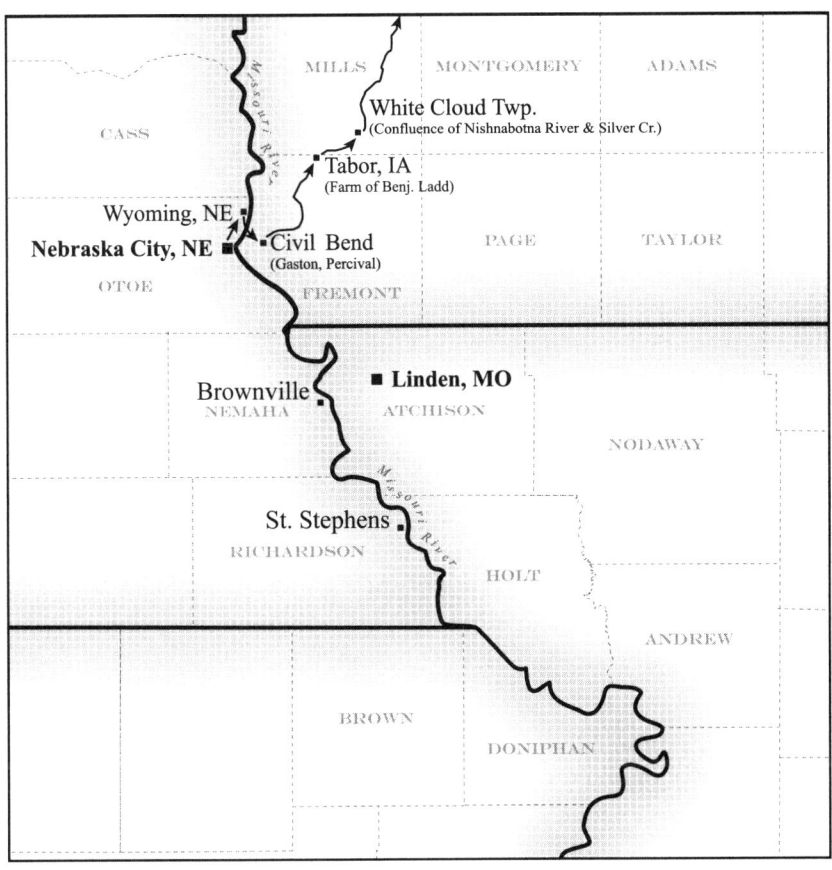

2. Four Corners geographic area. Map by Ben Kruse, History Nebraska.

Brown's Cave. Unfortunately, the cave's actual usage as a regular shelter for freedom seekers is more legendary than historical, although the abolitionist Mayhew family did "entertain" a number of freedom seekers in their cabin for an aboveground respite that included a meal. Nebraska historian James Potter allowed the possibility that "this was the [John] Brown party of February 1859." Today much of the site is unusable, damaged by flooding. Whether the attractions will be restored and reopened is unknown.[14]

In contrast to Nebraska City's celebrated folklore surrounding its participation in helping freedom seekers, the town also served as the nexus of Nebraska slavery. One writer reported in 1855 great "excitement" in Nebraska City about slavery, "in way of street debates, door-step discussions; and the question is, 'Shall Nebraska south of the Platte river be a slave state?'" Nowhere in the territory was the question posed with more intensity.[15]

Indeed, by 1858 most enslaved people in Nebraska Territory lived in and near Nebraska City. Beautifully situated on a bluff with ample room for a town and a natural landing for steamboats to dock, the frontier town grew rapidly as it vied to become a river metropolis that would grow and flourish as a transportation hub. Celia and Eliza were among the first recorded enslaved residents in Nebraska Territory, arriving in 1854 when their enslaver, Virginian Stephen F. Nuckolls, crossed over the Missouri River to make Nebraska City his home.[16]

As Nuckolls moved West with enslaved people in his company, he was also moving into the great debate. Whenever the United States expanded into new territories, the contentious issue of whether enslavement would enter into those territories surfaced. As historian Christopher Lehman persuasively argues, despite laws prohibiting enslavement in the North, in reality slavery continued to exist in pockets of Illinois, Iowa, Wisconsin, and Minnesota Territory.[17]

While debating the Kansas-Nebraska Act of 1854, Senator Stephen Douglas of Illinois admitted that slavery continued to exist in Northern climes "in a small way." This admission was meant to smooth the furious debate centered on the slavery question that arose as Congress considered opening new territories. Douglas proposed popular sovereignty—local self-government—as a solution to the ongoing struggle: let the people of the territory decide whether slavery would be legal in their area.

Popular sovereignty had long existed as a political theory, yet as the United States expanded westward, the issue of slavery surfaced at every turn. And as it did, questions involving popular sovereignty arose. Should territorial governments be subject to greater federal control until ready to become full-fledged states? Or should newly organized territories decide the issue of slavery through their representative vote in the territorial legislature? Both Kansas and Nebraska Territories were test cases for popular sovereignty at the territorial level—a solution explicitly put forward to calm the clash over enslavement.

But popular sovereignty failed to calm the proslavery and antislavery factions, and not only in Kansas Territory. The slavery issue hung over all the towns along the Nebraska side of the Missouri River, inviting argument as settlers from different regions of the United States streamed into the territory. In the early years, the land north of the Platte River tended to be settled by Northerners. But south of the Platte, particularly in the southeastern districts, many settlers flowed in from Missouri and the Upper South, some of them determined to exercise their right as U.S. citizens to hold people in bondage.

The situation created a contested boundary over slavery, which was uncertain and volatile as sectarian tensions between North and South played out. The possible extension of slave power westward into these transitional and diverse spaces caused great ferment all along the Missouri Valley, with direct citizen engagement from all four directions.

Popular sovereignty apologists dismissed the potential of Nebraska as a place where slavery could flourish. They argued, "There is no slavery in Nebraska," denying its very existence. When concrete examples of enslavement were pointed out, some, but not all, proslavery Nebraskans grudgingly admitted its existence, then argued that enslavement in the territory was on such a small scale that it did not matter. Their position was that slavery did not "practically" exist in Nebraska.[18]

It was in the midst of this controversy that Eliza and Celia Grayson's much-publicized flight and their enslaver Stephen Nuckolls's hot pursuit took place, demonstrating to the naysayers that slavery in Nebraska was an important reality. Moreover, the Graysons' flight highlighted the failure of popular sovereignty. The territorial legislature moved to prohibit slavery only to see bills delayed, tabled, and vetoed. Eliza and Celia's resistance became a vital part of the ongoing legislative debate. As Nebraskans argued, the nation watched and joined in. Through Celia and Eliza's actions, Americans saw Nebraska's experience as evidence of heightened division and disunion.

Nebraska Territory as a Society with Slaves

Historian Ira Berlin broke new analytical ground when he distinguished slave societies from societies with slaves—a distinction based on how ubiquitous enslaved labor was in the local economy. In slave societies, slave labor was dominant. In societies with slaves, slave labor was a smaller part of the overall labor force. As new territories opened up in the West, the question of enslavement entered into the calculus of how the "peculiar institution" might grow or diminish through new settlement. Thus the small foothold of enslavement in southeast Nebraska fit into Berlin's idea of an emerging "society *with* slaves," where slave labor would be accepted as just one form of economic production.[19]

In escaping Nebraska Territory, Celia and Eliza left a society with slaves. The enslaved labor force was indeed small. But those who supported the institution of slavery in Nebraska furthered the notion that its smaller scale was an advantage. By leaving slave states, slaves had bettered their situation.[20] Many scholars, including Wilma Dunaway, Diane Mutti Burke, and Kristen Epps, have challenged this common belief in the benignity of more "domestic" enslavement on smallholdings.

Born in the Appalachians of Grayson County, Virginia, Celia and Eliza spent their early years in domestic smallholder enslavement similar to what they later experienced farther west. Some historians have suggested that antislavery feelings ran high among nonslaveholders, explaining why some Upper South areas chose the Union side during the Civil War. However, recent histories have challenged this view, proposing that enslavement was an accepted part of life even where enslavers and the enslaved were a minority. Celia and Eliza were born in one of these contested areas into a form of bondage that historian Wilma Dunaway has dubbed "mountain slavery."[21]

The Nuckolls family who enslaved Celia and Eliza was typical of the Appalachian slaveholding class. Grayson County had no large plantations with hundreds of slaves. Yet the minority slaveholding class were better off than most white people in the county. This minority dominated the political and legal landscape, and the majority who did not own slaves went beyond tolerating the practice.[22]

The Nuckolls clan held important positions in commerce, local government, and the courts. They brought this Appalachian cultural capital with them when they moved west into Missouri, Iowa, and Nebraska. They platted towns, bought large tracts of land, established banks, and held public office. They extended their influence into almost every aspect of frontier life, including the promotion of tacit acceptance of enslavement in Nebraska Territory. In Missouri, Iowa, and Nebraska, they formed a plains slavery analogous to mountain slavery in its societal and political impact.

The Grayson story also blends themes of smallholdings and urban enslavement. The size of a farm and its location could influence the experience of slavery and slaveholding.[23] Where enslavers were a minority and the holdings small, an intimacy could arise between enslaver and enslaved, who often shared living quarters and worked side by side. Some historians have deduced that enslavement was likely more benign in these situations, an image that historians Diane Mutti Burke and Kristen Epps, writing about Kansas and Missouri, have challenged as too simple in the face of "the more complex picture painted by the individuals who actually endured enslavement."[24]

Like Appalachia, slaveholders were a minority in western Missouri, but slavery was still central to Missouri society. Indeed, "most white Missourians considered racially based slavery to be the foundation of the society that they helped to create."[25] Yet the familial closeness in smallholdings did not always equal benevolence; punishment on these farms often resembled that on larger plantations. As they did in other regions, enslaved people resisted in various ways, including active escape.[26]

Bondage in northwest Missouri resembled slavery as it had developed in Upper South states, such as Kentucky and Tennessee, perhaps because the area was settled primarily by people from those regions.[27] Despite the persistence of large plantations as representative of enslavement in America in the public discourse, Burke points out that "88 percent of slaveholding families owned fewer than ten slaves."[28] Slaveholders Stephen Nuckolls and his father, Ezra, fit well into the aspiring smallholding class—a class that contributed much to the national debate over slavery in the United States.

As early historians had done regarding Appalachian regions, borderland regions like Missouri, Kansas, and Nebraska were sometimes portrayed as places where slavery could be milder because the enslaved were "part of the family." As Gen. John G. Haskell stated in his address to the Kansas State Historical Society in 1901, "Slavery in western Missouri was like slavery in northern Kentucky—much more a domestic than commercial institution."²⁹ Nuckolls himself emphasized that Celia and Eliza were part of the Nuckolls family, "scarcely regarded as slaves," and as such, they must have been "enticed away" to leave their home.³⁰

But leave they did, and when they left, their legal status as slaves was in dispute. Celia and Eliza's public flight to freedom challenged Nebraska Territory's legislators who either denied slavery's presence or minimized its importance and gave ammunition to those who wanted to prohibit slavery in the territory. In sum, Celia and Eliza represented slavery's potential for expansion even in a Northern, free-soil territory.

It is past time to place Nebraska's enslaved people at the center of their own history and recognize their courageous will in challenging their enslavement. The story of Celia and Eliza Grayson is an opportunity to give names and voices to these early freedom seekers and illuminate the ways they challenge Nebraskans to confront how their history intertwines with America's "peculiar institution."³¹

{ 1 }

Growing Up in Appalachian Mountain Slavery

Born in 1836 and 1838, Celia and Eliza Grayson grew up in Grayson County, nestled in the Blue Ridge highlands in southwest Virginia's Appalachian range. Still wild and sparsely settled, the county shared a border with North Carolina.[1] Although breathtakingly beautiful, the rocky terrain was suited only to small-scale agriculture and pasture. The people who lived in the Blue Ridge were not "moonlight and magnolia" plantation owners. They were pioneer smallholders, and their lifestyles showed it.

Celia and Eliza's original enslaver was farmer and merchant Ezra Nuckolls. The Nuckolls family arrived in Virginia from England before 1685 and lived primarily in Louisa County until some branches moved west into Grayson County in the late 1790s and early 1800s.[2] The Nuckolls clan and other, more prosperous families occupied the best land along the river bottoms in "old Grayson," as they called it. Ezra farmed about two hundred acres, raising Indian corn, wheat, and oats, much of it for private and local consumption. Because of the mountainous landscape, livestock raising was integral to the economy. Cattle, sheep, and hogs ranged freely and foraged but were brought in at night to protect them from wild animals. Nuckolls family members also invested in nearby mines in the "Virginia Copper Region," though with little success.[3]

Ezra Nuckolls and Lucinda Hail (or Hale), married in Grayson County in 1823.[4] Ezra was the son of John Nuckolls, a fourth-generation Virginian, and Mary Garland, both from Louisa County. In a 1914 history celebrating the stalwart and brave pioneers of Grayson County, descendant Benjamin Floyd Nuckolls wrote with a touch of pride that the family had "a record given of the births of fifteen negroes belonging to John Nuckolls, and twelve negroes belonging to Mary Garland. Of this number, none were sold out

3. Grayson County, Virginia. Photo by Famartin, Wikimedia Commons.

of the Nuckolls family, except two men who were sold to men who owned the wives of these two negro men."[5]

Early records from Louisa County paint a different portrait of the John and Mary Nuckolls family. In 1787 John Nuckolds appears on the Louisa County tax list with a total of four taxable enslaved persons: one African American over sixteen and three under sixteen.[6] From there the Nuckolls and Garland families engaged in complex transactions including both real estate and enslaved people. Mary Garland Nuckolls's brother Charles, a single man, granted land and enslaved people to his nieces and nephews. Some of these legacies were to be held in trust until John and Mary's youngest child, Ezra, came of age, at which point property—including enslaved people—should be sold and the proceeds distributed.[7]

Missing from the pioneer narrative was that John and Mary's marriage was not a happy one. It was marked by enough strife and abuse that Mary sought relief from the authorities, and the Louisa County Court granted her that relief in the form of a legal separation. In 1805 the local court extracted John Nuckolls's acknowledgment of the "abuse and ill treatment he hath lately inflicted on his wife, Mary Nuckolls." The court further ordered that John transfer the land on which he lived, an African American woman named Amey, and other property to Mary for her lifetime use, reserving a workshop on the land for him. If Mary died before John, only the land would revert to him—the rest of the property would go straight to their children.[8] Ezra Nuckolls would have been age seven at the time of his parents' separation. He likely lived with his mother in Louisa County for at least a few more years before his move to Grayson County under the sponsorship of his older brother, Robert.

Ezra's father, John, may have been a wheelwright to supplement his farming income. In 1806 John Nuckolls was indebted to George Pottie and executed a trust deed that included "Negro Ned who has been bred to the wheelwright's business," along with an African American named Stephen, age twelve.[9] Although it is not known whether John met the deed's terms, the language indicates that he was ready to leverage his slaves to escape his financial difficulties, raising questions about the assertion that enslaved people were never sold out of the family.[10]

John Nuckolls continued to buy and sell land in Louisa County, but he may not have been considered entirely reliable. His father, James Nuckolls, left John only $10 in his 1810 will (although John may have already received his portion) and left "Negro Martha" to his grandsons Asa and Ezra Nuckolls.[11] In all, James's will divided nineteen enslaved people among his heirs, suggesting a fluid household size typical of smallholdings. As numbers approached what might be deemed a "middling" plantation (twenty to forty-nine enslaved people), transfers to children and others started the process over again, keeping the Nuckolls family in the smallholding class.[12]

Various Nuckolls family members moved from Louisa County southwest to Grayson County in the late 1790s and early 1800s. Large-scale plantations were not the norm, so their smallholder status was typical of other families in the area. Whether Ezra received any enslaved people as a gift upon his marriage or whether his wife, Lucinda Hail, brought any as a part of her dowry is unknown.

Ezra Nuckolls appeared on the Grayson County tax list for the first time in 1824, with one enslaved person age twelve to sixteen (born circa

Growing Up in Slavery 13

1808–12). The gender is unknown, but this could have been Martha, left to Ezra in his grandfather's will.[13] Indeed, there was often a preference for a new couple starting out to have an enslaved woman of childbearing age. As historian Stephanie E. Jones-Rogers writes, "With both enslaved males and females as inheritances upon marriage, they more frequently gave them female slaves."[14] Thus a young family could add to its enslaved property through the enslaved women's children.[15] Not surprisingly, the four enslaved people mentioned in the Nuckolls family records as having been transferred from Ezra Nuckolls to his children were all young girls.[16]

By 1828 Ezra Nuckolls and his wife, Lucinda, had three children: Mary, called Polly; Stephen Friel; and Frances. Their enslaved household also grew. Ezra appears on the personal property tax list that year with three Black enslaved persons, two over age sixteen and one between twelve and sixteen. To jump from one enslaved person age twelve to sixteen to two enslaved people over sixteen in four years suggests Ezra bought a person over sixteen, perhaps to form a couple. Enslaved children under age twelve were not taxable and would not be represented on the list. A later list of enslaved people showed births starting in 1820. Thus the 1828 tax list does not furnish a full picture of the growing enslaved family held by Ezra Nuckolls.[17]

By 1850 the number of enslaved people in his household grew to eleven, while the average for a slaveholding household in Grayson County was three or four enslaved persons. Thus Ezra moved from the lower to the higher property bracket in a steady progression. Comparing the pattern of births in his account book to enumerations in tax lists and censuses suggests that almost all this growth was through births to the enslaved women in his household. Ezra also increased his landholdings and business interests to the point where he was now considered wealthy.[18]

Ezra's uncle Charles Garland's trust deed had designated that a portion of the proceeds from Charles's estate sale should go to Ezra, who would have had an opportunity to purchase an enslaved person from that sale. More importantly, James Nuckolls left a female named Martha to Ezra and his brother Asa—a woman who could be the Graysons' progenitor. However, it was often the tradition that a Southern woman was given an enslaved person upon her marriage to help set up the household, so the first enslaved person in his household may have come from his wife, Lucinda Hail's, side of the family.[19]

The birth and death entries in Ezra Nuckolls's account book for most of the enslaved people are precise. Celia was born on February 13, 1836, at 1:30, and Eliza was born on January 24, 1838, at 11:00 p.m. Births occurred roughly every two years, leading to a near certainty that Celia and Eliza were sisters, part of a larger Grayson family with births ranging from 1820 through 1842, including a likely sister Edith born in 1830, who was also brought west.[20] In addition, because a Nuckolls-inspired editorial explained that Celia and Eliza "belonged to a family, formerly owned by Mr. N.'s parents in Missouri," this book considers Celia and Eliza to have been sisters.[21] The name of Celia and Eliza's father remains unknown, but he could have been one of the older men that appeared in Ezra's 1850 tax list or a man from a neighbor's farm.

Life in Grayson County among the Nuckolls family was certainly full of hard work, especially for the enslaved people. Ezra recalled the difficulty of making "a living by scratching and scraping in those hills, rocks, stumps, and roots." But Ezra was also a storekeeper who exchanged goods for farmers' surplus produce, extending credit in the surrounding communities, and in these activities he was more successful.[22] Enslaved people probably split their time between domestic tasks, field work, caring for livestock, gardening, planting, tilling, hoeing, hauling goods, stocking shelves, and carrying purchases out to buyers' wagons.

With no record from either Celia's or Eliza's point of view, other accounts provide context for their experience. Grayson County's legacy of slavery has only a few stories, including that of an African-born woman named Beck, who, along with her daughter Aimy, was purchased in Richmond by William Bourne, the grandfather of Stephen Nuckolls's wife, also named Lucinda. As Beck aged, she became known as Granny Beck and "took charge of the cattle and stock out on the range; salted and watched after them," while Aimy was the "house girl," who "waited on her master and mistress as long as they lived, and was very much attached to all the family." Bourne's wife, Rosamond, was reported to be "always kind to their negroes and provided well for them. She was their doctor when sick, their comfort in trouble."[23]

Bourne oral history quotes William Bourne as requesting that Aimy "not be sold and could choose where she would live" after his death, citing her position as a valuable servant who had "raised for me 18 children." Since Bourne and his wife had nine children, Aimy may have raised his children alongside nine enslaved children, at least some of whom were probably her own. This positive account of slavery dominates the picture of enslavement in the area, with an emphasis on "servants" as an important part of the family, cared for by kindly and paternalistic owners.[24]

But a Works Progress Administration interview of Ohioan freedwoman Sarah Woods Burke presents a less glowing report. Grayson County born and raised, Burke relates a vivid description of enslavement for that area. Her experience may not reflect Celia and Eliza's existence with the Nuckolls family, but given the lack of records about their day-to-day lives there, interviews such as Burke's can help provide a partial landscape of their childhood enslavement in Grayson County.

Born in 1842, Sarah Woods Burke was a few years younger than Celia and Eliza. David Woods and his wife enslaved Burke and her family, who lived in a log cabin with dirt floors and beds "built against the walls, jus' like bunks." They never had enough to eat, receiving only leftovers or whatever the slaveholder chose to give. At times they sneaked out and killed a pig or sheep, buried the skins and feet, and brought the meat back to their cabin piecemeal to avoid detection.[25]

The family who enslaved Sarah Woods Burke was not as well off as the Nuckolls clan and resided in the poorer, more mountainous area of Grayson County. Still, enslaved people lived close to their enslavers in a domestic form of slavery often assumed to be gentler than plantation-style. Yet for Burke and others, punishment was almost certainly common, even for small infractions. Indeed, punishment could be every bit as severe on smallholdings as they were on larger plantations.[26] Sarah reported that it was common that "slaves were tied to a whipping stake and whipped with a blacksnake until the blood would run down their bodies."[27]

Another account of enslavement in Grayson County is even more troubling. Hannah Moore reported that the man who held her in bondage, Conrad Hackler, was "a poor man and had no other slave but me." Treated more as a "brute" than a human being, she was fed with the dogs out of an

4. Lewis Hale's old kitchen/cabin with Clarke and Charlotte.
From Nuckolls, *Pioneer Settlers of Grayson County*, 1914.

old wooden tanning trough. She slept on a bed of rags, and once Hannah was grown, Hackler "thought nothing" of taking her clothes off to whip her until the blood ran. The only thing that saved her was that her owners "got religion" when she was about twenty-five years old, and the physical punishments stopped. Hannah, like Celia and Eliza, was taken along when the family moved to Missouri. When her mistress died, Hannah was sold to a succession of enslavers, some of whom were quite brutal. She finally escaped enslavement when she was traveling with a mistress in Philadelphia.[28]

Two reports cannot be considered representative of slavery in Grayson County. However, while day-to-day interaction may have created closer relationships in some cases, these interviews reveal that the violent nature of enslavement could be as bad as what was reported from the Deep South.

What may have helped Celia and Eliza in their early childhood was the presence of family members around them, with the protections that having a supportive group nearby can provide. When they were very young, they may have played with white children and performed small assigned tasks on the farm. The enslaved family was large enough that it is likely Ezra Nuckolls had at least one separate dwelling for them. Probably rough, these quarters still would have afforded a measure of family privacy.[29]

Growing Up in Slavery 17

5. Nuckolls homestead built by Robert Nuckolls and Charles Garland.
From Nuckolls, *Pioneer Settlers of Grayson County*, 1914.

Marie Jenkins Schwartz's study of enslaved childhood suggests that slaveholders interacted with young children with an eye to raising servants that would be loyal and biddable. As Celia and Eliza approached their middle years, which Schwartz defines as age five to ten, they probably began to perform varied tasks and chores, while their white counterparts started learning to be masters and mistresses rather than playmates. Schwartz describes the enslaved children's tasks: "Both girls and boys drove the master's cows to pasture, fed his chickens, and gathered eggs. They fetched water and wood for the mistress . . . raked leaves, husked corn, and worked in the kitchen garden."[30]

Schwartz also suggests the middle years were times when slaveholders used more punishments, particularly for infractions such as "not working, for disobeying arbitrary rules, for disrupting the plantation, for demonstrating insolence and for destroying property."[31] Given Nuckolls's choice to take Celia and Eliza to Missouri to help set up a new household at the end of their "middle years," it seems likely they were identified early to work inside the house. They may have even been living in the main house, although much of their work would still have been overseen by other enslaved people. Not surprisingly, when dealing with enslaved children, slaveholders tended to emphasize behavior that would uphold the owners' social and economic position, while enslaved family members around them imparted ways to "ensure their individual survival and that of the slave community."[32] When Celia and Eliza were taken away from their family to Missouri, they had only each other for support.

A Pleasant Mission Field and Grayson County Excitement

Further insight can be gained from looking at how Grayson County citizens reacted to challenges to their brand of mountain slavery. Even in this county, in what seemed like a stable society with smallholder enslavement firmly entrenched, change was in the air. Feelings about enslavement were not monolithic. Although many, if not most, of the whites living here accepted slavery, antislavery sentiments were also present. How these close-knit mountain communities handled these tensions became part of the Nuckolls family experience.

In 1848, about the time that Celia and Eliza were preparing to go west, a newly minted minister from Ohio named Jarvis C. Bacon appeared in Grayson County as a missionary and church planter. His Wesleyan Methodist compatriot Adam Crooks had already begun work in Grayson County, moving to nearby Guilford, North Carolina. Bacon joined Crooks to further his work "to plant the standard of reform, on the tops of the mountains of Grayson County, Virginia."[33]

Several years before Bacon's arrival, the Methodists in Grayson County tried to avoid dissension over slavery. After early wrangling over the question, regional conferences were allowed to have their own rules. Yet the moral issues remained thorny, and controversy erupted again when many felt that a Southern Methodist bishop who held slaves in Georgia should not remain in office unless he emancipated his slaves. In 1844 the Methodist General Conference finally voted to begin a plan of separation. When asked to vote in 1844 on whether the local congregation wanted to belong to the North or South Methodist Church, Grayson County's presiding elder "refused to allow the vote." But at the Methodist regional level, the Holston conference, to which Grayson County belonged, voted to adopt the South division. As a result, a small Wesleyan breakaway group formed in Grayson County, with the conference expelling those members who would not follow the Southern rule.[34]

Historian Clifton Johnson distinguishes between "Christian abolitionists" and "antislavery Christians." Around the 1830s many Protestant churches began to require their parishes to sever all connections between the church and slavery. These church bodies, who felt that slaveholding members and their supporters should be excommunicated, were the "Christian abolitionists." "Antislavery Christians" were those who condemned the institution of slavery as an evil and wanted to promote emancipation but would not exclude those who disagreed with them from Christian fellowship.[35] The Wesleyan Methodists, including Adam Crooks and Jarvis Bacon, adopted the abolitionist line.

Bacon was a young and eager preacher, good-mannered and pleasant. He succeeded in making fourteen conversions to his new congregation. But it was not long before he caught the authorities' attention. During one of his sermons, he quoted the Bible passage regarding Jesus driving the moneychangers from the temple. Bacon announced that thieves and robbers were in church that day. He explained that if a man stole his neighbor's corn, he was a thief, but there were places where he could steal the labor of another human being with impunity. The congregation could hardly have missed his point: slaveholders were thieves in the eyes of God. Although most of the worshippers were likely aware of Bacon's antislavery views, the comparison to thieves may have still come as a shock.[36]

Despite his popularity as a preacher, or perhaps because of it, reports of Bacon's doings flowed out of the open meetings and into the wider community. In addition to his preaching, Bacon had apparently lent out antislavery reading material. Perhaps unwittingly, he had run afoul of a recent 1848 Virginia statute that punished a free person who wrote or circulated a book or pamphlet intending to incite Black people to rebellion or that denied the right of slaveholders to own enslaved people as property.[37]

On April 3, 1849, the Grayson County grand jury met to review the evidence gathered to indict Bacon based on the 1848 statute. A local newspaper called Bacon "The Destroyer in Our Midst," painting him as a firebrand of "dangerous, destructive and illegal doctrines," who had whipped up "gangs of negros and a few whites," while also congratulating Grayson

County citizens for their "patient forbearance" in allowing the matter to be settled in the courts. Ezra Nuckolls was one of the three magistrates who examined Bacon, recommending he face trial. Ezra's father-in-law, Col. Stephen Hale, a Southern Methodist who in 1850 had fourteen slaves, was the grand jury foreman. After the grand jury's decision to allow the charges to go forward, Judge James E. Brown issued a bench warrant for Bacon's arrest. Bacon had to give bond for his appearance for the next phase of the trial the following month.[38]

On the morning of May 28 a crowd gathered outside the brick courthouse in the town of Greenville, later known as Old Town.[39] Court days in the South were important in the life of the town and surrounding area, treated as both a holiday and a time to do business. Stores, taverns, and street vendors often took advantage of the opportunity that a court day offered with increased numbers of people in town. Drinking, horse trading, and general "idleness" were common. Court cases themselves were events that provided entertainment, almost like stage plays, especially when the case was of interest to the community. Bacon's trial would naturally have attracted a large crowd.[40]

On this particular morning, feelings were intense on both sides of the issue. When the courthouse door opened at 11:00 a.m., the throng pressed into the central hall and squeezed into the courtroom wing, jostling for places in "great excitement." Bacon's supporters and detractors prepared to watch the show.

At 12:00 noon Bacon's case began. Mine owner and lawyer Samuel McCamant of Grayson and William H. Cook of Carroll County prosecuted the case on behalf of the commonwealth of Virginia. Bacon, an island of calm and dignified assurance in the middle of the charged atmosphere, heard the charges. He pleaded not guilty to circulating material with the intent to incite insurrection.

During the arguments, it came out that Bacon had lent *Narrative of the Life of Frederick Douglass* to a young lady. Her brother had discovered the book among her things. Not sharing his sister's sympathies, he had secretly delivered it to the slaveholding authorities. The second count against Bacon was the circulation of a sermon pamphlet by fellow Ohio abolitionist Edward Smith. The attorneys for both sides agreed that the same arguments regarding the Douglass book should apply to the sermon pamphlet. Prosecutor Cook, playing on already high emotions, cried that Bacon's actions would deliver "our throats... to the butcher knife, our houses to the torch, and our wives and daughters to—." The report let readers imagine the terrible fate awaiting Grayson County wives and daughters.[41]

The case proceeded with much argument and little evidence that Bacon had circulated anything widely. Bacon's attorneys, Virginians Peregrine Buckingham of Montgomery County and Andrew Steele Fulton of Wythe County, pointed out that the works had not been shared with any "colored people," so there was no criminal intent.[42]

The magistrates decided there was enough evidence to indict Bacon for "feloniously circulating a pointed pamphlet addressing and inciting persons of color within this Commonwealth to rebel, make insurrection, denying the rights of masters to property in their slaves, and inculcating the duty of resistance to such right."[43] Both counts were referred to the superior court, to be held in September.[44]

Grayson County slaveholder John Cornutt (spelled Cornett in some records) was among those who posted Bacon's bail, drawing more than a little local ire. Cornutt, whose wife was childless, had a number of mixed-race children through a liaison with his enslaved woman, Rebecca, a fact well known throughout the county. Once released on bail, Bacon returned to working and preaching in Grayson County through the summer, achieving more conversions and building a congregation. Cornutt and others continued to support Bacon's work.

Bacon's criminal trial in September featured a familiar face: that of Ezra Nuckolls's father-in-law, Stephen Hale, who had been the foreman of the first Grand Jury in April. Even so, the jury had trouble finding Bacon guilty.[45] There was a lack of evidence that his tracts had been circulated to Black people or that he had directly incited enslaved people to leave their condition. The verdict was that Bacon was not guilty.

Judge Brown was surprised by the acquittal and used his power to inflict retribution despite the case's outcome. He remonstrated with the jury, "How could the guilt of the prisoner be made to appear more plain? It was proven he circulated the book." He announced that Bacon was guilty of violating the law and fined Bacon $400. Brown further announced that he would burn the book and pamphlet (effectively burning the evidence). The antislavery *Pennsylvania Freeman* asked if Judge Brown thought "the truth and the facts which it told would be annihilated when the paper turned to ashes."[46]

Judge Brown also required Bacon to give $1,000 bond for good behavior for the next twelve months. Bacon appealed the ruling, arguing that he had not denied the legal right to property but had counseled as a minister that slavery was a moral sin. The Virginia Supreme Court agreed with Bacon, ruling that restricting freedom of speech "should be strictly construed" and that a minister could "counsel a member of his flock" to avoid keeping or taking human beings in slavery, at least as a matter of morality.[47]

Grayson County citizens, previously described as examples of "patient forbearance," did not take the ruling kindly. Bacon continued his mission work there, but under constant threat and danger. It did not take long for another event to capture the public's attention, bringing Bacon back under the societal microscope.

Slave Catching in Grayson County

Celia and Eliza's Grayson County roots and their courageous decision to self-emancipate are thrown into relief when considering the nature of the enslavement into which they were born. Ezra Nuckolls, portrayed as a benign paternal figure to his enslaved people, was also firm in his support of slavery. In 1851 four enslaved men sought their freedom in an ill-fated and deadly escape. According to court records, Simon and Lewis were enslaved by John Reeves of Grayson County, Jack was enslaved by David Cox, and Henry was enslaved by Reeves Cox of nearby Ashe County, North Carolina. The men had obtained a canoe and were paddling up the New River, hoping to reach Ohio and freedom. When they stopped to rest near Clements Mills in Grayson County on August 11, they built a small campfire. John Clements saw the smoke and spied the men in the woods. Clements drummed up a slave patrol, armed with "guns and a bulldog, to help him apprehend the men," although the extant court testimony did not mention the bulldog.[48]

The slave catchers who assembled at Clements's house included Samuel Bartlett (sometimes written as Bartlet) and his brother Alfred, both men in their thirties; Cyrus Wilcox; Ezra Nuckolls's brother-in-law, William B. Hail; and William's son Curran Hail. (John Clements and William and Curran Hail all later moved to Nebraska City.)

According to William Hail's testimony, he joined the group at Clements's house, and they walked to a small hollow in the woods where the enslaved men were camped. Clements was already there, talking to the men and asking what they were doing there in a friendly tone, to keep them off guard. But when the African American men saw the rest of the group approach, they rose to their feet, understanding that this was a "slave patrol." One of them was armed with a scythe, another with a knife. William Hail yelled, "Lay down your weapons!"[49]

The slave catchers spread out. Alfred Bartlett and Cyrus Wilcox moved to one side of the hollow, while William Hail and his son went to the other. Reports of what happened next differ in detail, but when Hail shouted, "Lay down your weapons!" only the smallest, Henry, surrendered. The others were undaunted. Lewis raised his scythe and advanced on Bartlett and Wilcox. Hail yelled twice, "Shoot him down!" Wilcox fired and may have hit Lewis, but the enslaved man still advanced, so it may have been only a grazing wound. His shot having failed, he told Alfred Bartlett to shoot, but Bartlett's rifle, "easy on the trigger," misfired, and Lewis "made slick with his scythe at Alfred," who parried the blow aimed at him, severely injuring his wrist. In the meantime, Hail had turned his gaze on the knife-wielding Simon and yelled at him to put up his knife or he would be shot. Simon answered, "Shoot me if you want to."

Around this time, Jack threw a well-aimed rock at Hail and hit him square in the head, stunning him for a moment. It was during this chaotic interlude that Samuel Bartlett was knifed and mortally wounded, and perhaps this was also when Clements suffered a critical head wound, but Hail's testimony does not include these moments. Hail did remember Simon knifing Wilcox in the neck and Alfred Bartlett, then striking Simon in the back to protect Wilcox from further injury.

Hail's testimony became even more confused from there, probably because so much happened in the heat of the action. But Hail and another man (perhaps his son Curran) captured Henry and Jack. The other two enslaved men slipped away but were eventually caught. The details of Lewis's capture are unknown, but Jack Lambert arrested Simon on his farm in neighboring Wythe County on September 4. Also uncertain is how Samuel Bartlett received his mortal wound on that fateful day, but he died six to eight hours later. The four freedom seekers ended up in the Grayson County jail. Because Henry had not participated in the fight, he was eventually released back to his enslaver.[50]

The news about the murder of a white man by "fugitive slaves" spread like wildfire through the entire vicinity, then the story spread nationwide. The main newspaper account appeared in the *Wytheville (VA) Republican* and was quoted and misquoted throughout the country, with some editors identifying the murdered man as Alfred Bartlett, rather than Samuel.

The Grayson County Vigilance Committee also met to blame the "destroyers" in their midst, such as Jarvis Bacon, who they believed had incited the enslaved men to "elope." The group went in hunt of abolitionists. They were unable to locate Jarvis Bacon, nor did they find his Wesleyan colleagues Rev. Jesse McBride or Rev. Adam Crooks. But rage needs an outlet, and on September 13, 1851, a mob of "near two hundred" visited the farm of John Cornutt, who had posted bond for Bacon during his trials. They demanded that Cornutt forswear abolitionism. He refused. The men stripped off his clothes, blindfolded him, tied him to a tree, and whipped him "till the blood ran down to his feet." Apparently, his wife tried to reason with them, and they tied her up so she could not interfere. Cornutt finally broke and promised to obey the laws of Virginia, sell his slaves, and leave the state. The committee then rode off "in pursuit of others."[51] These lawless actions broke into the national news, with opinions like "a resort to Lynch law is to be deeply deprecated, but Abolitionism is worse than Lynch law," on one side and "We make a great ado (not unreasonably) about Italian despotism, but wherein is it more atrocious than this?" on the other.[52]

Ten days after Cornutt's assault, it was time for the freedom seekers' trial in what was then the new county seat in Independence.[53] The morning of September 23, 1851, the courtroom in Independence was packed. Ezra Nuckolls, Shadrack Greer, Samuel Fulton, Fielden Young, and Garland Anderson were the justices in the matter. The charges against Simon, Lewis, and Jack were grave. They were accused of having "feloniously plotted and conspired the murder" of Samuel Bartlett, Cyrus Wilcox, John Clements,

Alfred Bartlett, and William B. Hail. If convicted, the sentence was death by hanging.[54]

The five justices, including Ezra Nuckolls, were all slaveholders. After hearing the evidence, the jurors exited, but their deliberations did not take long. Samuel Bartlett was dead, and there were plenty of witnesses. Hail's testimony insisted the enslaved men were the aggressors in the bloody fracas that had ensued. The judge probably asked Simon, Lewis, and Jack to rise to hear the verdict. Even though the outcome may have been assured, one can still imagine the crowd growing quiet, leaning in to hear the words. Guilty as charged. The three men would hang by the neck until dead.

Which enslaved man dealt the mortal blow to Samuel Bartlett and at what point in the fight? The record is unclear. The charges drew no distinction between the murderer and any accessories to the deed. Simon, Lewis, and Jack were all charged with "murder with malice aforethought," although how the enslaved men, surprised in the woods, could have plotted ahead for Samuel Bartlett's demise defies logic. A close reading of the record suggests that it did not matter who actually killed Samuel Bartlett. Nailing down the facts was not of prime importance.

After the trial, a large number of citizens, including Ezra Nuckolls and his father-in-law, Stephen Hale, remained at the courthouse and called a meeting of the Grayson County Vigilance Committee. The slaves would hang, but the committee wanted more. In their opinion, Simon, Jack, Lewis, and Henry had been seduced to leave their homes and families. Bacon was the real murderer. He might as well have committed the crime himself.

The Vigilance Committee passed several resolutions, one to raise a $1,000 reward by subscription among the citizens of Grayson, Wythe, Carroll, and Smyth Counties for Bacon's apprehension and delivery to Grayson County. They also resolved that Grayson County merchants like Ezra Nuckolls would no longer purchase goods from any nonslaveholding states until they were confident that the Northern states would respect their legal and constitutional rights to own slave property.[55]

Meanwhile, the condemned freedom seekers went back to jail for a little over a week. They may have been able to hear the staccato beat of hammers as the scaffold for their execution was built nearby. The day of their execution was Saturday, November 1, 1851. Ezra Nuckolls's store probably did brisk business as people poured into tiny Independence. They came from all over Grayson and adjoining counties, from the gorges, hollows, and mountains. They came in wagons, on foot, on horses, and on mules. They came for the show.[56]

One woman later recalled "thousands" there, although her memory may have been exaggerated, since she was a little girl at the time. No doubt it was a large number. Simon, Jack, and Lewis sang hymns as they were brought by wagon to the scaffold, with a "vast throng of curious people pushing along in eager excitement to witness their contortions."[57]

None of the slave catchers in the case owned enslaved people themselves, illustrating that enslavement was more widely accepted in Appalachia than sometimes assumed. In places like Grayson County, with smaller overall populations, family, social, and economic ties were strong regardless of slaveholding status. For instance, William B. Hail never appears in a record as an enslaver, but his parents and family members do. John Clements had no slaves, but he was Hail's neighbor, and he was also in heavy debt to Ezra Nuckolls. Within this tight and tangled web of economic and social obligations, even those uneasy with the institution of slavery may have felt accommodation was necessary.[58]

After the trial and hanging, instead of leaving Grayson County, John Cornutt emancipated the people he held in bondage, Rebecca and her children George, Francis, Tate, and Clark. He then sued his tormentors for the attack on him. The trial was to convene in April 1852, but again the members of the local Vigilance Committee had other plans. They plotted to disrupt and deny Cornutt his day in court. And it was no secret—the committee asked that their threats, called "resolutions," be published in the Abingdon and Wytheville newspapers and copied throughout the state of Virginia.[59] Local newspapers complied and served as the committee's mouthpiece, warning that any attorneys who dared to take up Cornutt's case would be tarred and feathered. Their list of extralegal means was long.

In this highly charged atmosphere, Judge James E. Brown (the same judge as in the earlier book burning) still tried to open court proceedings in April 1852, with Cornutt's case on the docket. But the Vigilance Committee arrived en masse, firing their guns, while those present scattered to safety. No one was hurt, but Ezra Nuckolls's friend and relation, Garland

Anderson, strategically resigned his appointment as clerk of the court to protest the proceedings. No one else would step up and take the office, forcing Judge Brown to adjourn. The vigilantes carried the day.⁶⁰

Newspaper editors weighed in. The editor for the *Salem (NC) People's Press* approved of the Vigilance Committee's action, warning that other "obnoxious" people might "spread desolation and death in our midst." Resorting to courts would not be as effective to remedy the situation as the Grayson County Vigilance Committee's "summary process"—an interesting euphemism for mob justice.⁶¹

Although some editors had egged Graysonites on, the editors of the *Staunton (VA) Spectator* excoriated the mob action, declaring that "some of the most respectable people of the County" were no better than a "band of outlaws." They concluded that the persecutors' refusal to "confront him [Cornutt] in a Court of justice" was an acknowledgment of their guilt. A separate item above this critique discussed magistrates and stated that not every man was fit to be one. Although the piece was general in nature, its placement may have been aimed at magistrates like Ezra Nuckolls, who joined in the lawlessness and blocked a fellow citizen's right to his day in court.⁶²

The *Pennsylvania Freeman* warned that Northerners should learn from Grayson County how much "slaveholders are ready to do," with their "villainous despotism" outside the bounds of law and order. The wrongs perpetrated were steps that were "necessary to the downfall of the institution itself," and free states should "ponder well over this Grayson County action."⁶³

Although Celia and Eliza were already in Missouri with Stephen and Lucinda Nuckolls during these dramatic events, their former enslaver, Ezra Nuckolls, was connected to the Bacon trial, the persecution of John Cornutt, and the hanging trial of the three enslaved men discovered at Clements Mills. The enslaved among the Nuckolls clan certainly must have been aware of these demonstrations of violence, punishment, and control. Other than the small band of Wesleyan Methodists, the nonslaveholding majority in Grayson County did not seem to object in any appreciable way; they had joined in the hunt and then celebrated the executions.⁶⁴

The lessons to Grayson County's remaining enslaved people were clear: self-emancipation would be met with violence, torture, and even death.

These events demonstrate that the Nuckolls clan hailed from a place of mountain slavery—a society with slaves. Although a minority, slaveholders held the reins of power and wielded considerable clout in all aspects of local life. Moreover, they did not hesitate to use force and extralegal means to uphold what they saw as their property rights to the enslaved people in their midst.

This was part of the cultural capital the Nuckolls family brought with them as they migrated west to settle during a time of ferment over the extension of slavery into the territories. If Celia and Eliza were unaware of the events that took place in Grayson County after their removal to Missouri, it is almost certain that their relatives who were brought into Atchison County a few years later related what happened in detail. Thus as African Americans helped occupy the West, they brought their experiences, memories, and narratives into their new environments—traditions from their close-knit society that incorporated varied forms of resistance with a keen awareness of slavery's backdrop of control, intimidation, and violence.

6. Many migrants west traveled by steamboat. Photo by Mathew Benjamin Brady, NARA 5289791. Wikimedia Commons.

{ 2 }

Adjusting to New Lives in Missouri

In the fall of 1848 eleven-year-old Celia and nine-year-old Eliza Grayson, probably with their relative Shack, who was about thirteen years old, stood at a steamboat landing on the Ohio River. Had they been white, the experience may have revealed a taste for adventure and opportunity. Instead, they were being taken west to Missouri, involuntary migrants separated from their family and the familiar hills, valleys, and forests of Grayson County.

If Celia and Eliza had ever been in a boat before, it was likely a small ferry. Steamboats were another thing altogether. Constructed like a layer cake perched on a shallow hull, the boat had levels for machinery, goods, and passengers, with the smallest layer, the pilot house, on top. The girls may have wondered at a "long close line of woodladen" Black men that resembled "a moving woodpile," as they loaded wood onto the ship for the boilers. More familiar to them may have been the songs of the "Negro deckhands," which to one hearer carried "a weird and not unmelodious effect."[1]

Celia and Eliza's journey west started with their new enslaver, Stephen Nuckolls. He was one of eleven children, the oldest son born to Ezra and Lucinda (Hail) Nuckolls in Grayson County. Not much is known about his early education; perhaps it consisted of a mix of home tutoring and an established local school. But he eventually went away to a classical academy, the newly established Virginia Institute (later Roanoke College), nestled in the Blue Ridge Mountains near Staunton, Virginia. Two Lutheran pastors, David Bittle and Christopher C. Baughman, founded the school to provide a full Christian education to the up-and-coming generation of leaders in southwest Virginia.[2]

Nuckolls returned home from his studies in about 1846 to work in the family store. Ambitious and driven, he looked west for an opportunity to establish a mercantile business of his own, as well as to take advantage of the

West's major draw—real estate. In October Stephen left home and walked two hundred miles to the village of Guyandotte, Virginia (near present-day Huntington, West Virginia), and took deck passage on the steamboat *Swatara* to St. Louis. Onboard, he met settler and farmer William Lambert, who offered Stephen free board at his house near "Hog Thief Bend," in Atchison County, Missouri. From St. Louis, the pair made their way by land to Lambert's place. Not afraid of hard work, Stephen took Lambert up on his offer to "grit," helping Lambert mill corn by hand while scouting the area for business opportunities.[3]

At a local horse race, Nuckolls met a man who would become a staunch Democrat ally and friend, attorney Allen A. Bradford. Described as eccentric, grotesque, and peculiar, the rotund Bradford sported a heavy beard and had small eyes. Although lacking the finer social graces, he was a man of ability and not to be trifled with. His shrewd and cunning cynicism occasionally devolved into bitter invective aimed at his enemies.[4]

Bradford was also an Atchison County resident. Atchison was Missouri's northwesternmost county, bordered by Iowa on the north. To the west was the Missouri River and Indian Country. Bradford exhibited enough charm at his first meeting with Nuckolls to persuade him to open a store in the town of Linden. Linden was home to thirty inhabitants, one general store, a blacksmith shop, and a church. With such a promising start, Lindenites hoped to make their new home the permanent county seat. The county had fields of undulating prairie mixed with rolling hills of fertile loess—soils richer than Stephen had ever known back home. Although Missouri attracted emigrants from all over the United States, its status as a slave state may have been an extra draw to Nuckolls and his fellow Southerners. Indeed, the majority of emigrants attracted to Missouri's northern tier of counties were from Upper South border areas like Kentucky, Virginia, and Tennessee. Linden's location must have seemed ideal for Stephen's mercantile concerns.[5]

After choosing his new western residence, Stephen returned to Virginia to prepare for a permanent move. He married his mother's young cousin Lucinda Bourne on October 7, 1847. Contemporary photographs of Lucinda Bourne Nuckolls show her dark hair pulled back in a severe bun. Shadows were ever present under her light eyes, giving her a worn and faded look, even in her youth. The corners of her thin mouth turned slightly down. In repose, she looked melancholy. She could read and write but with less facility than her husband. By contrast, Stephen, although already balding, radiated vitality and intelligence, with an upright posture that exuded confidence. After the wedding, the couple prepared for their move west. Among the arrangements were decisions about which enslaved people would accompany them. In addition to Celia and Eliza, Shack Grayson, likely their brother and older than Celia by a year or two, probably joined them on the trip west with Stephen and his bride in 1847–48.[6]

Celia and Eliza likely helped prepare and pack for the move with more than a little trepidation. At ages nine and eleven, it is almost certain that they had never traveled far from Grayson County. Moreover, even though Lucinda Bourne was from a Grayson County family that was known to them, having a new mistress to accommodate may have added to their worries. Worst of all was the impending separation from their family members who would remain behind in Ezra Nuckolls's Virginia household.

Stephen and Lucinda, accompanied by the three young Graysons, may have taken the same route to Missouri that Stephen had scouted out the year before. Any carriage or wagon was likely reserved for Lucinda and the household goods. On his prior trip, Stephen had walked all the way to the Guyandotte port, but whether he joined Lucinda in riding this time is unknown. Shack and the two girls probably walked most of the way before boarding the steamboat. On deck, the odors from the goods, barrels, and livestock stored on the lower levels would have wafted up, permeating the atmosphere as the family prepared to embark.

Nuckolls likely procured a cabin for Lucinda and himself, while letting Celia, Eliza, and Shack stay on the crowded, dirty, and smelly upper decks, open to the elements. Private cabin passengers ate in a dining room and were served food reminiscent of that offered by good hotels, while the other class of passengers had to make their own meals from their personal food supplies.

Their steamboat wound its way down the Ohio River to St. Louis, where they probably switched boats to travel up the Missouri. The trip would not have been without its challenges or charms. One writer described the late-fall river scenery after departing St. Louis. His steamboat passed "between

Adjusting to New Lives 33

7. Stephen Friel Nuckolls. Brett Conover Collection.
Used with permission from Brett Conover.

shores heavily timbered with cottonwood," their whitish, bare branches looking "dead and dreary." The Missouri River was also famous for "eating" steamboats with its numerous snags and snarls, often obscured by muddy and tossing waters. The Graysons may have looked with some curiosity on the constant sounding of the Missouri's depths, with men calling out "Ten feet!" or "Eight and a half!" or "Three feet, scant!" at which depth the pilot would halt the boat and study the river.[7]

8. Lucinda Bourne Nuckolls. Brett Conover Collection. Used with permission from Brett Conover.

Slowly and cautiously, the boat would have steamed along in the uncertain channel, paddlewheels churning. Abolitionist John Todd of Iowa made the trip in 1848, and he found the going difficult. He related, "Boats passed up only at irregular intervals . . . and not unfrequently remained for weeks upon sandbars and snags." A poetic diarist once described coming upon a shoal: "The boat walked right over on stilts. The chandeliers rattled as though we were stumbling over the hump of an earthquake."[8] As

Adjusting to New Lives

fascinating as all these sights and sounds may have been to the Grayson sisters' young minds, with every mile the steamboat floated, their hearts had to have been heavy with sorrow and loss.

As they neared their destination, they would have passed rocky heights and hills that receded "in long wooded slopes, indented with shadowy ravines through which some spring sent forth a little brawling stream to break the solitude," as well as log cabins and "towns being built among the bluffs." Perhaps they, like others, noticed an air of "shiftlessness" about the people and the towns, a thrown-together temporary feeling that their old home in Grayson had outgrown.[9]

How the Nuckolls group felt when they first laid eyes on their new home in Linden, Missouri, cannot be known, but their living arrangements in these earliest years were probably a far cry from their more settled existence in Grayson County. Atchison County had been organized for just a few years and still had a frontier feel. Wildlife was plentiful in those years, with deer, turkey, ducks, geese, squirrels, otters, beavers, mink, muskrats, raccoons, panthers, foxes, wolves, wildcats, and even bears. And natural beehives could be found along the streams throughout the county, making honey one of the area's most important products.[10]

Once in Linden, Celia, Eliza, and Shack probably had little time for anything but work as they helped Lucinda with unpacking and setting up the new household. The old adage "A man may work from sun to sun, but a woman's work is never done" may have ruled Celia and Eliza's days well into the evenings. The sisters may have begun to understand that their lives were forever changed.

Nuckolls plunged into merchandizing and real estate investments from his new home in tiny Linden. His Cheap Cash Store sat on a road that led north into Iowa, with an eye to serving a wider area.[11] And the family grew. By 1850 he and Lucinda had a two-year-old son, William, called Billy, and a newborn daughter, Virginia Ann. Celia and Eliza likely added minding the children to their list of household duties.[12]

Around this time Stephen's sister Rosamond, called Rosa, joined him and Lucinda in Missouri. According to family sources, she helped in the Linden store, where she met a German immigrant clerking for Stephen, Henry Augustus "Gus" Borchers. Rosa and Gus married in Sidney, Iowa, in

1851. After their marriage, they operated a general store linked to Stephen's business and located on the same road.[13]

The Borcherses helped found the town of Hamburg, Iowa, whose limits extended with within half a mile of Atchison County. Stephen Nuckolls was one of the major investors. Gus's brother George also worked with Nuckolls as a merchant and appeared in the 1850 slave schedule of Atchison County as having one enslaved thirty-year-old woman, perhaps a woman that his Missouri-born wife brought to the marriage.[14] As the Nuckolls family members spread out, they established mercantile businesses, blending their resources. These businesses acted as a chain of related stores that served northern Missouri and southwestern Iowa.[15]

In addition to their Virginia friends and family, the Nuckollses lived among people who brought similar values with them from the Upper South. They naturally perpetuated a system of human bondage marked by a smallholder minority that turned to enslavement as another form of labor. These white emigrants sought upward mobility, and their goals of increased prosperity and landownership unified them regardless of their place of origin.

Thirty-two Black persons were counted in the Atchison County slave schedule in 1850, distributed among just ten enslavers, out of a total population of 3,428. As busy as life was, the other enslaved people in the area had to be of more than passing interest to those living in the Nuckolls household. However, it is uncertain what opportunities there might have been to meet them.[16]

Celia and Eliza may have welcomed any chance to broaden their social network, whether accompanying Lucinda Bourne Nuckolls outside the house, helping at the Linden store, or going to large gatherings where they may have been called to serve. If Celia and Eliza attended religious services, it may have been in a private capacity or when a visiting minister passed through the town. Even then, Celia, Eliza, and Shack may have had to sit in a separate area in the back of the church with any other enslaved people allowed to attend.

The sisters' new lives reflected the expansion of slavery into new areas of the growing nation. Those emigrants who held people in bondage developed strategies for their migration westward, including which enslaved

Adjusting to New Lives

people would move along with them. Although the Nuckolls clan later couched their choices as a benign consideration of older slaves not wanting to make the trip, clearly young and strong enslaved people would enhance their chances of economic success. For Stephen and Lucinda Nuckolls, the Graysons fit the bill. The average age of the thirty-two enslaved persons listed in the 1850 slave schedule was fifteen, with a preponderance of young enslaved women, 59 percent of the total.[17]

Different crops, different living conditions, and greater proximity to free territory meant that the adjustment process for Celia, Eliza, and Shack diverged from that of involuntary migrants whose enslavers had taken them or sold them from the Atlantic states into the Deep South. The 1850 statistics for Atchison County reveal agriculture's slow start there, with the county producing 5,652 pounds of beeswax and honey, 862 pounds of flax, 350 pounds of butter, and 24 tons of hay.[18]

With their new home in Missouri blending elements of a frontier small town with a rural location, it is likely Celia and Eliza's duties were mostly domestic, while the enslaved males in the household may have worked around the house, on the farms, and in the Linden store. But Stephen's activities may have lent more mobility to their lives, particularly for males. Evidence suggests that enslaved males during Nuckolls's Missouri sojourn had a measure of autonomy. Graysonite William M. Norman, who came to Missouri in 1855 with Ezra Nuckolls, got a clerking job located at Stephen's Sonora, Missouri, store and one of Nuckolls's "servants" drove him there in a carriage. It seems likely that Shack and other enslaved males who joined them later may have run errands and carried messages on their own, depending on Stephen Nuckolls's needs.[19]

Apologists for domestic slavery in the West abounded.[20] For instance, one Missouri newspaper offered this assessment: "Western people are always ready to assist their neighbors in time of need; and we think many crazy abolitionists would be cured of their nonsense if they would push their way to the West and see slavery as it exists, and not depend on what they hear. The slaves of the west are better cared for than a large portion of the white population in the East."[21]

Although no interviews or oral histories of former slaves exist for Atchison County, two WPA interviews were conducted with individuals in neighboring counties and can provide some perspective on the local Missouri culture in which Celia, Eliza, and Shack lived. One, ninety-three-year-old Aunt Sarah Waggoner of Savannah, Andrew County, Missouri, recalled in 1937 that in her youth she had migrated up to Missouri from Kentucky, an Upper South location. The trip took "six weeks to come with oxen."[22] Waggoner's enslavers were Mr. and Mrs. Jim Howard, and her mother, also enslaved by the Howards, had the surname Waggoner.

Like Celia and Eliza, Sarah was taken to Missouri before the Civil War, where she noted "Indians, buffalo, deer and quail was thick." She had only two dresses, a muslin one for Sunday and a work dress. Waggoner washed and cooked for the entire household, milked eight cows in the mornings, and had plenty to eat, albeit leftovers. She and her brother slept on a trundle bed in the kitchen. She also reported that she was sometimes hired out to work at other farms, "but we didn't get no money for dat ourselves. Dey drawed de wages."[23]

Church attendance was required, and Sarah washed her Sunday dress every Saturday. Thus attired, she went to "the white folks' church, and part of the time I was de only n—— gal there." She admitted that she was "whopped" but not "very often, 'cause I done my work bes' I could." Only Mr. Howard administered punishment, not his wife. She also recalled that she had a cousin named June who was "sold here at de courthouse door in Savannah. Him and another boy was sold down South."[24]

Another interviewee, Sarah Frances Shaw Graves, was from neighboring Nodaway County and was also Kentucky born. She gave her 1937 interview from her farm home near Skidmore. Described as "still rugged and healthy" at age eighty-seven, she welcomed the chance to talk. She related that her enslaver hired her out to another person, where she was whipped, sometimes "for no good reason." Unlike Sarah Waggoner, who never worked in the fields, Graves worked grueling days, stacking corn into shocks and carrying water for the field hands. Her mother and stepfather had a small plot they were allowed to tend on their own time, and they could sell the crop for some of their own money. But like Sarah Waggoner, she attended church.[25]

Graves related, "Some masters was good an' some was bad. My mama's master whipped his slaves for pastime. . . . I've had many a whippin', some I deserved, an' some I got for being blamed for doin' things the master's children did." Even though she said her master was not as bad as some, she went on to say he used a cat-o'-nine-tails for whipping, and she remembered having "stripes of blood" running down her back. But the worst whipping she ever received came from her "mistress," Emily Graves Crowdes, and she still had the marks on her body.[26]

Thus enslavement in northwest Missouri was a mix of domestic and field slavery. The area had no cotton or sugar fields, but life was hard nonetheless. There were fields to be broken, tilled, planted, and harvested, as well as the ever-present chores for those employed in the house. Punishment for infractions was usually swift and hard, and it seems likely this was the case for the Graysons as well.

But Stephen F. Nuckolls had not come west to be a yeoman farmer. In addition to his store, Stephen had his hand in a number of projects. Buying, renting, and selling real estate became the foundation of what would quickly amount to a small fortune. By 1850 he had acquired 514 acres in Atchison County, of which just 6 acres were improved, along with two horses, three mules, three "milch" cows, twenty-two swine, and fifty pounds of beeswax and honey. He had not yet planted any crops.[27]

As Celia and Eliza grew into teenagers, their responsibilities presumably increased. In addition to housework and minding children, they may have milked the cows, cared for the other animals, and assisted in tilling and hoeing the 6-acre plot of land, which was probably dedicated more to a large garden than to cash crops. Starting out in a new and still small town, it seems likely that Celia and Eliza lived in the same house as the Nuckolls family, perhaps sleeping in a trundle bed as Waggoner described, ready to watch over the small children throughout the day and night.

Their duties also grew in surroundings where few other enslaved people lived, making them more socially and economically dependent on the Nuckolls family than they would have been in Grayson County—a kind of "dependence through isolation."[28] With three to five enslaved persons in his household, Nuckolls was re-creating another smallholder "society with slaves" like the one he had known in Grayson County. In doing so, the Nuckolls family also extended their business and personal network. They had been intimately connected with the exercise of power in Grayson

County, maintaining slavery's place as a small but integral part of their society. During these early building years in Missouri, Stephen and his family members made powerful friends and accumulated large tracts of land. Stephen also expanded his holdings north into Iowa, buying large parcels of land near Hamburg.[29]

The family makeup was also changing. In 1852 Stephen and Lucinda had a third child, a daughter named Alice, who joined young Billy and Virginia Ann in the household. But not long after Alice was born, Virginia Ann died at age two.[30] It was a sad group, which probably included the Graysons, that attended the funeral at the newly established Elmwood Cemetery, perched on a hill south of town. Alice joined Virginia Ann there in August 1854. Lucinda accompanied Stephen on a buying trip the next month, writing home, "How could I stay and no Alice there?"[31]

In 1854, even with his new stores prospering and his family settling in, Stephen Nuckolls's attention was drawn farther west. Everyone was talking about the Nebraska bill that would open the territory west of the Missouri River for settlement, and he wanted in on the action. His brother-in-law Harvey Gordon Bourne, by then living in Sidney, Iowa, wrote a letter to his brothers Stephen and Alexander Bourne, back in Grayson County, with all the news, including the imminent opening of Nebraska Territory. Harvey Bourne mentioned old Fort Kearny, which became the site of Nebraska City:

> It is said to be a great country and there is more excitement about it than any other one thing in this country. Old Fort Carney is opisite Sidney [Iowa] 12 miles distant there will be a Town there of some importance perhaps. . . . I have a claim adjoining the Fort. I cannot hold it only by what we term Club Law that is the neighbors agree among themselves that if a man will do or have $60 Worth of work done on his clame annually they will protect him and keep his clame from being jumped.[32]

He went on to explain that he had no intention of actually settling on this claim. He would give the land to Alexander if his brother would come west, otherwise he would "sell it to some one who has more Money than Brains." While Bourne clearly wanted to remain in Iowa, and "flip" his Nebraska land, his brother-in-law Stephen Nuckolls began to plan for bigger things. He would make Nebraska City his home. As Bourne's letter shows, people were already staking claims, even before the territory was officially open. Nuckolls would position himself to become a major landowner to profit from the coming inflow of settlers.[33]

The potential opening for Nebraska settlement also encouraged more chain migration. Back in Grayson County, there was a "great excitement about the advantages" of Nebraska Territory. Stephen's brothers Heath and Houston, as well as his uncle William B. Hail, had come to Missouri and planned to cross into Nebraska as soon as it opened. Stephen's married sisters had also migrated: Polly and her husband, Wrice D. Schooler, to Missouri and Frances and her husband, Harvey G. Bourne, to Iowa. Ezra's brother-in-law Ira Coltrane wrote to Ezra in Missouri to report that Stephen's uncle Fielden L. Hail "thinks he has got the Nebraska fever, as it is called here, but whether it will terminate mortally I can not tell."[34]

What Bourne's letter home in 1854 did not mention was the controversy surrounding what was known as the Nebraska bill—a controversy that centered on the extension of slavery into the territories. In fact, the question of slavery haunted Nebraska Territory from its inception. After the Mexican War, Pennsylvania senator David Wilmot put forward an unsuccessful bill that echoed the old Northwest Ordinance that "neither slavery nor involuntary servitude shall ever exist in any part" of territory obtained with congressional funds. Southerners were predictably against it. Democrats then backed the idea of nonintervention put forth by presidential candidate from Michigan Lewis Cass, which was a form of vague popular sovereignty.[35]

But Northerners and Southerners each interpreted nonintervention in their own way. Northerners assumed that territories could prohibit slavery immediately upon organization, while Southerners thought slavery would be allowed during the territorial period. As historian Stephen Maizlish notes, the Northern position would "block slavery from gaining a foothold from which it could not be easily removed." The Southern construal would let slavery become established before the issue was subjected to popular vote.³⁶ To avert a crisis over the extension of slavery as the country expanded, Kentucky senator Henry Clay introduced resolutions designed to mitigate the situation, albeit without clarifying the territorial conundrum.³⁷

In the Compromise of 1850, Congress admitted the state of California into the Union, established the territory of Utah, and established boundaries for the state of Texas. The compromise also ended the traffic in human bondage in the District of Columbia and then enacted its most controversial provision: amendments and supplements to the Fugitive Slave Law of 1793.

Since that time, Northern states had enacted "personal liberty laws" that allowed alleged escaped slaves a trial by jury. At the same time, some jurisdictions prohibited local officials from helping with the return of "fugitive slaves." In 1842 the U.S. Supreme Court ruled in *Prigg v. Pennsylvania* that states did not have to offer aid in hunting and capturing slaves. Southern states had been in an uproar over the situation, arguing that their due property rights should be upheld everywhere in the United States.

Congress adopted Clay's proposals to amend the 1793 law in ways that favored the Southern position. The 1850 Fugitive Slave Law upheld the idea that people who "owed service" to masters and fled from their obligations, whether indentured servants or enslaved individuals, could be followed into free states and apprehended. Rather than settling the situation, the law exacerbated the ideological impasse over the extension of slavery into the rapidly expanding West.³⁸

The 1850 refinements allowed the appointment of federal commissioners with the power to issue warrants for freedom seekers' arrest without due process. Black people accused of being escapees would be brought to a hearing before a court, judge, or commissioner, who could issue a certificate establishing proof of identity and allow these people to be taken back to the state or territory from which they had fled. The accused could not testify, and local officials who failed to arrest a "runaway" bondsperson could be fined $1,000. Thus officials in free states and in the territories would be legally obligated to assist slave catchers, canceling the personal liberty laws that many states had adopted.³⁹

Because slaveholders or their agents only had to give an affidavit to capture an alleged bondsperson, the law resulted not only in the arrest and rendition of freedom seekers but also in the kidnapping of free Blacks into slavery. Northerners, even those who were tolerant of slavery in the South, resented being forced to cooperate with "slave hunting." The law subjected anyone who hindered the arrest of fugitives, harbored them, aided them, or attempted to rescue them from custody to substantial fines and even imprisonment.[40]

The general response from Southern states was predictably favorable. Upon the act's passage, the Georgia convention declared that "the perpetuity of the Union depends upon the faithful execution of the Fugitive Slave Law."[41] However, not all Southerners agreed on the political strategy. As one proslavery Southern editor pointed out, the new law would lead to "increased hatred of slavery at home and abroad by its 'hard features and the barbarous enforcement of them.'"[42]

Giving voice to the opposition, Ohio senator Joshua R. Giddings railed that lawmakers were justifying their acts with talk of saving the Union from imminent danger: "To Save the Union, we annexed Texas," with "fifty thousand square miles of territory . . . delivered over to Texas and to slavery; to 'save the union' the people of the free States have been compelled to become slave catchers; and we are now told that 'to save the Union' this infamous law must be kept in force." Giddings predicted that the nation would soon have "but two political parties," a party of slavery and a party that "will contend for the emancipation of the free States and this Government from the control of the Slave Power."[43]

It was in this context that debate began on what became known as the Nebraska bill. Would the provisions of the Northwest Ordinance of 1787 apply to Kansas and Nebraska? The ordinance had prohibited slavery in the Northwest Territories: Ohio, Indiana, Michigan, Illinois, Wisconsin, and parts of Minnesota. As to governance, the ordinance had declared that when a territory had five thousand male voters, it could elect a territorial legislature and send a nonvoting delegate to Congress. The magic number for application to statehood had been sixty thousand inhabitants.

Others looked to the Missouri Compromise. Missouri had been part of the Louisiana Purchase, where slavery had long been legal. When Missouri applied for statehood in 1819, the controversial question of slavery's extension—a question that dominated the political landscape as the nation continued its westward march—once again arose. The Missouri controversy turned what had been an East-West debate over slavery into a North-South clash of ideologies. Both Northern restrictionists and Southern expansionists understood that slavery's future was at stake, not only in the West but in the Union itself. Then a young congressman, Kentuckian Henry Clay, worked on what would become the famous Missouri Compromise, barring slavery in the former Louisiana Purchase above Missouri's southern boundary at the 36°30' parallel, balancing Missouri's entrance into the Union as a slave state with Maine's entrance as a free state.[44]

By the 1850s the next logical step in western expansion seemed to make the passage of the Nebraska bill inevitable. What would become Kansas and Nebraska Territories lay above this parallel, and in theory, their territories would not allow enslavement. But Southerners once again reopened the question, asserting they had every right to migrate to the West with their property as other Americans did. With slave states dissatisfied with the Missouri Compromise, debate over the terms of Nebraska Territory's creation ensued. As usual, slavery was the sticking point, blocking prospects for the Nebraska bill's quick passage.

Illinois senator Stephen Douglas, full of presidential ambitions and with westward railroad expansion in his sights, loomed large in the discussion, promoting popular sovereignty as a solution to the debate and delay over the Nebraska bill. In 1848 he had proposed simply extending the 36°30' parallel, but that proposal went down in defeat. This time Douglas hoped that the right to self-determination would be a workable compromise to facilitate the creation of Kansas and Nebraska Territories. Under the theory of popular sovereignty, the people who lived in the territories would decide whether their jurisdiction would be slave or free.[45]

Stephen Douglas's proposal would effectively repeal the Missouri Compromise. It was alarming to many people because it opened up the possibility of "slave power" extending far into the North as well as into the West. A manifesto published in January 1854, the "Appeal of the Independent Democrats," asked whether slavery would be permitted in Nebraska, asserting that the bill would convert the territories "into a dreary region of despotism, inhabited by masters and slaves."[46]

In Linden, Stephen Nuckolls and his extended family and friends were also discussing the issues. The Graysons were likely listening carefully to all the conversations about Kansas and Nebraska that consumed the white people around them. It would have been clear to them that if Stephen Nuckolls took them across the river, it would be under the condition of slavery. Were they about to move once again? If so, what would their status be?

{ 3 }

The Opening of Kansas and Nebraska Territories

While the Kansas-Nebraska Act consumed politicians at the national level, the debate swirled among local movers and shakers in Iowa and Missouri. In late 1853 and into early 1854, citizens of Iowa and Missouri met in both Andrew County and St. Joseph, Missouri, to call for opening Nebraska Territory to settlement. Stephen Nuckolls attended the meetings, along with his friends Hiram P. Bennet, Allen A. Bradford, and Charles H. Cowles, all of whom subsequently moved to Nebraska City. Another future Nebraska City resident, Missouri enslaver Charles F. Holly, chaired the committee on resolutions and proposed language stating, "The emigrants in the territories ought to receive the same protection to property that they enjoyed in the states from which they emigrated."[1]

Everyone understood that Holly's reference to property included enslaved people. The effort was reminiscent of the period when Indiana and Illinois opened for white settlement in 1800, with proslavery leaders and settlers raising the same question. One candidate for Indiana's territorial legislature, John Hadden, stated that he backed "the emigration of citizens of any part of the United States, with any property they are permitted to possess." Thus even in areas where the Northwest Ordinance ruled, efforts to extend slavery had been ongoing and persistent, and enslavers looking west in 1854 continued to assert their right to bring all their "property" with them. Despite the precedents set by the Northwest Ordinance and the Missouri Compromise, the expansion of slavery into other areas remained unresolved. The same challenges about citizens' rights to bring their property into new territories would be repeated and antislavery precedents tested at every turn.[2]

The group that met in northern Missouri echoed the property rights pushback facing the federal government at each new territory's establish-

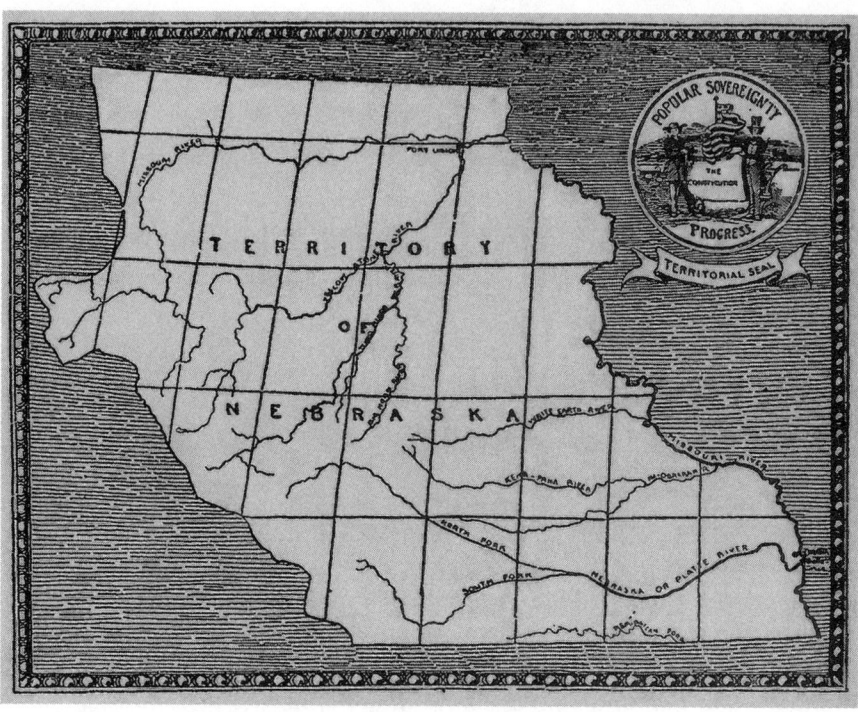

9. Map of Nebraska Territory. From Troup, *Once upon a Time in Nebraska*. Wikimedia Commons.

ment. However, even among this sympathetic group, the resolution stalled. Cowles, who was from Linden, Missouri, later recalled that at the St. Joseph meeting, they spent all night debating Holly's resolution about slavery. They decided to leave the issue unresolved because the committee was "nearly equally divided" on the question. Cowles said the group did not realize that they "were making a small ripple in the tidal wave which was soon to sweep over the bloody plains of historic Kansas, and finally culminating in a national wide-spread fratricidal strife."[3]

Despite the group's hesitation that night in passing a resolution that would explicitly assert settlers' rights to hold people as property, what became known as the St. Joseph Convention, representing the "people of northwestern Missouri, western Iowa and Nebraska Territory," passed resolutions similar to those discussed in Andrew County. They endorsed the popular sovereignty solution to the slavery question, as open-ended as it was. The resolutions decried the "agitation of the slavery question" that was preventing the Nebraska bill from smooth passage. The citizens noted that the controversy was "fatal to the best interests of Nebraska itself, and even threatening the harmony, if not the perpetuity of the whole Union."[4]

With the goal of Union harmony established, the following resolution stated "that in organizing Nebraska territory all who are now or may hereafter settle there should be protected in all their rights, leaving questions of local policy to be settled by the citizens of the territory when they form a state government."[5] The old Northern policy of slavery's containment to the South in hopes that it would gradually disappear was at stake. For those who attended the St. Joseph convention, all they needed was enough Southerners to move into these areas to ensure slavery's continuance.

While Congress continued to debate, Hiram P. Downs, a former sergeant at old Fort Kearny, acquired 160 acres of land surrounding the fort through the Preemption Act of 1841. This act allowed squatters who were already living on federal land to purchase the land they lived on. Knowing the site was ideal for development, Downs turned around and sold at least half his claim to Stephen Nuckolls.[6] The parcel encompassed the old military blockhouse and site of the fort, and on December 20, 1853, the Table Creek post office opened there for business, with Iowa ferryman John Boulware as postmaster. Seeking an early advantage to obtain the best property, Nuckolls and his friends planned to start building almost at once—technically squatting—with the assumption that their efforts would soon be a done deal.

In addition to encouraging building, Nuckolls was already establishing ties to expand his mercantile business into his new environs.[7] However, while he was on a buying trip to St. Louis for goods to be used in the new territory, Hiram Downs wrote to warn him that if whites settled on what was still Indian land, they would be ordered off, so Nuckolls returned early.[8] The area surrounding old Fort Kearny was still part of unceded Otoe-Missouria Indian lands, while north of the Platte, the Omaha people held sway. While discussion of slavery delayed the Nebraska bill, the government negotiated treaties with these tribes. The treaties needed to be finalized and signed before whites would be legally allowed to settle in the territory.[9]

Even before the treaties were signed, white people began crossing the Missouri to lodge claims and start building. Cowles was among the squatters and built a store in Table Creek. The squatters barely avoided eviction by delaying official efforts to dislodge them.

When Congress passed the Kansas-Nebraska Act in 1854, Nebraska Territory commanded a vast expanse that included the Dakotas, Wyoming, Montana, and part of what became Colorado. The issue of slavery was left to territorial governors and the people of the territory to decide. The debates over the Kansas-Nebraska Act had been fierce and disruptive, dividing Democrats and spurring the creation of the Republican Party. Historian G. G. Van Deusen wrote, "More than any other measure passed or threatened during the decade, this bill was responsible for the Civil War."[10]

Stephen Nuckolls and his relatives crossed the Missouri River from their Atchison County, Missouri, lands to take advantage of the opportunities that only a new territory could offer. On March 4, 1854, Table Creek changed its name to Nebraska City. According to the 1854 territorial census, Stephen had brought three enslaved persons with him to what was then known as Pierce County (changed to Otoe in 1855): no doubt Celia, Eliza, and Shack. His brother Heath Nuckolls is listed with two enslaved persons, and their brother-in-law Wrice Schooler brought four.[11] Thus Nebraska Territory tolerated slavery from the beginning. And the Southern strategy of gaining a foothold for enslavement during the territorial period had begun.

In addition to establishing Nebraska City, buying land, platting town lots for sale, and opening a store, Stephen Nuckolls is said to have immediately sought influence by offering a "wagon" to transport the first governor of Nebraska Territory, South Carolinian Francis Burt, to Bellevue, Nebraska, where his administration would be located.[12] The forty-seven-year-old Burt was spare and handsome, with a strong, square jaw and an aquiline profile that added to his air of distinction. An experienced politician in the old Southern tradition, he had served in the South Carolina state legislature and had voted in favor of the infamous 1832 nullification convention, which recognized a state's right to nullify—or defy—federal law in defense of slavery. In 1844 Burt's brother Armistead served in Congress. In response to the almost constant Northern petitions to abolish slavery, Armistead

Burt had poured out his scorn, saying, "The South would regard it as a declaration of war, and she would act accordingly." Francis Burt possessed solid proslavery credentials, and he brought at least one enslaved "female domestic" with him to Nebraska Territory.[13]

On the way to take up his new post, Burt had fallen sick in St. Louis. The further trip to Nebraska Territory did not improve his health. He arrived with some fanfare in October 1854, but two days after taking his oath of office, he died.[14] Despite Burt's and Nuckolls's differing opinions on where the territorial capital should be located (Nuckolls backed Nebraska City instead of Bellevue), Burt's death still may have been a blow to the Nuckolls family and their friends, given his firm proslavery stance.

The secretary of Nebraska Territory, Iowan Thomas B. Cuming, became the acting territorial governor. Cuming had substantial business and property interests in Omaha and immediately ordered a territorial census—a difficult job because the land surveys were not all complete. As people poured in, it was almost impossible to determine who was a legitimate resident. Some of the settlers originally credited to Nebraska were actually residing in Kansas.

At the same time, Iowa residents were eyeing what was happening next door. When he was running for governor, James Grimes had campaigned against the Kansas-Nebraska Act because it annulled the Missouri Compromise. He warned that Iowa could be bordered "on two sides by slave States." Without the 36°30' parallel drawn to protect the North, he predicted, "We shall be intersected with underground railroads and continually distracted by slave-hunts." In his December 1854 inaugural address, Grimes returned to the theme: "It becomes the State of Iowa—the only free child of the Missouri Compromise—to let the world know that she values the blessings that compromise has secured to her, and that she never will consent to become a party to the nationalization of slavery."[15]

While Nuckolls and other settlers had been positioned to stake their claims and establish residence, Sen. Stephen A. Douglas tried to calm continuing fears over the slavery question in Nebraska. He predicted that "when settlers rush in—when labor becomes plenty . . . it is worse than folly to think of its being a slaveholding country."[16] Douglas admitted that slaves "were then kept in Nebraska" but pointed out that states where enslavement had been legal during the colonial period, such as Massachusetts, Connecticut, Rhode Island, New Jersey, and Pennsylvania, had eventually emancipated enslaved people, while "no free state had adopted slavery." He expected Nebraska would follow the same course. His belief that popular sovereignty would work appeared to be sincere.[17]

Douglas's pronouncements were not the end of the discussion, nor did they calm the roiling waters over the fate of the West. An editorial appearing in the *Nebraska City News* in May 1855 challenged the airy dismissal of slavery's prospects there. The piece announced that slavery had arrived in Nebraska, contrasting the southern portion of the territory with the north. Many Missourians and Virginians had come into that area with their slaves and were "among our most enterprising and popular citizens." It noted, "Though they say but little in regard to the matter, they are bent upon establishing the 'peculiar institution' in Southern Nebraska."[18]

The editorial further stated that those who promulgated stereotypes of Southerners as "indolent and without any ambition, are silly-pated, foolish men.... We have seen as much enterprise in Nebraska, which originated in Southern heads ... as we have of Northern undertakings." The editors rejected the idea that slavery was impossible in Nebraska because of its geography; "on the contrary, we see no impossibility about it." Clearly Nuckolls and his allies were the main subjects of the piece, picked up by newspapers across the country. And the presence of Celia, Eliza, Shack, and the others enslaved in Nebraska City confirmed the editor's opinion that enslavement was possible.[19]

The editors of the *Nebraska City News* were not alone in questioning Nebraska's future. Far from dismissing slavery in Nebraska as a fantasy, a writer for the *Springfield Illinois Journal* asked some "solid citizens" of Missouri whether they would take slaves into the new territory and published their reply: "Of course we are, we must be great fools to make all this fuss with the North, if we didn't mean to make slave territory of it." The Missourians concluded that if Congress allowed them to take slaves into the territory, it would be "bound to protect us."[20] On the other side of the issue, the Northern *Biddeford Maine and Eastern Journal* opined that the Kansas-Nebraska Act was an "attempt to smuggle slavery into the territory," a view shared by many. Thus people on both sides agreed that slavery was possible in Nebraska, despite many official avowals to the contrary.[21]

The Kansas-Nebraska Act provided for Nebraska Territory's organization with a legislative assembly composed of a council (somewhat like an upper legislative house) elected for two-year terms and a house of representatives elected for one year. The council had thirteen members and the original house had twenty-six. In May 1854 Stephen Nuckolls persuaded lawyer Hiram Bennet to leave Glenwood, Iowa, for Nebraska City and promptly put him up for election to the territorial council while Bennet was still just boarding in the town. Bennet and another friend of Stephen's, Allen Bradford, became the first representatives for Otoe County (called Pierce in 1854) on the territorial council. Bennet later admitted that he owed his position "more to Stephen F. Nuckolls than to the fact of any long or well-known residence in Nebraska prior to the election."[22]

Although the 1854 census showed a greater number of people living south of the Platte, acting governor Cuming gave the territory north of the Platte seven councilmen and fourteen representatives and the south portion six councilmen and twelve representatives.[23] To add to the South Platters' complaints, the twenty-five-year-old Cuming then boldly announced that the first territorial legislature would be held in Omaha. This was one of the first instances, but not the last, in which a territorial governor imposed his will in stark contrast to the spirit of popular sovereignty. Bellevue's *Nebraska Palladium* editors called Cuming dishonorable and argued that Washington "never intended the Capital to be located by the Governor, but by the PEOPLE, the true and only sovereign. It was for the Governor to confirm the will of the people and not to defeat it."[24]

The next year, census returns still indicated a larger population south of the Platte, with sixteen hundred more people. The *Nebraska City News* complained, "Squatter sovereignty makes poor headway against the oligarchic rule of a few Government officers who have been sent here." The editorial railed about bribery, "official cupidity, and stupidity" in locating the capital north of the Platte, noting that the thirteen-member territorial council had six members from the area south of the Platte River, while the those living north of the Platte River had seven, even though the South Platters were in the majority.[25]

Unable to block the North Platters' influence on the capital's location, Nuckolls had other political cards in play during this early period. Joining his friends Hiram Bennet and Allen Bradford on the territorial council was a Georgia-born Democratic ally, Martin Riden. Stephen's younger brother Lafayette Nuckolls was elected to serve in the legislature, representing one of the other original counties, Cass. Stephen's uncle William B. Hail, who had been a slave catcher in Grayson County, was elected as a representative from Pierce County along with Charles Cowles.[26]

President Franklin Pierce's appointee as chief justice in Nebraska Territory, Judge Fenner Ferguson of Bellevue, took Hiram Bennet and Lafayette Nuckolls into another room to swear slightly altered oaths, dropping the salient parts regarding their eligibility because the newly arrived Bennet's legal residence was in question and Lafayette was not even twenty years of age.[27] When waiting to be sworn in, someone asked Lafayette Nuckolls how old he was. His answer: "Ask my constituents, as Henry Clay once said."[28] Although Lafayette was seated in the legislature, complaints about his eligibility persisted, and he resigned at the end of the first session. But with so many allies and relatives in the territorial government in 1855–56, a cycle of political influence and patronage was well in place, in many respects to the advantage of Stephen Nuckolls.

Nuckolls's influence did not go without public notice. In 1855 the *Omaha Nebraskian* charged that slaveholders Nuckolls, Hail, and federal appointee Judge Edward Randolph Harden, in addition to writing letters of endorsement for their favored proslavery candidates, also provided free dinners and whiskey to buy votes. The article jeered the "distinguished personages," one "all the way from Georgia [Harden], with his one N—— and stragglers from the F. F. V. [First Families of Virginia], with their several N——s," who were ensuring that Hiram P. Bennet would be elected. The *Nebraskian* added that Bennet, too, had been liberal with dinners, cigars, and apples and asked, "What think you of this, ye sober steady citizens of the Territory? Are free dinners and drinks going to buy your votes?" A year later a Nebraska Citian complained that "nearly all the towns are owned by proslavery men, who give employment to a great many of the lowest class of citizens, and on election days put tickets into their hands, and send them to the polls like sheep to the shambles."[29]

In late 1854 President Pierce had appointed Arkansas slaveholder Mark W. Izard as the second governor of Nebraska Territory to replace the late Burt. Izard was also sympathetic to the proslavery stance. Whether he brought enslaved people with him to Nebraska Territory is uncertain, but Washington DC's antislavery *National Era* newspaper reported the presence of enslaved people at his inaugural ball with some consternation.[30]

Another important federal appointee was Edward Randolph Harden, who became the district judge for Nebraska's Second District. Harden's correspondence makes no mention of Stephen F. Nuckolls during the judge's residence in the territory. He was unimpressed by Nebraska City's leaders and citizens, saying they were "of a different cast from those to whom I have been accustomed."[31]

Indeed, Harden may have been a little shocked by his new society's manners. His first court in early 1855 was held in a log house owned by Hiram Downs. During the proceedings, lawyers Hiram P. Bennet and Oliver P. Mason "engaged in physical combat," albeit without bloodshed. Stephen Nuckolls later recalled with some amusement that this was Judge Harden's introduction to "Western habits."[32]

Although Harden and Nuckolls were both Southerners, they were from different parts of society. Stephen Nuckolls was from Appalachia, while Harden was from the aristocratic old guard of Virginia planters. Indeed, Stephen's booster mentality and his Town Company, chain of stores, sawmill, quartz mill, and freighting company exhibited all the energy and ambition of the mercantile middle class—pursuits that many of the Southern old guard ascribed to grasping Yankees. Judge Harden, described as courteous, agreeable and affable in conversation, was a political ally.[33] He was probably polite to Nuckolls in his public dealings, while maintaining his personal distance.

The Graysons no doubt followed the local and territorial debates over slavery while noting Nuckolls's influence and political clout in their local area. The situation may have reminded them of how the Nuckolls clan operated in Old Grayson. Whatever their thinking, Celia, Eliza, and Shack surely kept their ears open as they worked hard, biding their time.

The Grayson trio had been in Nebraska Territory for a little over a year when they had happy news—Ezra Nuckolls and his family had arrived safely in Atchison County, Missouri, along with some of the Black Graysons. Ezra had been preparing to move to the Far West for over a year. The company left Grayson County on September 8. Ezra later wrote, "We were 62 days on the road from Elk Creek had 43 persons and 10 wagons 6 carriages in our croud."[34]

Just four days after his arrival in Atchison County, Ezra sold three horses and one of the wagons he had brought from Grayson. He was pleased with the move and happy that he received $475 for what had cost him only $400 in Grayson. He was already boosting his new position out west when he wrote back to Virginia, "I shall have more grain from the rent of my land than I ever raised in any one year in Grayson."[35]

Stephen Nuckolls had maintained his business in Missouri even as he installed himself in Nebraska. Ezra wrote that his brother-in-law William Hail and his son Stephen had already planted forty acres for him in the same field that Wrice Schooler had rented the year before—a field that now belonged to Ezra. Stephen also employed one of the young men who accompanied Ezra's group from Grayson, William M. Norman, in his Sonora, Missouri, store. Norman called it "a pleasant situation on the bank of the Missouri River." It is clear that Stephen Nuckolls was becoming the leader of a sprawling family enterprise.[36]

For Celia and Eliza, the arrival of the extended family group nearby after seven long years would have meant a joyful reunion with their own family members. Following the practice of bringing younger enslaved people west, Ezra and Lucinda brought Mary, age twenty-six; Rebecca, twenty-five; Henry, twenty; Calvin, thirteen; Jane, nine; Malinda, nine; Charles Raleigh, five; Clayton, three; and baby Eliza Caroline, who died during the trip. This group may have also included an enslaved man named Shade, who was likely Celia and Eliza's brother.[37]

Ezra was fifty-seven years old and Lucinda forty-nine when they moved to Atchison County. Despite being older, Ezra quickly became a leading citizen. He helped survey and plat the town of Rock Port, which eventually became the county seat.[38] Other family members who came in the larger group began to fan out into nearby areas. Stephen's brother Columbus "Lum" Nuckolls moved to Mills County, Iowa, starting a business in Pacific

City to coordinate with the family holdings in Nebraska City; Sidney and Hamburg, Iowa; and Linden and Sonora, Missouri.[39]

In 1855 the Nebraska territorial census shows that of the immediate Nuckolls family, only Stephen remained in Nebraska City, with his three enslaved persons.[40] In 1856 he was listed as S. F. Nuckolls, with four slaves. The addition was probably Shade, lent by or hired from Ezra.[41] Thus Celia, Eliza, and Shack formed the nucleus of Nuckolls's "servant" household in Nebraska City, with the occasional addition of Shade to help out.[42]

The census numbers do not mean that other enslaved people were not present in Nebraska City at different times. For instance, Stephen's brother-in-law Wrice Schooler had moved back across the river to Missouri with his enslaved people, but the Otoe County deed index shows that Schooler still owned considerable property in the area. By 1857 Houston Nuckolls resided in Richardson County, where he, Heath, and Stephen, along with other investors, organized the Yankton Town Company. The Nuckolls family members may have shuffled enslaved people back and forth across the river to work as needed. This strategy could have kept slaves' residential status in question if they spent as much time in Missouri, where slavery was legal, as they did in Nebraska Territory, where their status was ambiguous.[43]

Celia and Eliza may have been saddened by the removal of their likely sister Edith and her family from Nebraska City. Ezra Nuckolls had transferred Edith to his oldest daughter, Polly, possibly at the time of her marriage to Wrice Schooler in 1838. After the Schoolers returned to nearby Atchison County, it is likely that visits back and forth were fairly frequent when the river was open. Likewise, Stephen's brother Houston, after living in Missouri with regular travel back to Nebraska and Iowa for various business concerns, settled near the St. Stephens area in Richardson County, south of Nebraska City. Houston may have also had enslaved people in his household, but if so, they never made it into a census count. Moving enslaved people back and forth between Nebraska and Missouri would have been easy for Houston, who obtained ferry licenses for St. Stephens and the now-defunct town of Yankton, opposite Holt County, Missouri.[44]

Historians have noted that mobility among the enslaved was a common feature of life along the Kansas-Missouri border, and this may have also been common along the Nebraska-Missouri border.[45] The continued presence of Celia, Eliza, Shack, Shade, and other enslaved people on the borders between Nebraska, Missouri, and Iowa suggests that slavery in Nebraska, as it had been in northern Missouri, was "an extension of the small-scale slaveholding system that existed elsewhere in the Upper South."[46]

Celia, Eliza, and Shack were brought into Nebraska Territory in its earliest days. Joined from time to time by Shade, they were among the enslaved that Stephen Douglas admitted were kept in Nebraska. Whether willing or reluctant, these Black pioneers shouldered the hardships of building in a new country. They may have shared the Nebraska City southern contingent's view of Nebraska as a place where slavery could and would be accommodated; seeing "no impossibility about it."[47] Thus they lived and worked in bondage on the frontier, earning the dubious recognition of being the first recorded enslaved residents of Nebraska Territory.

{ 4 }

Life in Nebraska City, a Missouri River Town

When Celia and Eliza first clambered off the ferry onto the boat landing to survey their new Nebraska City home in 1854, they would have observed a few rough-hewn warehouses along the riverbank. They may have winced at hearing the screeching flocks of Carolina parakeets that inhabited the Missouri bottoms. Walking up and to the right along the Missouri, they would have crossed a creek, then made a left turn on a new road cut a hundred feet wide that led uphill from the river, a road that would become the community's main thoroughfare. They would have taken in the "city" blocks dotted here and there with wooden shanties before arriving at their first residence—the old military hospital. These quarters were temporary, a place to live and work until the two-story brick house Nuckolls was building on the corner of Fifth Street and Main Street (later Central Avenue) was ready.[1] How Celia and Eliza, as well as Lucinda Bourne Nuckolls, felt about living in such a busy location can only be surmised.

An 1868 Nebraska City map shows the two-story residence with small additions extending into the back of the lot, probably the additions Lucinda wrote home about in 1855: "Wee are building an addition to our House dinening room and kitchen we will have a very nice house when it is finished." An urban slavery study in Wilmington, North Carolina, indicates that in larger houses, walls shielded the "kitchen and cooks from dining room and diners," while outdoor or back staircases "allowed slaves to carry baskets of laundry and buckets of coal from the ground level to the parlor and bedrooms above." When the Graysons lived there, a small orchard had been planted behind the house. In all probability, there was also a kitchen garden with the orchard—a space where they may have been able to visit with passersby.[2]

10. Nebraska City Courthouse mural by Frank Zimmerer, 1952. Photo by author. Used with permission from Nebraska City Chamber of Commerce.

Given Stephen Nuckolls's prominence, the living spaces inside for the white people were probably comfortable and even luxurious. When the house was spared in an 1860 fire, it was described as one of the town's most "splendid." It seems likely that the front rooms were well-appointed public rooms where people who called might sit while visiting. Where the Nuckollses' enslaved people slept can only be guessed, perhaps an attic garret, a back room, or trundle beds in the kitchen or nursery.[3]

When the residence was complete is unknown, but it was likely by autumn. The family may have been living in the old military hospital in July 1854, when the fledgling settlement celebrated the "glorious Fourth." The Nuckolls clan was no doubt in attendance, and the Graysons were probably present as well. Early settler J. W. Pearman recalled the wonderful outdoor barbecue they enjoyed, with arbors provided for eating, speeches, and dancing. He reported "at least one thousand persons present," with "most of the white people" being from Atchison County, Missouri, and Fremont County, Iowa. Pearman added that the Nebraska City area "furnished many whites and a host of Indians," probably the local Otoe and Missouria peoples who had recently signed the treaties allowing for the creation of Nebraska and Kansas Territories.[4]

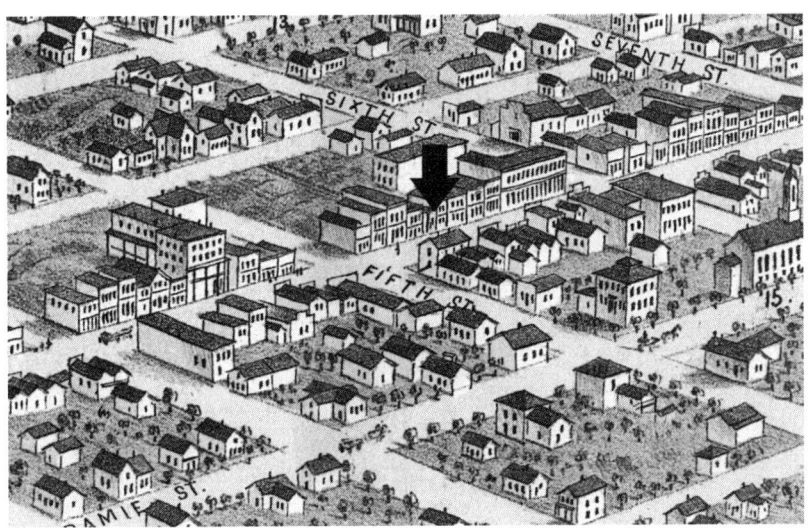

11. Close-up of map showing Nuckolls residence from 1868. A. Ruger and Merchant's Lithographing Company, *Bird's Eye View of the City of Nebraska City, Otoe County, Nebraska 1868*, Library of Congress, LCCN 73693494, https://www.loc.gov/item/73693494/.

Fourth of July celebrations were traditionally large public events in the United States. But the scale of this occasion may have been novel for those from the thinly settled "Old Grayson." Pearman enthused, "Dancing and eating commenced at about one o'clock of the 4th" and ended with a "'big Injun dance' on the evening of the 6th." Four days after the grand celebration, Stephen Nuckolls and his friend Allen Bradford drove the first stake for Nebraska City's survey and predicted that in a few years Nebraska City would have "at least twenty thousand inhabitants."[5]

Aspirations aside, there was little about the settlement that resembled a town, much less a city, when they first lived there, despite Stephen Nuckolls's boast in August 1854 that "Nebraska City is improving fast. There are about 100 families in the vicinity."[6] How the families were living he did not say. In the midst of plentiful deer and antelope, the settlement consisted of "about half a dozen rudely constructed houses and but one store." Indians were a common sight, often camping nearby and visiting what settlers deemed their "old hunting grounds." Celia and Eliza could not have failed to notice that the undulating ocean of prairie surrounding

Life in Nebraska City 61

their new home was what one settler called a "wild waste, where night was made hideous by the dismal howl of the wolf."[7]

Although the move from Virginia to northwest Missouri was almost certainly the most traumatic for Celia and Eliza, the move from Linden to Nebraska City presented its own set of challenges. After spending six years helping establish the family in Linden, the Nuckollses' enslaved people had to start over yet again in this new and raw environment. Now ages eighteen and sixteen, Celia and Eliza were more experienced after their Missouri sojourn and ready for what they would face. Still, many questions remained as they were uprooted once again. What would life be like in Nebraska City? Would they have more freedom of movement or less?

The timing of their move to Nebraska was fortuitous but deceptive, for the "winter of 1854–55 was so remarkably mild that everybody who had come to Nebraska, was thrown off his guard and imagined it enjoyed an Italian climate." A January 1855 arrival, Martin Riden from Georgia, wrote that the town was "thriving finely" and believed "there will be a great influx of immigration and business to this point next Spring." At the same time, he was shocked by the "rough-hewn set" and casual violence he had witnessed in the streets and hoped that the society would become "more refined." Despite the coarse society, he waxed eloquent over the "beautiful town sites."[8]

Stephen Nuckolls advertised those beautiful town sites in April 1855, predicting Nebraska City would be the "future emporium of Nebraska Territory." He extolled its advantageous situation on a "fine bluff," with a "picturesque view of the mighty Missouri," "excellent water, a temperate climate," and a rock landing for a regular steam ferry.[9]

By September 1855 the intense spring and summer building period had yielded results. Whereas a year before the settlement had scarcely more than one real building besides the blockhouse, one newspaper reported that Nebraska City could now "boast of near two hundred buildings, and an enterprising population of mechanics, professional men, merchants and laborers, with their shops and offices and stores, and a printing office."[10] The report may have stretched the truth or relied on quantity rather than quality, as another observer later noted that most of the structures were shacks with few buildings worthy of the name.[11]

12. Blockhouse where early press was located. Courtesy of Morton-James Public Library and Nebraska City Historical Society.

Also in 1855 Nuckolls's fellow Democrat J. Sterling Morton (who later established Arbor Day) was interested in editing the Nebraska City newspaper. Nuckolls had sponsored its first printing in Sidney, Iowa, in November 1854, making it one of Nebraska's first newspapers. He moved the press to Nebraska City soon after.[12] The newspaper office was in the second story of the fort's old blockhouse, overlooking the Missouri. According to Nuckolls, "Upon his [Morton's] first arrival with his estimable wife, they visited the printing office—finding Shack Grayson the sole person in charge."[13] What Nuckolls meant by "in charge" is unknown, as Shack's literacy at this time is in question. Morton accepted Nuckolls's offer of editing the *Nebraska City News* for a salary of $1,000 a year and made the move to Nebraska City. He probably continued to employ Shack, at least part-time.[14]

What was the atmosphere at the newspaper like for someone like Shack? He would have run errands, fed sheets into the printing press, and folded and packed newspapers, while Morton and later editors attended to reading, writing, and especially, visiting with patrons, gleaning all the news and subscribers they could find. Morton reminisced about his "untiring" work in the rough blockhouse alongside another editor, Welshman Thomas

Life in Nebraska City 63

Morton (no relation), overseeing what he called "the dawn of civilization on the west bank of the Missouri."[15]

In the newspaper office's close quarters, Shack would have overheard discussions and snatches of conversation that he could file away for later consideration. The debates about territorial policy that swirled throughout the region were hot topics, including efforts to pass laws outlawing slavery. Doubtless Shack would have shared this knowledge with Celia and Eliza. He may have also watered trees in Morton's orchard and helped plant seedlings, and he was almost certainly the enslaved person whose services one contemporary antislavery writer asserted that Nuckolls valued at "'one thousand dollars' per annum."[16] Whenever the Graysons were able to meet without white people around, in all likelihood they exchanged news both personal and political, helping one another gain their footing in new and challenging circumstances.

In the main, the Grayson sisters would have worked in the Nuckolls residence in town. Their duties would have been largely domestic, much as they had been in Linden. Now that they were older and stronger, their days may have also been more difficult than in Linden. They would have been responsible for laying the fire for the stove, preparing all or most of the meals, and scouring pots and pans. Scrubbing floors, dusting, and attending to any of Lucinda's needs were activities the two sisters may have split between them. Laundry was another task traditionally left to enslaved people. Most weekends, Celia and Eliza would have boiled water, then transferred it to washtubs, where they used washboards to scrub the clothes for the entire household. Starching and ironing bedclothes and other items would have consumed another large block of time. The work was hot and difficult, far from being light housework.[17]

Enslavement in a Small Frontier Town

What was the experience of the enslaved in Nebraska City? In addition to studying smallholders, historians have also begun to study enslavement in small towns as distinct from cities and rural landscapes. Celia, Eliza, Shack, and others hired out or living in Nebraska City were in a small frontier river town.[18] But Nebraska City was far from a sleepy backwater. Early settler Nahum Harwood recalled that for all Nebraska Missouri River towns, "the river boats and stages came in crowded and went away empty; hotels were full and crowded to the ridge pole; there were speculators on every hand, and prices of real estate were advancing by leaps and bounds."[19]

However, even after three years of vaunted growth, Nebraska City did not always impress, particularly when it came to women. A young Indiana girl, Mollie Dorsey, arrived in the spring of 1857 and commented that Nebraska City was "a nice name, but not much of a city." Her landlady, Mrs. Allen, warned the Dorsey family that the place was "full of gamblers, topers, and toughs of every description." Rude cabins and shanties still dominated the housing, with warehouses and stores scattered along Main Street. The town had so few women that the Dorsey women "could not step outside the door without being stared at by the loafers over at the hotel and the saloon."[20]

Dorsey's critique matches that of Ellen Kinney, who arrived in June 1858 to join her parents in Nebraska City after finishing her education back east. After hearing glowing reports, Kinney was a little surprised when she took her first tour, noting a "small one-storey hotel" and "the larger Frontier Hotel," among scattered and "indifferent buildings." She also mentioned passing the two-story brick Nuckolls residence before seeing the three-story bank, which Nuckolls also owned. After her tour, she asked her father where the town was.[21]

As she settled in, Kinney noted the rough mule whackers who crowded the noisy business district, and that as a consequence, "wives and daughters of the 'cultured class' rarely appeared on Main Street." But on Sundays, "the disorder and ribald jests of weekdays" that Kinney decried were absent, and the streets had a quiet dignity. The people out and about were well dressed as they headed to church services.[22]

For Celia, Eliza, Shack, and Shade, Nebraska City may have been particularly challenging. Grayson County and Linden, Missouri, did not have the same boomtown atmosphere Nebraska City did. Their Main Street home may not have been much of a sanctuary for either the Nuckolls family or for the Graysons. Celia and Eliza performed grueling domestic duties, with the constant sound of wagons clattering, oxen lowing, whips snapping, chains rattling, and men shouting during the migration season. Adding to the noise and pungent smell of sweat and dung, the lumbering wagons

Life in Nebraska City

would have churned up dust and mud, which no doubt seeped into their living quarters and contributed to their fight against dirt. Indeed, Lucinda later wrote to her brother, "You don't have any Idea how much dust blows in our house in one day our House in fronting South and the south wind is all ways blowing."[23] The hurly-burly atmosphere may have led to frayed nerves and occasional short tempers.

One question is how much freedom of movement Celia and Eliza may have had in the town. Few works have focused on slavery in small towns. Historian Lisa Tolbert's study of Franklin, Tennessee, concludes that small towns afforded more mobility to enslaved men than did rural locations. As female domestics, Celia and Eliza may not have had as much liberty in their movements. On the other hand, Shack Grayson probably enjoyed a good deal of freedom, as Tolbert's study suggests. He may have stopped for regular visits with other enslaved and free Blacks in moving from work at the press or on errands for Stephen or Lucinda Nuckolls. Shade, too, may have been a visible presence in the town. Later reports, although probably exaggerated to make Nebraska slavery look nonthreatening, mentioned that Shack and Shade were often seen hunting and fishing. Indeed, early recollections of slavery in Nebraska identified Shack and Shade by name, suggesting they were more visible, and therefore more familiar to the townspeople, than Celia and Eliza.[24]

Small-town environments also lacked the anonymity and isolation of farm life and even of larger urban areas. When Celia and Eliza were allowed to venture out, citizens no doubt knew who they were. They could not have wasted much time visiting without drawing attention and comment.

Although their surroundings would have affected their mobility and opportunities to socialize, the personalities of the individuals in the household likely had the greatest effect on the women, with the town's size exerting its own influence on the family's actions through the importance of reputation. Among the immediate family members, Stephen Nuckolls stands out. Aggressive and ambitious, he had high expectations for both quantity and quality of work. Quick tempered and bold, he probably did not shrink from corporal punishment. Yet with all his travel and activity, his attention was rarely focused on the home front. Thus Lucinda Bourne Nuckolls exerted the greatest control over Celia and Eliza's everyday lives. As

Diane Mutti Burke observes, women were "confined to the often-cramped quarters of small slaveholders' homes and lacked the space provided men in the fields and the greater community."[25] The domestic routines common to a small-town home would have colored Celia and Eliza's interactions with the Nuckolls family, creating further intimacy.

There are no contemporaneous reports of Lucinda's participation in the community, outside of being a founding member of the local Baptist church.[26] Stephen was not listed among the members along with his wife, which may have been of some concern to her. Lucinda may have experienced the same kind of "melancholy" that her sister-in-law Frances Nuckolls Bourne, close by in Sidney, Iowa, expressed in a letter home when her husband, Harvey, would not make his profession of faith: "Mother, I ask you not to let one day pass without asking God to give Harvey to see he is a sinner."[27]

Unfortunately, the early Nebraska newspapers have little social news, making it difficult to gauge whether Celia and Eliza had to serve large dinner parties. But even in the scant social news, Stephen and Lucinda Nuckolls are not mentioned as attendees at functions where they might be expected, such as the first inaugural ball given for Mark Izard.[28]

It may be that the Nuckollses were a bit clannish, with so many Virginia relatives nearby. Given local society's admitted roughness in the early years, the women may have remained somewhat sequestered. In all likelihood, Lucinda Nuckolls, and by extension Celia and Eliza, may have lived a very busy yet sheltered life, centered around the household. Indeed, Lucinda wrote, "I never stay away longer than three days without something is the matter that I cant leave home." In another note, she admitted, "I look so old and black," adding, "this is a hard country on women & children." An affectionate daughter, she always inquired after family members, sometimes adding greetings to family "both White and Black." She often longed to see her relatives, and without ever stating so, she may have suffered from homesickness.[29]

In addition to her participation in the Baptist church, Lucinda's main outside interest was in the sewing society, meeting every two weeks at private houses, with the money the ladies made going "towards building of the church." No doubt Celia and Eliza had extra tasks when Lucinda took her turn hosting the sewing circle. Despite her many "good neighbors," Lucinda often wrote that she was lonely.[30]

Whatever the reason, the Nuckolls family chose to miss social functions that one would normally expect a town leader and his wife to attend. Under these circumstances, would Lucinda have unburdened herself to Celia and Eliza when feeling homesick, lonely, or overwhelmed by the constant noise and activity? Might they have shared memories of Grayson County?[31]

Given Lucinda's longing to see her close relatives and friends in Grayson, Celia and Eliza's constant company may have provided psychological as well as physical relief as she met the challenges of setting up and keeping house in a frontier town. Another displaced Southerner in Nebraska City, Judge Edward Randolph Harden, wrote, "I am an exile from my native land … in an intemperate climate, without any society but my own thoughts, with no human but my old faithful servant to whom I can unbosom myself and reveal the workings of my mind."[32]

However, Lucinda Nuckolls was rarely alone, even if she was lonely. Offering a glimpse into the size of household that Celia and Eliza had to serve, Lucinda wrote to her brothers William and Richmond in November 1857, "[People] have been crossing the river every day, this winter there is but very little ice in it now the like has never bee known since I lived in the wist. Martha Anderson has been staying with me for the last six months wee also have four hurd boys, Mr. Wyatt, Reeves and two duck boys. Wyatt and Reeves are boath from Va."[33]

Thus the household that Celia and Eliza served went beyond the nuclear family, as hired people and relatives like Martha Anderson moved in and out. That Celia and Eliza shouldered much of the increased household burden is almost certain.[34] The inclusion of visiting Virginians along with other family workers may be one reason there are no reports of large dinner parties—the number of people to serve was already large enough.

When Lucinda did venture out to call on others or to shop, she probably did not go far without someone to accompany her. At times her companions must have been Celia or Eliza. Moreover, when Lucinda visited relatives in Iowa and Missouri, Celia and Eliza may have gone along, becoming familiar with the ferry crossings and travel conditions. If the sisters were allowed to make small autonomous trips, they could have met some of the other Black residents in the town. Moreover, for public gatherings and meetings, they may have been called on to serve along with other enslaved people, such as those that freighter Alexander Majors brought to town in the spring of 1858. Still, the town may not have had more than fifteen to twenty-five Black residents outside their family while they lived there. Their limited acquaintances and constant interactions with whites would have made a distinct Black society in the early years impossible.

As small-town living and individual personalities may give contours to Celia and Eliza's life in Nebraska City, Stephen Nuckolls's goal of establishing smallholder enslavement such as he had known in Virginia also had its effect. With such a mix of people from all over, whether immigrants, Southerners, or Northerners, he would have been careful to present domestic slavery in as good a light as possible. Small towns and neighborhoods could provide a social shield to the enslaved.

As Frederick Douglass noted, in his immediate neighborhood, keeping up with appearances ensured that punishments did not "lacerate" the enslaved, nor did enslavers want their neighbors to hear bondspeople cry out. "[The] slaveholder is anxious to have it known of him, that he feeds his slaves well."[35] African American abolitionist and writer Harriet Jacobs wrote of her time in bondage in the small town of Edenton, North Carolina. Living in a place where everyone knew each other afforded a kind of protection. She surmised, "If I had been on a remote plantation, or lost among the multitude in a crowded city, I should not be a living woman at this day."[36]

In both Linden and Nebraska City, Celia and Eliza lived near enough to others to experience the same kinds of social protection described by Douglass and Jacobs. As a prominent leader in both communities, Nuckolls would have been conscious of his reputation, taking particular care when he entered Nebraska Territory, where projecting a benign form of enslavement with an emphasis on a family atmosphere could lead to the institution's ultimate accommodation, if not acceptance.

Despite these positive images, the intimacy of everyday interactions between enslaver and enslaved did not necessarily equal friendship. Interviews reveal that enslaved people took care to hide their real feelings even as they lived and worked alongside their enslavers, aware of the inherent injustice in their situation. Celia and Eliza would not have forgotten the overriding fact that they were still slaves in Stephen and Lucinda Nuckolls's eyes.[37]

"Five Negroes for Sale at Nebraska City"

With Shack working regularly outside the household, he would have kept Celia and Eliza apprised of any town gossip, while the sisters would have known the inner workings of the Nuckolls family. They all would have been quite attentive to the debate over slavery in the territory. A year after Stephen Nuckolls drove the first stake for platting Nebraska City, he assessed the local situation. Labor was hard to come by, and he and the men in the town company wanted to build—and build big. On July 14, 1855, with J. Sterling Morton at the editorial helm, the *Nebraska City News* published an announcement that made a major news splash:

> Negroes For Sale at this Place: We call attention to the advertisement of negroes for sale, which appears in another column. A company of gentlemen from Missouri, who have large interests here, have imported them for the benefit of our young and growing city. Nebraska City is now about twice or three times larger than any other town in the Territory. Help is much needed and but little to be had; for this reason slave labor is required. We are authorized to state that the same company have twenty more in Missouri, which will be brought to Nebraska City if sufficient inducements are held out.[38]

On August 16 the *Fairfield Ledger* in Iowa announced:

> **Five Negroes for Sale at Nebraska City**
> FIVE SOUND, HEALTHY NEGROES are now offered for sale at this place—Three Girls, good house keepers, and two Boys, Rufe and Joe, fine field hands, compose the lot. Terms easy. For further particulars, enquire at the News office.[39]

Outside of Nebraska and Iowa, over forty newspapers, including the *New York Times*, picked up the slave sale story as big news in the ongoing debate about the extension of slavery. After the *Times* criticized the imminent sale, lawyer John S. Patterson wrote an anonymous letter to the editor identifying the Nebraska sellers as "NUCKOLLS & HAIL, owners of quite a share of the site of Nebraska City, and extensively engaged in business there. They own, severally, quite a number of slaves in Atchison County, Mo., in fact, a majority of slaves in that county."[40]

Patterson obviously had local sources on the ground, whether in Missouri or Nebraska. He pointed out that Nuckolls and his associates also owned the newspaper, with Morton editing the *News* to "reflect their views and interests." Yet Patterson also imagined that the majority of people in Missouri's northern counties, as well as those living in Nebraska Territory, were antislavery, and he dismissed the slave sale announcement as "bravado at home ... designed to find favor and approbation at the hands of those men in St. Louis, with whom they have business associations." Echoing Illinois senator Stephen Douglas, Patterson pressed on, saying there was "no danger of Nebraska becoming a slave territory, even if Kansas should." He concluded, "I am well persuaded that NUCKOLLS & HAIL have no faith in its being otherwise."[41]

In Iowa, the *Fairfield Ledger* editors were not nearly as sanguine as Patterson about slavery's impossibility in the territories, stating, "The friends of freedom have now two territories to watch—for Nebraska is now marching side by side with Kansas in supporting the hateful burden of human bondage." Countless papers simply pointed to the sale as evidence of slavery's spread.[42]

The proslavery *Squatter Sovereign* of Atchison, Kansas, took a different tack, although agreeing that slavery was possible. The editors were elated that "Southern institutions are spreading to our sister Territory," in spite of a "large band of cattle and negro thieves; slavery actually exists and is protected by territorial law."[43]

Regarding Celia and Eliza's position in this affair, Patterson also wrote, "For some time Nuckolls and Hail have had three or four slaves at Nebraska City, employed in household duties, and taking care of stock &c." There can be little doubt that Patterson was referring to Celia, Eliza, Shack, and Shade.[44]

Later that month Morton claimed that the slave sale advertisement was a hoax. He had published it to see what the response would be. He crowed about the rampant abolitionists and the "Southern fireaters" who had showered either abuse or praise upon news of the sale. As a "little" press, advertising was slow, and these "designing politicians" had actually helped him put Nebraska City on the news map. To add editorial insult to injury, Morton gloated that the "negroes" he had advertised "were all made of glass—one was called Rufe, from the fact that the rotundity of his corporality gave it a very striking resemblance to one Rufe Hosmer, an abolition editor of Detroit . . . while Joe was abused by being libeled as a namesake of Joseph Warren, another frothy abolition editor."[45]

The *Burlington (IA) Daily Hawk-Eye* accepted Morton's account, explaining that the "whole thing was a fiction of its own coinage," with little else to say.[46] A few other newspapers followed suit, deciding to take the position that the abolitionists were "hoaxed" and that Morton was holding "constitutional middle ground" by laughing at the extremes on both sides. One editor wrote with approval that the notoriety and publicity the slave advertisement had "procured" for Morton "would have been cheap at any price."[47] The *Chicago Free Press* viewed these interpretations with skepticism, stating that a movement to extend slavery was afoot, despite the fact that the *News* "now declares that no such scheme is in contemplation and that the negro sale was a mere joke."[48]

Whether real or not, the joke fell flat. Morton's wordy and insulting explanation smacked of protesting too much, taking more column inches than the advertisement and announcement combined. In it, Morton scoffed at the real and serious tension over the potential extension of slavery, while portraying himself as a reasonable man who loved God and the Union—a man of "sense and moderation." Of moderation, there is little evidence. Morton called his fellow editors "magnificent blatherskites" when they responded to the items. And from his superior view, Morton rejoiced to "condemn them by their own words," deploring the "ruthless spirit of ambitious fanaticism" of what he called the "North-Mud Party."[49]

But Morton's advertisement contained no hint it was not serious. The wording indicated that this sale was private, rather than a public auction. The phrase "terms easy" suggests that the slaveholders were prepared to mortgage or even hire out enslaved laborers. Determining whether the ad was real would be difficult. The Otoe County Register of Deeds has no record of any slaves sold or mortgaged in the county during the era—only land. But recording a deed was not required, and many deeds remained in private hands. Hiring out was also usually a private transaction, rarely leaving a public record.

This July 1855 foray into a prospective Nebraska slave sale raises numerous questions. Perhaps it was a verbal bomb lobbed to explode on the battleground over slavery in the territories. More likely is that Morton penned the follow-up as a form of damage control. After the original article attracted so much negative attention, the answer could have been a weak effort to save face and calm roiling tensions. Moreover, national attention could have carried a political cost. Nebraskans may have been willing to let the slavery issue lie for the sake of peace among settlers, but not when the territory dipped into slave sales. If that was the case, would they have Bleeding Nebraska to go along with Bleeding Kansas?

A few months after the infamous ad appeared, a *Nebraska City News* article headlined "One Hundred Laborers and Mechanics Wanted at Nebraska City" promised good wages and steady employment, as "men of capital and taste" were building over thirty dwellings. Nuckolls and Morton may have been willing to test the waters for adding slave labor to the boomtown mix.[50] It also seems likely that Nuckolls and his family had other enslaved people across the river in Missouri, who were not their "family servants" but slaves whose owners were ready to hire them out in Nebraska City during a labor crunch. Given the uproar surrounding this potential slave transaction, Celia, Eliza, and Shack surely caught wind of it. The mere talk of a sale—even if brushed off later—would have sent a chill through them all, a grim reminder of their precarious position as "property." Was there anywhere they could be safe? They may have looked with increased longing across the river to Iowa.

Life settled down again once the ferment over the "fake" slave sale in Nebraska City subsided. However, this incident underscores some important points. The extended Nuckolls family had easy access to more enslaved people's labor than ever appeared in a census count. Enslaved people on both sides of the river were shuttled back and forth as needed, whether hired for money or lent out because of family ties. The nature of Stephen's family empire with outlets in three states meant that Celia, Eliza, Shack, and Shade were probably all familiar with the ferries and crossings. Indeed, the Nuckolls clan obtained ferry rights that may have lessened the expense of transporting enslaved people and other property.[51]

"Treat the Negroe Kind and Humanely & as a Negroe Should Be Treated"

Celia and Eliza's first enslaver, Ezra Nuckolls, often expressed concern for his "servants." When Ezra transferred the sisters to Stephen, he instructed his son not to dispose of them without his permission. Moreover, Ezra charged Stephen and his sisters, "Treat the negroe Kind and Humanely & as a negroe should be treated." If Stephen was "likely to sell" them, Ezra would take them back, repaying Stephen the $350 each his son had paid for them.[52]

For the Nuckolls clan, the wording of the agreements Ezra had with his children demonstrates that he considered himself a benign and paternal slaveholder.[53] Yet the Nuckolls correspondence also reveals the complexities of what enslavers considered humane. Ezra's inquiries into the situation of one enslaved person back in Virginia named Old Mose provide a glimpse of how families like the Nuckollses brought their cultural views on enslavement to southeast Nebraska.

In 1856 Ezra's sister-in-law Sophia Hail Mitchell wrote to him and his wife, Lucinda, that Old Mose said to tell them "he is well satisfied but he would be so glad to see you all both black and white." A year later Old Mose was no longer with Sophia Mitchell, and he may not have been "well satisfied." In an 1857 response to a letter from Ezra, his nephew James Anderson discussed Old Mose's situation. Ezra must have expressed concern that Old Mose was not being properly fed and clothed, because Anderson assured him that their friend and neighbor Jeremiah Jennings had agreed to take the aging servant and share Old Mose's time with another neighbor, Andrew Robinson. Jennings promised that Mose would have adequate food and clothing. Anderson added, "Mose says his old Mistress treated him the best & Kindest of any place he ever lived at," referring to Ezra's wife.[54]

Ezra's expressed concern for Old Mose meshes well with his self-concept as a father figure to his enslaved people. At the same time, Mose wanting to see the family, "both black and white," could have indicated that he would have preferred to go west. It cannot be known whether Old Mose's feelings were consulted, but emigrants often left older people behind when going west because they could contribute little to the hard work of establishing new homes and breaking new ground. Because of his age, Mose was probably "superannuated" and, in the eyes of potential buyers, of little monetary worth. Ezra Nuckolls had obviously made special arrangements for him.[55]

Fielden L. Hail wrote to his "brother and sister" Ezra and Lucinda Nuckolls contemplating his own move west. He wondered what to do with Uncle Harry and Charlotte, two of his enslaved people, who did "not want to go." Hail supposed that none of the "grown negroes will want to go. I suppose we will leave them & take the Young ones," soliciting Ezra's advice on what he should do with them.[56] That Ezra was familiar with Harry and Charlotte is clear. Possibly the two had a tie to Celia and Eliza, given the nature of slaveholding in Grayson County. In any case, the correspondence affirms historian Ira Berlin's work showing that enslavers preferred to take younger slaves when migrating and leave older ones behind.[57]

Old Mose's relationship to Celia, Eliza, and the rest of the enslaved people taken west to Missouri and Nebraska cannot be surmised from the fragmentary evidence. The 1850 Virginia slave schedule for Ezra Nuckolls shows he had two older enslaved men, one age fifty-four and another fifty, who did not make the trip to Missouri. Mose was still alive in 1857 and might have been the older man listed in the slave schedule for Andrew Robinson in the 1860 census, given the letter to Ezra saying that Mose would split his time between Jeremiah Jennings and Andrew Robinson. After that Mose is impossible to trace, and he does not appear in the 1865 Black Census for Grayson County.[58]

The Nuckolls correspondence also shows that hiring out and selling enslaved people were not unheard of in the family. For instance, Ezra Nuckolls's brother-in-law Martin Hail wrote to Missouri from Alabama in 1855 regarding Ezra's mother-in-law back in Grayson County: "I have a particular anxiety to make them negroes at Mothers leave that Country or bring a price. I acknowledge that negroes are flesh & blood and should be treated humane but have come to the conclusion it is not best to consult a negroes notions too much particularly when they are tampered with by unprincipled white persons."[59]

Martin Hail also shared his plan to acquire more enslaved people from an estate to which he was appointed guardian. After he settled these affairs, he hoped to visit Ezra and Lucinda, although he made clear his intent was just to visit, since he was content in his new Alabama home. Hail updated them later that he had bought "a negro man 22 Years old at $1200 & his wife 16 years old at $1110" from his wards' estate, saying, "The Grayson negroes need not be afraid of me now as I have as many negroes as I want."[60] In light of Ezra Nuckolls's insistence that his enslaved people be treated "as they ought to be" and that they not be sold out of the family, his brother-in-law's more cavalier attitude stands in some contrast.

Letters to Ezra and Lucinda confirm that many members of the Nuckolls clan were engaged in hiring out. Fielden Hail wrote in February 1856 that he intended to head west to join them. In the meantime, he had hired out "Black Fielden" to another relative, Clark Nuckolls, until the next Christmas for $60, while their mother had hired her "two boys" to Mastin and Eli Nuckolls for $100 a year each.[61]

Sophia Hail Mitchell complained the next month, "Mother hired Ballard for 100 dollars to Mastin and Wils," turning down another offer for $125. Eli Hail also had "black Sam for nothing." Another Black woman named Winney had been with Sophia most of the winter, but she had "been weaving for Fanny and Mother." Although she expected to at least have access to Winney's work the next summer, Sophia fretted, "Mother has hired her to Coltrane to cook for his road hands."[62]

Whether Sophia's complaints fell on sympathetic ears in Missouri remains unknown, but that the Virginia relatives were competing for enslaved persons' labor is clear. The process was not smooth or agreeable. Lucinda Hail Nuckolls's mother, Frances Hail, made deals without everyone having a chance to respond. Sophia was particularly irritated because after feeding Winney all winter long, the enslaved woman would be cooking for another relative during the summer, a season when she could have done more to lighten Sophia's household workload.

The practice of hiring out enslaved people carried over into northern Missouri and Nebraska. Nebraska City judge Harden wrote home to Georgia that his manservant Sam had "many applications to work" and apparently hired him out for $230.⁶³ Stephen's brother Heath wrote to "Dear Papa" in Atchison County about Shade in January 1857. On an errand, Shade had ridden a horse unshod from St. Stephens to Nebraska City, a forty- to forty-five-mile distance, endangering the horse's soundness. Stephen Nuckolls was not pleased, and Heath noted, "I think Friel will send Shade home. The reason Friel concluded to keep Shade he begged so that it made him and Lucinda sorry for him. He seemed to take it very hard when he heard he was to go home. He has not been worth anything to Friel for the last 3 or 4 months. When he is well he is a first rate negro."⁶⁴

The letter demonstrates that Shade had been lent by or hired from Ezra Nuckolls for an extended period of time. Moreover, Shade was trusted enough to go alone to retrieve the horse from Houston's home base in St. Stephens. Whether Shade was sent back to Ezra Nuckolls at that time, it is clear the Nuckolls clan continued to act as they did in Grayson County, hiring out their enslaved people to work for others, particularly family members.

Although hiring out could expose enslaved people to more cruelty and punishment than they received at home, the practice could also provide slaveholders "economic flexibility and profitability, and ultimately may have resulted in fewer slaves sold."⁶⁵ Indeed, Nuckolls's valuing Shack's labor at over $1,000 a year suggests he received wages for Shack's work on a regular basis. Shack was more than earning his keep.⁶⁶

In Celia and Eliza's case, this practice would have been more limited, although one or both of them may have been hired out or lent to trusted neighbors and family for a few days or for a special occasion. They may have helped at Nebraska City's first Christmas celebration at Stephen Nuckolls's uncle William B. Hail's house in the old military hospital, where Lucinda Bourne Nuckolls prepared "a fine supper." While they cooked and served, the rest of the small company danced.⁶⁷

Whether working in the Nuckolls household or elsewhere, Celia, Eliza, Shack, and Shade, all of whom lived with Stephen and Lucinda, were shouldering the burdens and hardships of early town-dwelling pioneers. With Stephen's concentration on land speculation, banking, and merchandising, farm duties were probably modest for his enslaved people during their time in Nebraska Territory. As in Missouri, Nuckolls's wealth in Nebraska was concentrated in unimproved land, with the addition of his stores and the Platte Valley Bank.[68]

In February 1856 the enslaved people in Nuckolls's households on both sides of the river may have heard about an Atchison County slave sale. A local farmer and slaveholder William Mann bought a woman named Mariah and three of her children, Thomas, Henry, and Samuel, while a fourth was sold to farmer Thomas Ely. The same day an African American woman named Sarah Ann, "belonging to the children of Abner Martin," was also sold. Again, William Mann was the purchaser, buying Sarah Ann for $600.[69] Both of these transactions were related to estate settlements.

The news of this sale doubtless circulated throughout Atchison County among enslaved people as well as free. Given the close ties that Celia and Eliza had there, they would have paid close attention. They may have felt not only sympathy for Mariah and the breakup of her family but also a frisson of fear. It was a stark reminder that a slaveholder's death was a time of uncertainty for enslaved people, who often faced separation, displacement, and sale. It highlighted their vulnerability while reminding them that the precarious balance of relationships that Celia and Eliza had achieved with family members nearby could be lost at any time. As former slave Lewis Hayden put it, "Intelligent colored people . . . felt no security whatever for their family ties." He explained that the slave trader, slave pens, rice swamps, and sugar and cotton plantations were ever present: "We had had them held before us as terrors by our masters and mistresses all our lives."[70]

{ 5 }

Politics Running High

As Celia, Eliza, Shack, and Shade adjusted to the ebb and flow of life in Nebraska City, discussion of slavery was a constant part of local social life. Abolitionist John Kagi reported to eastern newspapers on slavery's prospects in Nebraska Territory, complaining that "of the four newspapers in Nebraska, not one has ever dared to utter a single word in favor of freedom." Early on, he pronounced Governor Izard and other presidential appointees "warmly in favor of the introduction of slavery."[1]

Although Kagi hoped that an influx of more Northerners would turn the tide, the majority of residents seemed to be "in favor of ignoring freedom, if not directly establishing slavery." Kagi warned that more slaves were "on their way," and when Nebraska residents were asked, "What is to be done with the slaves of the territory when the constitution is formed?" they had no real answer, "for nearly all the southern people, and many from the North, would much prefer seeing slavery legalized, to having a few free negroes about them."[2] These attitudes filtered through Nebraska City society and probably reached the Graysons, who may have already been weighing their prospects for escape.

In 1856 newspapers were also full of the news of the upcoming presidential election. Pennsylvanian James Buchanan had defeated incumbent president Franklin Pierce to win the Democratic Party's nomination. John C. Frémont ran against Buchanan from the newly created Republican Party on an antislavery platform. Former president Millard Fillmore, who had permanently damaged his popularity when he signed the Fugitive Slave Act in 1850, ran as a third-party candidate for the American Party, and he received the endorsement of the anti-immigrant Know-Nothings. Although this situation looked like a three-way race, historian David M. Potter notes that there were actually two contests: "one between Buchanan and Frémont in the free states, the other between Buchanan and Fillmore in the slave states." Frémont was not even on the ballot in the slave states except Delaware, Kentucky, Maryland, and Virginia.³

"Politics never ran so high in the United States as at present," actor Harry Watkins wrote in his diary on October 12, 1856, and such was the case in the Missouri Valley region. In April of that year Ezra had written to his friend Ira Coltrane back in Virginia, noting with disgust that some of the Know-Nothings in Atchison County were Democrats. Buchanan was his man. After Buchanan's election, Ezra's friend Samuel McCamant (Jarvis Bacon's prosecutor) wrote and congratulated Ezra on the results.⁴

Nebraska Territory's *Bellevue Gazette* predicted that Buchanan's administration would restore the country to "peace and quiet," declaring that "fanaticism and disloyalty to our glorious Union" had been defeated, sentiments the Nuckolls family surely shared. However, instead of peace and quiet, Buchanan's 1857 inaugural address stirred up controversy when he stated that the "issue of slavery in the territories was a 'judicial question which legitimately belongs to the Supreme Court of the United States, before whom it is now pending.'"⁵

Buchanan's address effectively put Douglas's popular sovereignty solution in further disarray while signaling to the court his desired outcome. Although the court had almost certainly already decided the case, Buchanan's speech was widely seen as improper and raised accusations of a conspiracy between the president and the Supreme Court over the slavery question.⁶ Even some Democrats looked askance at Buchanan's dismissal of popular sovereignty. If Congress did not have the power to regulate slavery in the territories, it could not have delegated that power to territorial legislatures in the Kansas-Nebraska Act, rendering popular sovereignty null.

Buchanan's speech also denied prospects of freedom to enslaved people like Celia and Eliza. He said that only when a territory had enough residents to "justify the formation of a constitution" on the way to statehood could it prohibit slavery. He left out what the legal status of the enslaved in territories would be until that day. In the absence of a prohibition, it seemed that slavery would be legal.⁷

With President Buchanan appointing proslavery territorial officials, many of whom would bring enslaved people with them, it seemed that

Nebraska Territory's nascent society with slaves would be safe. Thus a year after the "fictional" Nebraska City slave sale, Buchanan's election assured the continued tolerance of domestic borderland slavery and its expansion into the West.

Closer to home, Stephen's uncle William B. Hail defeated J. Sterling Morton in his 1856 bid for the territory's House of Representatives by twenty votes, in an intensely bitter campaign. Morton had gone to Omaha in 1855 as a representative from Otoe County, but in some Nebraska Citians' eyes, he had sold out to the North Platters, especially when he threw his support to their proposed banking reforms.[8]

Hints of a rupture in the warm relations between Morton and the Nuckolls family appear in a letter from Hiram Bennet to Morton in July 1856. Bennet expressed his sorrow that Morton had experienced "discouragement" in his "Nebraska speculations and 'mercantile friendships.'" At least one of the mercantile friends Bennet referred to was Stephen Nuckolls, who "has ever used me well," Bennet avowed. "I owe much of what little property I have to his counsel and kindness. You and he are both my friends, and it does not become me a friend to do ought else than try to reconcile you."[9]

The degree to which Morton and Nuckolls were reconciled is difficult to judge. Morton blamed his 1856 election loss on his 1855 vote in the territorial legislature against wildcat banking schemes, a vote that was "vigorously criticized at home." And Stephen Nuckolls was head of the wildcat Platte Valley Bank. But the damage to Morton was temporary. He weathered this early storm to be reelected in 1857, this time joining William B. Hail in the territory's house.[10]

In the autumn of 1857 several large New York and Ohio banks collapsed, beginning a chain of bank failures throughout the West. Nebraska Territory's new and emerging economy was vulnerable to the panic that ensued. By December almost every bank in Nebraska had failed. Stephen Nuckolls's Platte Valley Bank was one of the only institutions to survive, and that with a last-minute loan from his fellow Nebraska Citian John Boulware.[11]

Even with the banking situation settling down, feelings between the North Platters and South Platters continued to run high. Stephen's brother Columbus Nuckolls wrote to Morton in January 1858, charging him with uniting "with the Omaha corruption party" and acting "the sh——t towards your best friends the Nuckolls." Morton replied to these insults, "If the Nuckolls are my best friends or ever were I am certainly hard up and truly a suspicious character." Columbus may have regretted his written outburst when President Buchanan appointed Morton secretary of the territory in July 1858.[12]

If Stephen Nuckolls shared his brother's bitter feelings, he did not show it. Although Morton's territorial policies may not have always aligned with his, the two men were both Buchanan Democrats and loyal to the party. And if Morton regretted his early association with the Nuckolls clan, he was still entangled with them both politically and economically. Morton and Stephen Nuckolls's correspondence remained businesslike.[13]

Nuckolls emerged from the banking debacle relatively unscathed, but land prices began to suffer, and money continued to be scarce. Yet in 1858 the discovery of gold in Cherry Creek, Colorado, set the stage for a quick recovery as miners began to pass through towns lining the Nebraska side of the Missouri River, adding to the flow of settlers headed west. Nebraska City also scored an economic victory when Missouri-based Alexander Majors, flush with lucrative government contracts, decided to expand and move his freighting business, Majors, Russell and Company, choosing Nebraska City as his main shipping point west.[14]

Meanwhile, the Nuckolls household in Nebraska City was buzzing with work. As a major investor in the town, Stephen engaged in constant boosterism, lauding Nebraska City's attractions as a hub not only for transportation and business but also for agriculture. For instance, an Illinois newspaper announced that S. F. Nuckolls of Nebraska was raising "gigantic" vegetables, including a 12-pound radish and a squash that weighed 155 pounds.[15]

In April 1858 hotelier John Armstrong completed a lavishly furnished four-story hotel called the Nuckolls House at Sixth and Main (now Central), opposite the bank buildings. The name honored Stephen Nuckolls, "whose capital, enterprise and indomitable perseverance" had contributed so much to the town that, Armstrong declared, "'Nuckolls' and 'Nebraska City' are almost synonymous terms." The hotel was a "magnificent structure," with a fine brick stable and icehouse, and its reputed cost was $20,000.[16]

Nuckolls's boosterism may have even extended to questions of slavery. When an emigrant train passed through Nebraska City headed for Kansas, one of the emigrants addressed "a man of considerable influence" there, saying, "I've got sick of trying to farm it in the North; they won't allow a fellow to hold slaves, or let him treat a white laborer otherwise than as an equal." The emigrant added that he was heading to Kansas because it would be a slave state. The gentleman replied, "You need have no fear of stopping in Nebraska, if that is your politics, for there is a strong determination here to make Nebraska a slave state, and I've no kind of doubt but that we shall triumphantly succeed." Even if not Stephen Nuckolls, the sentiments expressed matched his.[17]

In 1858 and into 1859 Majors, Russell and Company built large storehouses that were expected to prevent high prices, precluding "the necessity for sending to St. Joseph or St. Louis for articles which should be kept and purchased at home." In November 1858 S. F. Nuckolls and Company advertised that it needed three thousand hogs for Nuckolls's packing establishment, while one of his other enterprises, Nuckolls and Wyatt, was offering for sale four thousand acres in Atchison County, Missouri; four hundred acres in Iowa; forty-five hundred acres in Richardson County, Nebraska; and two thousand acres in Nemaha County, Nebraska.[18]

With all this growth, the amount of work Celia, Eliza, and Shack had to do likely expanded along with Nuckolls's ambitions. By the summer of 1858 hundreds of wagons were passing through the town. As described by one observer, "All is a commotion, the hallowing of the drivers, the clanking of chains and wagon masters giving orders."[19] Whereas in 1854–55 Nebraska City had only "wooden shanties breaking the solitude," by 1859 the "luxuries of civilization" were everywhere, with "hotels, mansions, and storehouses." The mansions may have been the "fine houses" of Alexander Majors, Judge John F. Kinney, Stephen Nuckolls, and Nuckolls's business partner Robert Hawke.[20]

Lucinda Bourne Nuckolls's letters reveal that she accompanied Stephen on at least one buying trip, but whether Celia and Eliza went with them remains unknown. Family letters during this period tended to talk of illness, sewing, housework, and news about extended family. Lucinda's correspondence reflects these ordinary concerns. Her comments on health and sickness are frequent, and it was common for "both white and black women" to be called on to help attend the ill. It may be that Celia and

Eliza helped Lucinda care for others when sick, whether family, friends, or neighbors.[21]

Lucinda rarely wrote about the enslaved people in her life, which is not surprising. Diane Mutti Burke's analysis of letters from enslaver households notes that for the most part, "Missouri slaveholders were silent about the enslaved people who worked, and often lived, in their homes." She theorizes that enslavement was such a normal part of life that unless something notable happened with the enslaved people, letter writers kept the focus on their own families.[22]

At the same time, Celia and Eliza's situation would have provided opportunities to resist their circumstances. Burke remarks that enslaved people like Celia and Eliza "were well placed to understand the personalities of their owners and used this knowledge to their advantage." They may have performed some tasks slowly, broken dishes, or resisted Lucinda's control in other ways.[23]

Celia and Eliza were not only in a growing frontier town but also in a river town. The Missouri River brought many people to the steamboat and overland freighting hub, some of them Blacks working on the boats or for freighting companies. Indeed, the arrival of a steamboat was an event in itself. Correspondent Mortimer Q. Thomsen, writing under his alias of Q. K. Doesticks, described the arrival of outfitter Alexander Majors in Nebraska City in April 1858 with caustic humor. While at the Nebraska City real estate office, Doesticks "heard a small boy say 'steamboat.'" Everyone dropped what they were doing to head down to the levee. Doesticks then launched into biting satire that played with names (like changing Majors to Bajors) and more: "Boat landed, Bajors aboard—(eighteen trunks, twenty boxes—ten sons fifteen daughters—eleven darkies—one wife—all labelled and paid for)—landed.... H. kissed Bajors seventeen times—Nuckolls tried to shake hands with Bajors—H. wouldn't let him.... Went up in the evening, tried to see Bajors—couldn't do it—K. on one side—H. on the other, S. in the rear, L. in front, all labelled, 'Keep off, gentlemen—this is sacred goods, we have charge of keeping and fleecing him.'"[24]

The satire captures the essential details. In addition to highlighting Majors's fawning reception and undignified jostling for attention, Doesticks also attacked his religion, the political spoils system that furnished him with his government contract, and the institution of slavery. Notably, Stephen Nuckolls did not merit a hidden identity.

The arrival of a steamboat was an opportunity in an entertainment-starved town. Mark Twain describes a similar scene in which the words "S-t-e-a-m-boat a' comin'!" was followed by a "furious clatter," with men and boys pouring out of "every house and store" to assemble at the landing with carts, drays, and wagons.[25]

Although Stephen Nuckolls was clearly present when Majors arrived, what about Lucinda and, by extension, Celia and Eliza? Would they have joined the carnival atmosphere? Probably not. Diarist Mollie Dorsey Sanford noted that when her boat arrived in Nebraska City in April 1857, they were greeted by the "boom of artillery" and "the levee was full of people," but they were "mostly men and boys."[26]

Serving a large household on the main thoroughfare of a busy transportation hub had to have been demanding. While Celia and Eliza's escape suggests the violent conditions of slavery and the inherent abuse the women suffered under the controlling eyes of their enslavers, evidence surrounding their treatment in the Nuckolls household is scant. And their treatment may not have been the deciding factor. As one former enslaved person, James Bradley, put it in 1834, "I was never acquainted with a slave, however well he was treated, who did not long to be free."[27]

Freedom seekers' accounts, based on earlier work by African Americans William Still and Sydney Howard Gay, showed that the most common motive for escape was brutal treatment at the hands of owners or overseers. The second reason freedom seekers cited was the threat of sale. Location also played a role; places that bordered free states had long seen greater numbers of freedom seekers.[28]

For Celia and Eliza, their situation suggests a confluence of factors. Opportunity beckoned. Whenever they looked east across the river, they saw Iowa's bluffs and loess hills where freedom reigned. And Iowa was not only a free state but also one with an abolitionist network already in place. Given this strategic location, Nuckolls's enslaved people probably discussed their prospects for a successful escape.[29]

Moreover, Nebraska City was a station on the Underground Railroad. Free Blacks and antislavery residents may have pulled Shack or Shade aside to inform them of their options. Yet the local agents, as willing as they may have been to help enslaved people passing through, may have hesitated to interfere in the case of Stephen Nuckolls's enslaved people. As Nuckolls was the founder of Nebraska City, an investor, and a banker and had powerful friends and family members, local abolitionists may have been reluctant to take him on personally and thereby risk endangering their activities.[30]

Another factor in Celia and Eliza's decision-making may have been events in the extended Nuckolls family after Ezra's move to Missouri in 1855. The winter of 1856–57 was harsh, with "freezing into ninety solid blocks of ice all the days of that month and the succeeding ones of January and February, 1857."[31] Deep snow covered the area, and the usual supplement of wild game at settlers' tables diminished. When the spring of 1857 finally arrived, so did bad news. Ezra Nuckolls died on May 4, and his wife, Lucinda Hail Nuckolls, died on May 17. They left eleven surviving children. Stephen's youngest siblings, Sena, Emmett, and Elizabeth, were still minors when their parents died.

In June, Lucinda Bourne Nuckolls went to Atchison County, perhaps to help sort out the household in the wake of these deaths. She took her now two-year-old son, Richmond, with her. Richmond fell deathly ill, and Heath Nuckolls wrote to Stephen back in Nebraska City that Richmond's condition was deteriorating so much that "Lucinda thinks you ought to come down."[32] Young Richmond died soon after. So Stephen Nuckolls lost both of his parents and a child in the space of six weeks. Richmond's death left Lucinda truly bereft. She wrote home that Billy was old enough "to wait on himself" and was going to school. With no child "about the house," Lucinda wrote she had not missed "Pinkey or Alice as I do Richey, go upstairs there is too little wagons three little chairs and trunk of his cloaths and these hats and bonnets scattered in every drawer oh it is too hard and to be where I cant see any of you."[33]

The death of a family patriarch was an important event, and for enslaved people, it was a time of increased vulnerability and danger. Ezra Nuckolls's will specified that his nine slaves not "be distributed sold, or hired out to any other person except some of my heirs, unless sutsch Slaves may be of bad character."[34] Notably, Ezra included "hiring out" as among the prohibited uses of his enslaved persons, perhaps after noticing how his mother-in-law and others used hiring out during probate to defray expenses and pay down debt. That he felt compelled to put his wishes in writing could also mean he was not convinced all his children would follow his general practice.

Ezra Nuckolls's 1857 estate appraisal (over $23,000 in assets) listed eight enslaved persons, including Shade, who had often been hired or lent to Stephen. They were valued as follows:

> One Negro Man Henry $1,000
> One Negro Man Richard $1,200
> One Negro Man Shade $500
> One Woman Mary and child $800
> One Boy Rolly $600
> One Boy Clayton $450
> One Girl Jane $500
> One Girl Rebecca $350[35]

Shade's lower valuation in comparison with Henry's and Richard's suggests that he may not have been strong or healthy, as all three were young men. Heath's comment to Ezra in early 1857 that when Shade was "well" he was a "first-rate Negro" indicated that he may not have been much help to Stephen Nuckolls. Despite Ezra's testamentary wishes, in September 1857 Stephen Nuckolls and his adult siblings applied to the Atchison County District Court for permission to hold a slave sale. One of Ezra's nine slaves, Henry, had died in the interim, making "a distribution in kind impracticable," given Ezra's provision for an equal division of slaves.[36]

Perhaps a hidden motive for the heirs to choose a sale rather than a straight division was that some of the Nuckolls clan lived in the free state of Iowa. They may have felt forced either to free or to sell their enslaved people, whereas the Nuckolls clan in Missouri and Nebraska would be able to retain theirs.[37] The sale bill dated October 24, 1857, furnishes the results:

> One boy Clayton $450 to C. Nuckolls
> One boy Raleigh $500 to S. F. Nuckolls
> One girl Jane $600 to A. Borchers
> One girl Rebecca $300 to Houston Nuckolls

Politics Running High 87

> One woman Mary and child $750 to Houston Nuckolls
> One boy Richard $950 to Houston Nuckolls
> One boy Shade $600 to L. Nuckolls[38]

Afterward, Lucinda Bourne Nuckolls wrote home, "Every thing sold very well the children bought all the negroes. Heath got one of the little boys Mr Borchers got a girl about 12 years old Columbus got one boy Lafayett got Shade Houston got all the balance of them. Borchers and Lafayitt took their negroes to Ioway."[39] Comparing the sale bill with Lucinda's letter, the "boy" that Heath got had to be Raleigh, bought by Stephen Nuckolls but clearly not for himself. It may be that Stephen and Heath had some account to be settled. That Houston Nuckolls received half of the eight enslaved people suggests that the four may have been a group they wanted to keep together.

Indeed, Ezra's will, written in 1855, demonstrates that Heath was not in Ezra's good graces. Heath was willed $5 and no more. Regarding Houston, Stephen Nuckolls was to hold his portion in trust until Houston was age twenty-two and then transfer the property to him only if Stephen deemed him of "good habits & morals & not addicted to gambling nor drinking." Apparently, Houston had passed the test, since he was allowed his share of property, including most of Ezra's enslaved people.[40]

For Celia and Eliza, it may have been that Ezra's death and the subsequent sale kicked off a series of discussions that put self-emancipation at the forefront of their thinking. As Ezra's household broke apart, the rest of the Graysons were separated. None of the previous generation was left to observe how well the heirs followed Ezra's provisions for their treatment. Celia and Eliza, although already held by Stephen Nuckolls, might have feared the further division of their family, raising the possibility of their own separation and sale.

In addition, the constant debates over slavery in the territory also continued to eddy about them. Stephen and his siblings navigated their position in society to maintain the status quo, hoping to make their corner of Nebraska Territory a place like Grayson County, a society where enslaved people lived in smallholdings or in private homes, with an ongoing acceptance, or at least tolerance, of slavery from their neighbors. Having lived through Nebraska City's "fake" slave sale in 1855 and the probate sales of enslaved people in Atchison County in 1856–57, they may have felt their situation was less secure than ever before.

Celia and Eliza knew that leaving was risky. They were well aware of slave hunters, men who fanned out through Kansas and Missouri and into Iowa to pursue fugitives to reenslave them. Indeed, their prior home of Grayson County had been one of the inspirations for *Uncle Tom's Cabin* in the use of slave hunters and vigilantes, who meted out extralegal punishment to freedom seekers and abolitionists.[41]

Without a doubt, they had heard about the 1857 incident a few miles south of nearby Brownville, Nebraska. A local farmer named Handley had spied three Blacks headed north and got a group together to hunt for them in the willows lining the Missouri River bottoms. Handley, joined by J. R. Davis, T. Williams, and Missourian William Myers, came across the Black men, and violence ensued. One of the Blacks shot Myers, who was from the Nuckollses' former county of Atchison. He died of his wounds an hour later. Two of the Blacks escaped on their would-be captors' horses. The third was shot in the arm by Davis and got away on foot, but he did not get far. He was taken to Brownville by local farmer William Kelley. His arm was amputated and he was held for trial.[42]

A mob of Missourians crossed the river demanding to take the Black man and hang him. Deputy Sheriff Thompson refused, stating that if they attacked, "there would be several funerals in Missouri in the next few days." The excitement subsided, and the wounded man was transferred to Nebraska City pending trial, while the Black man who shot Myers was found and killed along the Missouri River in Iowa. The wounded Black man was released to his "master without a trial."[43] Once again, the issues of slavery and freedom seekers entered into the public discourse.

Moreover, just as the *Nebraska City News* had said there was no question that slavery could exist in southeastern Nebraska, Celia and Eliza may have also believed it.[44] Although talk of prohibiting slavery in the territory was common, efforts had thus far been defeated. In fact, the week before Celia and Eliza escaped, a piece ran in the *News* headlined "Slavery Not Abolished in Nebraska: Slavery Still Here. The N——s Coming!" The legislature had postponed the bill to abolish slavery indefinitely, and the item mocked the abolitionist "Black Republicans":

People will do as they have a mind to and they will have n——s where it pays and where it suits their convenience.... [S]lavery has existed here from the organization of the Territory, notwithstanding that people bring as many 'servants' here as they choose without regard to color.... [N]——ism has about died out; negrophilism won't go down: it doesn't suit the popular taste ... [a]nd since no body cares about this little matter of negro slavery in Nebraska let us all hush it up and say no more about it.[45]

Although Celia and Eliza's plan for freedom may have already been in place, the outcome of the bill in Nebraska Territory's legislature and the crowing headlines may have strengthened their determination to take the risks of capture, re-enslavement, and punishment. It is difficult to discern when the sisters may have first contemplated their journey to freedom or how long they had discussed their possibilities. Historians John Hope Franklin and Loren Schweninger emphasize that the enslaved, even when they "lived or worked so close to freedom," exercised great caution and patience in their timing. If Ezra's estate sale was the deciding factor, that would have meant they bided their time for a year, perhaps considering the Nuckolls family routines as well as those of Nebraska City.[46]

Celia and Eliza must have weighed their opportunities against the risks. Despite committees of vigilance, slave hunters, and mobs, they were close to a network of abolitionists just a boat ride away. Adding to the mix, the "fake" slave sale of 1855 would have raised questions about their long-term prospects, while the death of the family patriarch in 1857 and the slave sale that followed may have aroused fears of being sold south.

The stakes were high. Violence and punishment of "runaways" were commonplace and widely publicized. Celia and Eliza's capture would mean whipping, at the least. Depending on Nuckolls's reaction, they also faced possible separation and being sold south. Failure was not an option.

{ 6 }

Fugitive Slave Excitement in Nebraska

On the night of November 25, 1858, the Nuckolls household slept. And all of Nebraska City, so lively in the daytime, slept. But Celia and Eliza Grayson did not. This was the night they would take their first steps toward freedom. As they prepared to leave, every little rustle of clothing or creak of the floorboards would have made the sisters stop and hold their breath. As they crept toward the door and exited the house, they would have been dressed in as many warm clothes as they owned and may have carried bundles packed for the journey. Then they quietly shut the door to the only life they had ever known.

The crunch of their feet on the frozen and deserted road would have echoed in their ears, the cold amplifying every sound. In late November the streets would not have been crowded, as they were in the summer and early fall, when masses of people passed through the town heading west and single men congregated to carouse along the riverfront and in the business district. Gone too were the muck, mire, and mosquitoes that plagued travelers along the Missouri bottoms. Quick and silent, they slipped to the north edge of the growing town to meet Black Cherokee John Williamson, their guide to the Wyoming Station ferry and freedom.[1]

At what point Williamson joined them is uncertain, but the sisters would have headed north from Nebraska City seven or eight miles. If on foot, they would have stumbled and picked their way through the darkness, probably staying on or near the rutted track that followed the winding bluffs contoured by the waters of the Missouri River.

Though Wyoming Station was only a hamlet, founder Jacob Dawson had once dreamed of its competing with Nebraska City and Omaha to be a Missouri River transportation hub. But Stephen Nuckolls and some of his friends joined Dawson as proprietors of the Wyoming Town Company, with the secret intent of blocking their potential rival town from success. Their scheme worked, and the population of Wyoming, Nebraska, never exceeded 151.[2]

For freedom seekers, this was an advantage, especially in the off season for ferries. Wyoming was a much quieter place for Celia and Eliza to cross, and it may be that Dawson and others were well aware that the proslavery leaders south of them kept a stranglehold on the community's growth. It would make sense that even if residents of the tiny place were aware of occasional nighttime crossings, they chose to look the other way.[3]

Once near the ferry crossing, Williamson and the women would have scrambled down the steep bluffs to the river. Since they crossed in a skiff, the river must not have been completely frozen over, but it would have had floating ice. In the 1850s the Missouri River was quite different from the narrow and controlled watercourse it is today. Muddy and treacherous, it was full of twists, turns, and snarls, and many an experienced boatman turned over, even in the best of conditions. Although Celia and Eliza were clearly determined, their hearts may have quailed as they stood on the Nebraska side of the Missouri that night. Despite knowing the danger, they lowered themselves into the boat. There was no going back. They wanted to be free.[4]

It is clear that Celia and Eliza had a solid plan; perhaps they and the abolitionists who helped them drew inspiration from Black abolition activist Harriet Tubman, who famously preferred the winter months to help freedom seekers in their journeys. Longer nights afforded more time to travel while shielded in darkness and meant fewer people out and about to observe freedom seekers' movements. She also favored days that would provide a lag time before the fugitive slave announcements appeared in the next newspaper.[5]

One can only imagine their small boat launching into the wintry river, waves and ice chunks dashing against and banging into the hull, shaking the small craft's timbers. A lantern light would have bobbed up and down, as Celia and Eliza shivered with cold and fright while they clung to whatever might steady them as they crossed the wide expanse of water.[6]

Civil Bend, Iowa, was almost directly across the river from Wyoming, Nebraska. The community was less a town than a string of houses perched along the river's east bank. Called a "colony of Oberlin," the town had been established by former missionaries and abolitionists in 1849–50 with plans to replicate their beloved alma mater Oberlin College in Ohio, famous for its stance on abolition.[7] But the town "on the bend" was too close to the river, so some of the residents left to found its sister town of Tabor as a more healthful site for a college. Among the settlers in Civil Bend who stayed was a former Christian missionary, Dr. Ira Blanchard.

Blanchard had considerable experience in the West, having served the Delaware and Kaw tribes in Kansas in the late 1830s and 1840s, when it was still Indian Country. However, in 1848 the Baptist Mission Board of Boston dismissed the married Blanchard because of rumors that he had had intimate relations with another woman. Blanchard, his wife, and four daughters moved north to Civil Bend, bringing the African American Garner family with them. In addition to duties as a "frontier doctor" (largely self-taught), Blanchard organized a temperance league. But by 1853 or 1854, he ran afoul of authority once again. The Union Church of Civil Bend, which he had helped to found, suspended his membership, and again rumors circulated, this time about an affair with a married woman.[8] Nevertheless, Blanchard was still one of Civil Bend's principal citizens, as well as a reliable agent for the Underground Railroad, so Celia and Eliza were entrusted to his care. They probably hid in his house, recovering from the cold before moving to the next stop.[9]

Blanchard's house was just a few blocks from the river, near a commons area in the town. The house may have featured a trapdoor, possibly in an enclosed porch, covered by a rug and trunk. Blanchard's great-grandson recalled that "slaves were hidden in the basement behind a secret fireplace in the home. They were fed and given medical care by the Blanchards before continuing on their way to freedom."[10] How long Blanchard hid Celia and Eliza may never be known, but presumably the sisters were moved north to Tabor and beyond as quickly as the Civil Bend agents could safely achieve it.

The morning after Celia and Eliza left Nebraska City, the Nuckolls household awoke to find their "servants" gone. Lucinda Bourne Nuckolls's heart may have sunk as she realized that the full burden of housework would now fall on her, while Stephen gave full vent to his anger. He sent word to Iowa friends and associates to be on the lookout for the two women. He also placed an announcement in the *Nebraska City News* about their

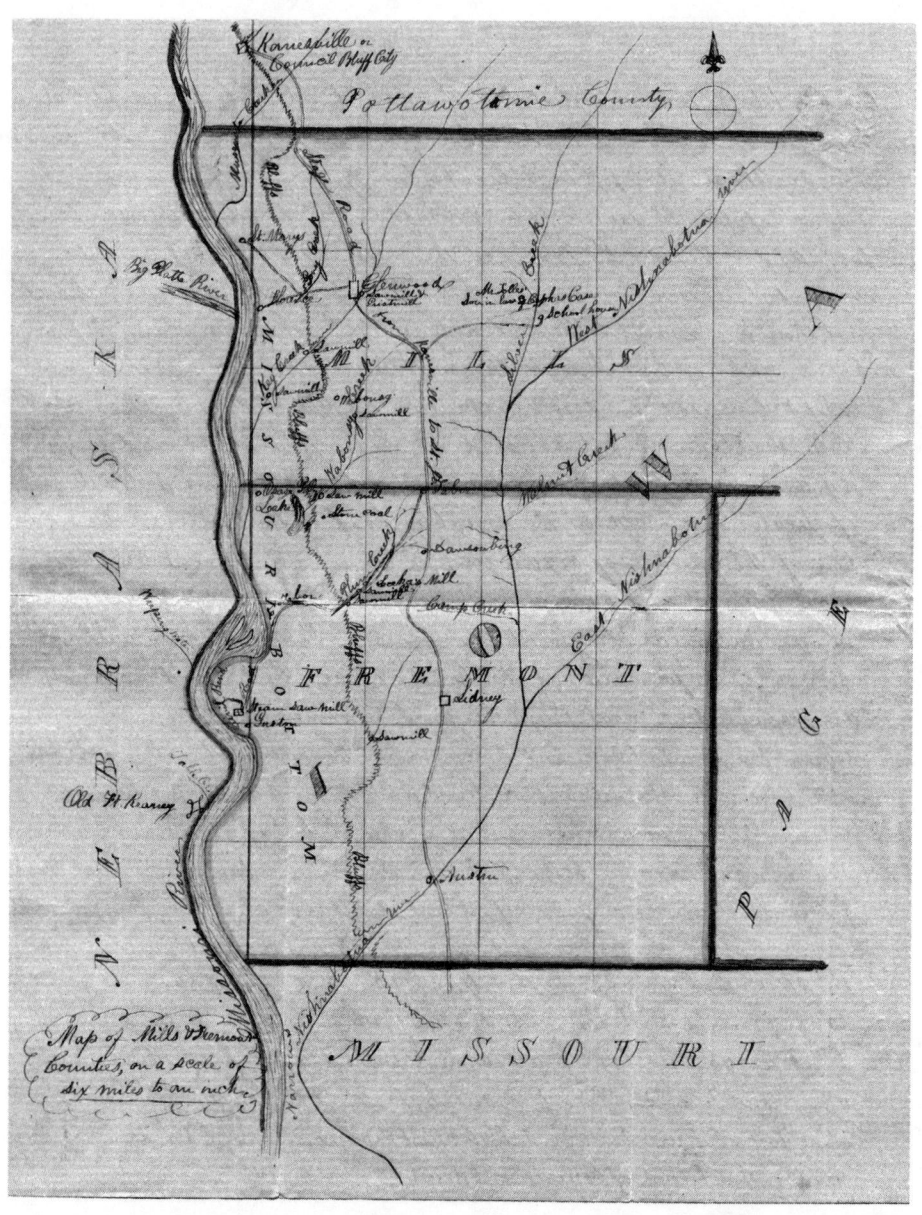

13. Map by Rev. John Todd, 1854. Courtesy of Tabor County Historical Society.

flight, complete with a reward. The typesetter would have sprung to action to ensure the news would be published the following day.[11]

On November 27, 1858, the *Nebraska City News* reported, "Quite a sensation was created in town yesterday morning by the fact being known that two female servants had been enticed away from our townsman, Mr. S. F. Nuckolls, by some vile, white-livered Abolitionists."[12] Celia and Eliza's act of resistance soon prompted newspapers across the country to weigh in on their fate, along with commentary on slavery's morality from both antislavery and proslavery perspectives.

It is unknown whether Shack was elsewhere or whether he witnessed the family's reaction as disbelief and anger set in. Why he chose to stay behind is difficult to discern. Perhaps it was because Stephen Nuckolls valued him highly and trusted him enough to allow him a measure of freedom. Shack might have even been promised eventual emancipation. A later account indicated that he "had money in the bank and didn't want to leave it."[13] Whatever the reason, in 1859 Lucinda wrote to her brother that they suspected Shack had helped Celia and Eliza, a deed that did not go unpunished: "Friel has sold Shack he got twelve hundred & fifty dollars for him. I suppose he is in the cotton country before this time wee think he had a hand in helping Liza and Celia off I think he would have went with them but he was making mony as fast as he wanted & he thought he would stay awhile & get all he could and then leave."[14] Thus Shack, so valuable to Stephen Nuckolls and regarded as a "part of the family," was sold south. His decision to stay cost him dearly.

"Beaten by the Hell Hounds of Slavery"

Stephen Nuckolls knew that the residents of both Civil Bend and Tabor, Iowa, had abolition sentiments. According to Civil Bender Elvira Gaston Platt, the day after Celia and Eliza left, Nuckolls gathered a group of men, crossed the river, and went to Doc Blanchard's home. Nuckolls explained to Blanchard that two of his "slave girls—unthankful for past favors and unmindful of the benevolent things which he would do for them in the future—had made their escape" the night before. He asked that Blanchard send the girls back to him if he saw them. Blanchard responded that he would not use force and thus would not send them back, but he would inform Nuckolls if he saw them.[15]

Nuckolls and his men then went to Tabor and scoured the town. From there, Nuckolls "sent out 'spies' in different directions," all to no avail. The women did not seem to have reached Tabor. He and his men rode back to Civil Bend, convinced that Celia and Eliza were still there and determined "that they should not leave the Missouri Bottom without being caught." He stationed men to watch different parts of the town. That night his men set the prairie grass surrounding the town on fire "so that no object could move without being visible."[16]

A correspondent to the *St. Joseph Gazette* wrote that the day after Celia and Eliza left, Nuckolls and a search party pursued the women. The piece used hunting terms that equated the women with game animals. The correspondent wrote playfully that "after scouting a few n—— holes started the game, and the prospect seemed fair to bag it." The story was sparse on details, and the writer lamented that "the trail was lost."[17]

Weary of watching without success, on December 1 Stephen Nuckolls and another search party—estimated to be forty to seventy men strong and armed with revolvers and clubs—once again combed Civil Bend and its environs for Celia and Eliza. Witnesses recalled that many were the worse for drink. Nuckolls's hatred of abolitionists boiled over, and his "search party" became a veritable mob. He set his sights on the Garners, the free African American family that had moved to Civil Bend with the Blanchards. The family of seven had recently lost their widowed father, and the remaining children, ranging in age from twelve to twenty, were in the house. The gang pulled down the outhouse, invaded the home, and tore it apart. The men were certain the Garners either knew where Celia and Eliza were or had been involved in their escape. They dragged Joseph Garner, age twenty, and Henry Garner, age nineteen, into the woods for "questioning" that soon became torture. In a nightmarish scene, the men whipped the brothers until they bled. Nuckolls and his men then choked the young men, yelling for them to give up what they knew. As the two held out, Stephen Nuckolls put a rope around Henry's neck and "hauled him up once or twice to make him confess." Henry probably thought he was going to die, but the rope was loosened and he tumbled to the ground.[18]

A few men started a fire—suggesting that even burning might be in store for the brothers unless they confessed. Fearing for their very lives, the Garners still denied knowing Celia and Eliza's whereabouts but identified John Williamson as having brought the women across the Missouri River. Versions of the story differ, but one of them may have even suggested places where Celia and Eliza might be concealed. The mob then mounted their horses and dashed to the house of a man named Smith, one of Civil Bend's oldest settlers. They surrounded the house, pounded on the door, and demanded to search it. Smith asked under what authority, and one of the men hit the door with a cane, crying, "This is our authority!" Smith answered, "I shall not fight, but if you search my house, it will be without my permission." Once again, the men searched every nook and cranny, as well as the outhouses and sheds. They stomped all over Smith's hay and thrust pitchforks into it.[19]

Incensed, they moved on to abolitionist Reuben Williams's house. Williams was working in the field, but his alarmed wife and sister stood by while the men inspected the cellar as well as every room. Williams saw the crowd and hurried back to his house as the searchers emerged. "Upon being informed what their business was," Williams said, "it was a mean piece of business." One of Stephen Nuckolls's brothers struck Williams with his cane, knocking him almost senseless, while Stephen drew his pistol, insisting he had every right to "hunt his runaways in any place he chose."[20]

Not far away, a young farmer named Julius F. Merritt had just sat down to write a letter to his brother, Rev. William W. Merritt of Montgomery County, Iowa, when a neighbor came into his house and said, "They are after you." Merritt gathered some gear and ran two miles to "get to a place of security." But the mob found him anyway. The mounted "border ruffians" chased him and surrounded him. Six days later he finished the letter to his brother. Declaring himself "beaten by the hell hounds of slavery," he described the mob's torture of the Garners and his own brush with death: "They smashed me with clubs and fists, until I broke and run, when S. Nuckols fired at me, the ball passed to the right of my head." He ended his missive by saying, "Don't let Mother see this letter."[21]

Given Nuckolls's quick and violent reaction, in all likelihood the Civil Benders had not had time to move Celia and Eliza to Tabor. Although

Fugitive Slave Excitement 97

the details are scant, at some point Nuckolls or members of his party even entered the house where the two women were concealed.[22] One can only imagine the fear and dread they felt when they heard the searchers overhead. They had put themselves in the hands of their agents, and now they had to hide when told to hide and move when told to move—all in unfamiliar surroundings and under the cover of darkness. Knowing their enslaver, Celia and Eliza may have expected that he would come after them, but they may not have fathomed the depths to which he would go in his pursuit.

The illegal searches continued on December 2. The mob first returned to the Garner house, but the family had been removed to Dr. Blanchard's for safety. After all the slave catchers' efforts, the women were still missing. Frustration may have fueled their fury, and the posse continued to search the area, "abusing and insulting everyone who had the manhood to oppose in word or deed their lawless conduct." Although the mob was less violent than the day before, still someone knocked an Irish-born laborer to the ground. In addition to torture and assault, Civil Bend had seen their homes invaded, feather beds ripped open and the contents strewn across their floors, "pans of milk poured upon them," and clothing scattered about. Enough was enough. That evening local magistrate J. C. Larimore issued an arrest warrant for fifteen or sixteen people for riot and assault, including Stephen Nuckolls. The constable served the warrant, and Nuckolls and some of his men "gave themselves up and accompanied the constable to the magistrate's office." Because of the late hour, a full examination was postponed until the next day. Nuckolls somehow got permission to return home for the night, leaving some of the men to remain as prisoners.[23]

On December 3 the "wind blew strong. Gray clouds obscured the sky, and stray flakes of snow were falling." The court convened with only a few prisoners present; later lore named two of Stephen Nuckolls's relatives among them. Somewhere between fifty and sixty citizens were in also in attendance, likely including some Taborites who traveled down to ensure that no Nebraska mob would disturb the proceedings.[24]

The defendants asked the court to issue a subpoena for John Williamson on suspicion of aiding the fugitives. Justice Larimore granted the subpoena but became wary of their motives. Perhaps it was a ruse to smoke Williamson out and get him into the mob's hands. He sent an extra guard with the officer to find Williamson. Williamson was brought in, but by then Nuckolls had sent a letter that he and the others charged could not cross the river. They asked for another postponement. The remaining defendants then waived the examination and gave bond for their appearance, and the proceeding was postponed for the next day, with the rest of the defendants put under guard.[25]

The evening of December 3 may have been when Celia and Eliza emerged from their hiding place. The *Nebraska City News* reported that "a man came to the river and hallooed across that the fugitives under an escort of thirty armed men had been transported to Tabor, another abolition hole a few miles distant."[26] Whatever the exact date, in early December Ira Blanchard took Celia and Eliza to Tabor, one account noting that "when capture seemed imminent a large dry goods box was secured and placed in a hayrack—with the negroes under the box and hay piled high above, they drove serenely on."[27] Traveling in a hayrack must have been bone-wrenching at best, similar to what one fugitive from Kansas described when he hid under a wagon seat with his "head repeatedly bumping against the wagon's floor," willing himself with every ounce of strength to remain quiet through the painful ordeal.[28]

The report of an armed thirty-man escort for Celia and Eliza to Tabor is dubious, given the abolitionist network's usual secrecy. A letter to the editor of the *Fremont Herald* signed E. R. of Civil Bend denied the assertion, stating that the armed escort "was either reported by some of their [Nuckolls's] own men, or some one wishing to curry favor [with them] even at the expense of the truth."[29] Moreover, such a large group would have attracted attention, even at night, a risk they likely would have avoided since not all Iowans supported the abolitionist cause. After all, the 1850 Fugitive Slave Law called for punishing anyone who helped fugitives. Although Nuckolls had men stationed at strategic spots to intercept the women, a week later Celia and Eliza were still free. Thus the later recollections of a few men who accompanied them on each leg of their journey are almost certainly accurate.[30]

December 4 was a busy day. According to the Civil Bender's timeline, the court in Fremont County, Iowa, convened once again. Stephen Nuckolls and his attorneys, Allen A. Bradford, and Oliver P. Mason, along with some forty or fifty more men, crossed the Missouri River from Nebraska into Iowa "by laying boards on the ice." Bradford and Mason asked for another postponement, which was granted. The attorneys may have then sworn out a warrant "for the arrest of the runaways under the Fugitive Slave Law," although another account states the court did not issue a warrant, so the paper Nuckolls produced was "bogus." Nuckolls spent the rest of the day searching Civil Bend again.[31]

On December 5 the Nuckolls group appeared in court. They would face a trial for the assaults on the Garners and Reuben Williams. The prosecutions for the remaining defendants for riot were dismissed.[32]

Meanwhile, near Tabor, perhaps on December 4, Celia and Eliza stayed with farmer Benjamin Ladd during the daylight hours. They waited until nightfall for the next transfer, then rode with Ladd during a "dismal, dark night, moonless, cloudy and misty." The small group crossed Silver Creek near the Nishnabotna River's mouth at White Cloud.[33]

Nuckolls had every reason to be confident that he might either recover "his property" or receive damages. Three years before Celia and Eliza's flight to freedom, Iowa had its own legal case that challenged the 1850 Fugitive Slave Law. In June 1855 two slave catchers from Missouri pounced on abolitionist Edwin James of Burlington, who had an African American man in his carriage. The slave catchers identified the man as a fugitive from Missouri called Dick, who belonged to a farmer named Thomas Rutherford, of Clark County. Dick was put in jail to await his fate.[34]

Dick's much-anticipated trial took a surprising turn. Rutherford could not attend the trial but sent his son to identify Dick and prove ownership. As local historian George Frazee later wrote, "It had been taken for granted that the men who had fallen upon 'Dick' before them had not been mistaken." Yet Rutherford's son said he had never before seen the Black man he encountered in the courtroom.[35]

The man was set free. But all agreed that had he been Rutherford's enslaved man, even those officials sympathetic to his plight would have been duty-bound to turn him over. Although many Northerners resented the law, it was largely enforced.[36] Thus slaveholders like Nuckolls knew that if they could capture their enslaved people and establish ownership, the enslaved people would be returned to them, even in free states. Then they could mete out whatever private punishment they deemed proper.

"As Soon as the River Will Do to Cross"

After the violence in Iowa, the *Nebraska City News* countered with the headline "Nebraska City About to Be Sacked," warning that Civil Bend's sister town of Tabor had passed a resolution to attack the Nebraska town "as soon as the river will do to cross."[37] Still another account reported that the Tabor "black scamps" passed a resolution "to run off all the negroes at Nebraska City and then sack the place!" adding with sarcasm, "So you see we are doomed!"[38]

Tabor did hold a meeting after the attacks to discuss their friends in Civil Bend. On December 4, 1858, "in consequence of a liability to have our dwellings and premises forcibly and illegally searched for fugitive slaves, as had been done at Civil Bend," they passed a resolution of mutual defense between Tabor and Civil Bend. They voted that each member would keep a rifle ready for use, with at least twelve rounds of cartridges, and if needed, members could check out a rifle from those stored for the Kansas Aid Society.[39] The assembly did not discuss an offensive or sacking of Nebraska City, but if violence came their way, Taborites were ready. Meanwhile, the *Nebraska City News* seemed to revel in the prospect of violence: "If we should hear of some fighting and some fun we shouldn't be at all surprised." As far as sacking Nebraska City, the newspapers taunted the Taborites that "they had better come over and try it. Come ye cuffies all."[40]

Alongside the Civil Bender's account of the trouble, the *Fremont Herald* noted that the *Nebraska City News* seemed "fearful that the citizens of Tabor will . . . go over to their city and search the houses." The item assured Nebraska City residents that Taborites would not do such a thing unless in a "legal and rightful manner, and having law and right to shield them," drawing a stark contrast between the upright citizens of Tabor and the drunken and abusive men who had sacked Civil Bend.[41]

This particular issue of the *Fremont Herald* had an interesting mix of news. The editors ran stories about the best route to the Cherry Creek, Colorado, gold mines; the "Civil Bend War" account; and an editorial about Tabor standing on the law. On the same page, they placed a piece about three free "colored persons" who were tried and convicted in Frederick County, Maryland, for the crime of enticing slaves away from their master. They were sentenced to be "sold out of the state as slaves for life."[42]

The timing and placement of this announcement may have brought John Williamson and the Garners of Civil Bend to mind for all the local Iowa readers. For these free Black abolitionists, the consequences of helping Celia and Eliza were even more dire than fines and jail—helping freedom seekers could result in their enslavement.

But the abolitionist network they chose to trust held fast. After Celia and Eliza crossed the Nishnabotna River, abolitionists Benedict Hill and John Hunter transported them to Lewis, Iowa.[43] The chase remained hot. Abolitionist Oliver Mills "told the girls that it would be unsafe for them to stop at either his place or Mr. Hitchcock's and sent them three miles northeast of Lewis. . . . James Baxter started to Quaker Divide with them."[44] Their likely route from there passed through Des Moines, ran east to Grinnell and Iowa City, and went through Springdale and the Pee Dee Quaker settlement to their last documented stop in Clinton County, Iowa, near the Mississippi River.[45]

Celia and Eliza's choice of a late November escape two days before the next issue of the *Nebraska City News* seems to have worked. Yet even with the advantages afforded by traveling during this time of year, every moment of their November-December sojourn had to have been fraught with fear and even indecision. Had they made the right choice? What did their future hold?

Celia and Eliza's journey and Nuckolls's determination to find them had further repercussions. Nuckolls apparently hired a professional slave catcher to continue the hunt. Amos and Augusta Bixby of Grinnell, Iowa, had been sheltering an earlier freedom seeker named Eliza, who had adopted the alias Frances Overton. Frances had fled slavery in Missouri and traveled on the Underground Railroad through Kansas and Nebraska into the relative safety of Iowa. She was staying with the Bixbys, learning to read while receiving religious instruction. The Bixbys later recalled that "two slave girls ran away from their master in Western [*sic*] Nebraska," which brought a professional slave hunter to the area who heard that "a nice piece of property known as Frances was unlawfully harbored in Grinnell." The Bixbys made a "fortress" of their garret and prepared to defend her. However, the danger of her discovery was so great that they moved her to a Quaker neighborhood "some 50 miles distant," and from there, the Bixbys lost track of her.[46]

Newspaper editors in the area entered the fray with gusto. As news of Celia and Eliza's flight spread, the *Burlington (IA) Daily State Gazette* inveighed against abolitionists, opining that "a fiend, under the garb of philanthropy, has induced them to escape, leave their happy homes and trust to the cold and uncertain charity of misguided fanatics in the Northern States, or perish with the cold of an inhospitable Canadian winter." Moreover, the *Gazette* described the easy lives that Celia, Eliza, Shack, and Shade had been leading (without naming them), with "nothing to do but housework and such chores as pertained to housekeeping—the men went a hunting or fishing at pleasure, either in Nebraska or on this side of the river in Iowa." Their lives had been "easy and comfortable, having good homes and but little to do." They had been reared with Mr. Nuckolls's father, "and were greatly attached to the family . . . with whom they lived without any restraint whatsoever." They had clearly been "meddled with by the fell spirit of abolitionism."[47]

The *Burlington (IA) Weekly Hawk-Eye* responded with a column dripping with sarcasm, critiquing the *Gazette*'s portrait of the Nebraska escapees as living in "the happy patriarchal condition of slavery in the free territory of Nebraska" and "as happy as our first parents in Eden before they transgressed." Now, instead of "having Mr. N to clothe and feed and educate and Christianize them," they would be "reduced to the beggarly condition of laboring like white folks—for their own support and maintenance." Invoking the violent mob attacks at Civil Bend, the *Hawk-Eye* invited the editor of the *Gazette*, William Thompson, as a colonel with military experience, to "put himself at the head of the lively and enterprising negro catchers of Burlington and at once proceed to the scene of action."[48]

Nuckolls himself may have turned to sympathetic newspapers for damage control. In January 1859 the *Iowa Gazette* reported that the escaped "negroes belonged to a family, formerly owned by Mr. N's parents in Missouri, and were scarcely regarded as slaves." The editorial added that "one of the same family is now living with Capt. L. Nuckolls, in Pacific City, Iowa," suggesting not only that the freedom seekers were considered a part of the Nuckolls family, but also that Celia, Eliza, and Shade (who was the enslaved man living in Pacific City) were siblings. The item opined further in Nuckolls's defense, "We do not believe Mr. Nuckolls ever thought of forcibly detaining these Negroes in Nebraska as slaves," concluding, "The negroes are free, Mr. Nuckolls is rid of them, and nobody cares, except a few agitators."[49] This gloss defied all logic, given Nuckolls's much-publicized pursuit of the women and the acts of violence and torture at Civil Bend.

Further "proof" that Celia and Eliza had been enticed away was Nuckolls's assertion that he had promised to free them in a year and a half, along with a donation of property "amounting to two or three thousand dollars" to set them up. As Ira Berlin notes, "The promise of freedom contingent on good behavior was a useful weapon in managing slaves during a period of slavery's decline," particularly in regions that bordered free territory. It cannot be known whether Nuckolls ever made such an offer to the women. A contrary and more probable account claimed that Nuckolls was about to send them "south on a steamboat."[50]

The theme of white meddlers influencing enslaved people to leave their happy homes was a common one. Masters regularly attributed their enslaved people's actions to outside interference. Many enslavers subscribed to conspiracy theories and blamed malign outside influences to explain how even the "most skilled and privileged among" their slaves could "leave without a word."[51] The thought that Celia and Eliza could have surveyed their options, weighed their opportunities and risks, and made up their own minds may not have occurred to Nuckolls or, for that matter, many white newspaper editors. And like his father before him, Stephen Nuckolls turned his rage on abolitionists nearby with his Virginia-style vigilance committee.

Having passed through most of Iowa with pursuers in their wake, Celia and Eliza faced heightened dangers in Clinton County, Iowa. Near the Mississippi River, it was a "logical place for slave-catchers to lie in wait."[52] Here the women stayed with Robert Lee Smith, south of Dewitt. Smith's son William later recalled, "The first black persons I ever saw were two girls, whose names were Celia and Eliza and who stayed at our house for weeks, waiting for the river to freeze over at Camanche so it would be safe

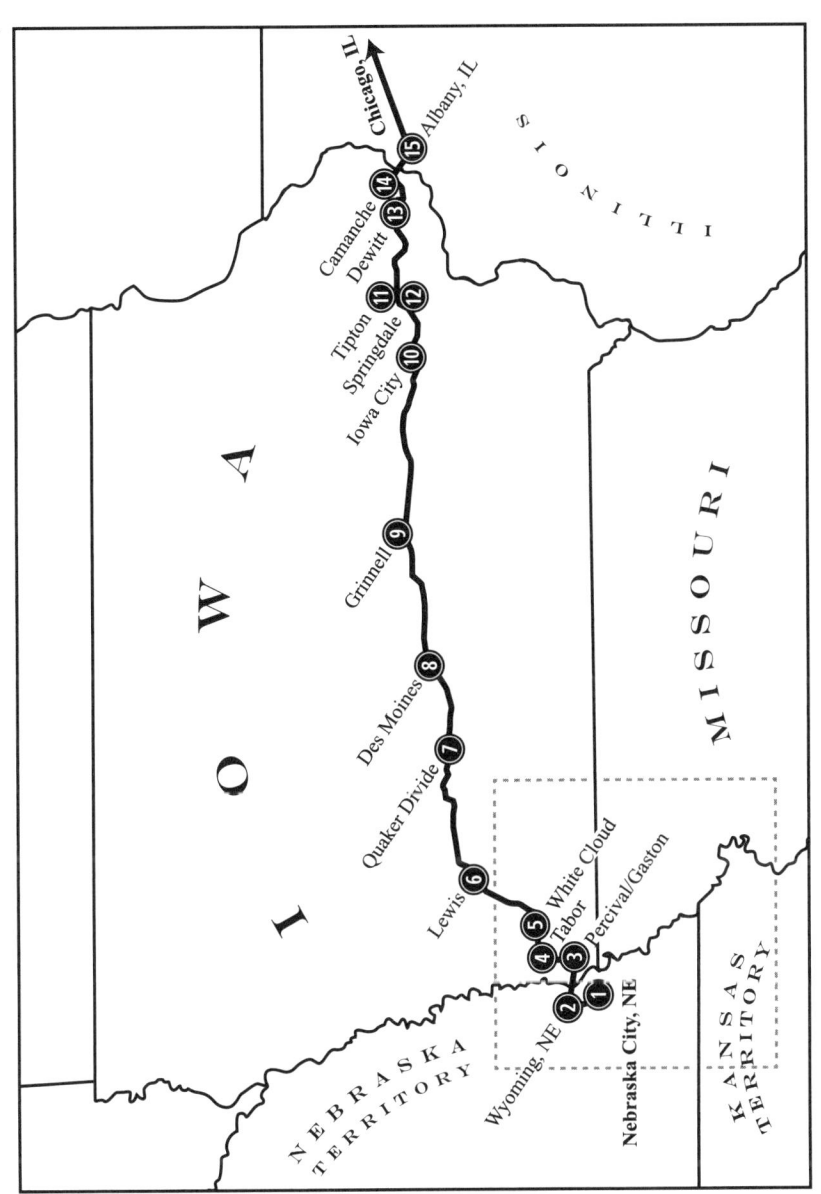

14. Celia and Eliza's likely route through Iowa. Map by Ben Kruse, History Nebraska.

to cross the ice."⁵³ Celia and Eliza cooked some dinners for their hosts during their stay, hiding whenever anyone came near in case visitors were not sympathetic to their cause.⁵⁴

Neighboring abolitionist John McDougall also remembered Celia and Eliza. After spending considerable time at Smith's home, McDougall advised Smith to see if sympathizer Horace Anthony, who lived on the river at Camanche, could help Celia and Eliza across the ice once the river was frozen over. Anthony agreed, and Celia, Eliza, and Smith went to his house one frigid evening at midnight. Horace Anthony and his friend Samuel S. Burdett would accompany them—armed and ready for action.⁵⁵

McDougall's story evokes images of Harriet Beecher Stowe's *Uncle Tom's Cabin*, in which a freedom seeker also named Eliza crossed the Ohio River, jumping from ice floe to ice floe.⁵⁶ Instead of ice floes, however, they waited until they thought the surface of the Mississippi would be solid. For Celia and Eliza, having crossed the icy Missouri in the relative safety of a skiff, walking across the frozen waterway posed new risks. Falling through into the frigid water would be an ever-present danger. The two women may have edged tentatively onto the rough and intimidating expanse with their protectors. Would the ice hold?

Anthony went "in advance with his cane to try the ice," followed closely by Burdett, "with one of the women on his arm," and Smith, who aided the other woman. In the darkness, there was little way to tell how safe they were, although Anthony may have scouted the safest route during the daytime. The small party probably listened to the *tap, tap, tap* of Anthony's cane, straining to hear any difference in sound—any telltale crackling or crunch. The ice may have been singing to Celia and Eliza of freedom and danger with every step.⁵⁷

How long their journey across the icy stretch lasted is unknown, but it probably seemed much longer than it was. Once they reached the other shore, their relief would have been palpable, but they had little time to rest. The group traveled in darkness to a Methodist minister's house in Albany, Illinois. The minister's son conveyed the women to their next stop in a carriage.⁵⁸

From there, Celia and Eliza made their way to Chicago. Their journey to freedom seemed secure.

{ 7 }

The Consequences of "Villainy and Meanness"

Newspapers far and wide carried versions of Celia and Eliza's escape into Iowa from the end of 1858 well into 1859. The story even made it into British newspapers. Headlines blared, "Another Speck of War," "Fugitive Slave Excitement in Western Iowa," and "Fugitive Slave Excitement at Nebraska."[1] Commenting on Nuckolls's efforts to capture Celia and Eliza, the American Anti-Slavery Society, no stranger to stories of violence, reported that "the outrages perpetrated in searching for these slaves exceed, if possible, in villainy and meanness, those recorded in most of the cases in this tract."[2]

The *Waverly (NE) Republican* immediately called attention to the issues Celia and Eliza's actions highlighted while the women were still crossing Iowa. The Nebraska Territorial Legislature had just indefinitely postponed a bill to abolish slavery, based on their assertion that "slavery does not exist in this Territory in any practicable form, and cannot so exist without affirmative legislation recognizing the right of property in slaves." The *Republican* pointed out that this official denial of slavery's existence flew in the face of Nuckolls's handbill offering $200 for "the return of 'my two negro women, who were enticed away from my house on the night of Nov. 25.'" The editors ventured that Nuckolls was "standing on the Dred Scott decision," rather than the legislative report they quoted.[3]

Indeed, the year before, the U.S. Supreme Court had ruled on the case of Dred Scott and his wife, who had sued for their freedom based on his long residence in free territory. Enslaved in Missouri, Scott was taken by his enslaver to live on military posts in the free state of Illinois and at Fort Snelling in Wisconsin Territory (today in Minnesota). The state of Missouri, where he lodged his suit, had a "once free, always free," judicial standard for freedom suits. As historian Don E. Fehrenbacher notes, "Again and again, the highest court in the state [of Missouri] had ruled that a master who took his slave to reside in a state or territory where slavery was prohibited thereby emancipated him."[4]

Though Dred Scott was first declared free, the case went through a number of appeals that took years to unravel. One of the questions injected into the legal argument was a new angle: once Scott returned to a slave state, his condition as a slave was "reattached" to him. In other words, if he had wanted to be free, he should have petitioned during his residence in a free jurisdiction. Another issue brought up but not emphasized was that military jurisdictions, as federal installations, did not have to follow the slavery prohibitions of the Northwest Ordinance or the Missouri Compromise. Ultimately, the case was appealed to the U.S. Supreme Court. Chief Justice Roger B. Taney wrote the majority opinion, ruling that Scott had no standing to sue for his freedom because slaves were not citizens, disregarding years of precedent set by freedom suits throughout the country. The opinion also stated that Scott's term of residence in Illinois and Wisconsin Territory did not free him because he was once again under Missouri law, which allowed slavery. Neither the Northwest Ordinance nor the Missouri Compromise applied, and he was not free. Taney remanded the case back to Missouri's Circuit Court with instructions for dismissal, while affirming the Southern interpretation of popular sovereignty.[5]

Celia and Eliza's status was analogous to Dred Scott's in some ways, but instead of residing on a U.S. military post, where people retained residency in their home states, they had lived in Nebraska City. And while Scott had been returned to the slave state of Missouri, Celia and Eliza continued to reside in Nebraska Territory. But was Nebraska slave or free? Was the Southern position that territories had to allow slavery until ready for statehood correct, or would the Northern understanding of popular sovereignty rule the day? These were the arguments that Celia and Eliza's flight prompted among proslavery and antislavery forces across the country.

Although it did not rise to the level of hostilities in "Bleeding Kansas," the violence surrounding Celia and Eliza's flight resembled the border ruffian tactics that had earned Kansas its nickname. Upon learning of Celia and Eliza's escape, Stephen Nuckolls drew on his background in his response—a response that may have been normal in his native Virginia but caused an uproar in Iowa, even among those Iowans who were inclined to tolerate slavery across the river. Indeed, the attacks on Civil Bend and the treatment of the Garner brothers went to an extreme that prompted newspapers from Iowa to New York and from Illinois to Mississippi to comment.[6]

Thus, even in the relative peace of Nebraska and Iowa, simmering tensions over slavery and freedom could be unleashed in vigilante-style violence. Celia and Eliza's escape prompted large groups of men in Nebraska and Iowa to arm themselves in preparation for battle. So-called upstanding citizens engaged in torture, assault, and illegal searches. Only the arrest of Nuckolls and some of his compatriots dampened the fuse of this borderland powder keg.

Back in Nebraska City, Nebraska's Second Territorial Court pursued some of the leaders for their role in the Iowa violence with alacrity. During the December term, which began the week of December 7, 1858, the assembled jury indicted Stephen F. Nuckolls, William B. Hail, Hiram P. Bennet, William Bennet, John O. B. Dunning, Stephen F. Hail, and Curran C. Hail for rioting. Except for William Bennet and Curran Hail, the men pleaded guilty, and the court fined them $5 plus court costs of $36.88. The defendants would be committed to the custody of the Otoe County sheriff until the fines and costs were paid. The jury did not find enough evidence to indict William Bennet or Curran Hail. The docket indicates the fines were paid, probably by Nuckolls, so it is doubtful that any of them spent time in jail.[7]

The *Nebraska City News*, which had blatantly encouraged and supported the violence, remained silent on these legal proceedings. Instead, a short report on the district court announced that a grand jury had been seated, and although there were "some in this county who are not good and law-abiding citizens; yet they are gratified that no very flagrant offences have been brought to their notice." No details surrounding the Nuckolls incident were furnished on the cases before the jury. Apparently, riot was not a "flagrant offence."[8]

Some accounts relate that Stephen Nuckolls pursued Celia and Eliza all the way across Iowa, but it seems unlikely. His multifaceted business interests needed his attention. The same December he was indicted for riot, the *Nebraska City News* announced he was "making all preparations for starting early in the spring" for the Cherry Creek, Colorado, mines. There had been much excitement about gold in the area, but rather than mining gold himself, Nuckolls's focus was on selling goods to miners. His large trains would transport "a saw mill, a blacksmith shop, and large quantities of goods."[9]

But he had by no means given up on recovering Celia and Eliza. His reward still stood, and there were men in Kansas and Missouri who had no qualms over slave catching. Stephen Nuckolls's determination may have also been affected by Lucinda's wishes. Eight months after Celia and Eliza left the Nuckolls household, she wrote to her parents about how hard she was working. After the common complaint about not receiving enough mail, she added, perhaps in answer to an inquiry, "Mother, we have the girl we hired last winter when Liza and Celia went off." She added that they had also taken in twelve-year-old Mary Long (presumably white) to help around the house. Still, Lucinda was "pritty busy" with "no less than ten work hands all summer," and as many as fifteen. Her time was filled with cooking, cleaning the house, and making butter while she did all her own sewing. Later, she wrote that she still had Susan Wright and Mary Long there to help, and there were "12 in the family now."[10]

"A Wholesome Lesson to Slaveholders in All the Western Territories"

Nuckolls, his relatives, and friends who had participated in the violence in Civil Bend faced both criminal and civil suits in Iowa. At the criminal level, the State of Iowa charged Nuckolls with assault with intent to commit great bodily injury. The case was decided during the September term of the Fremont County District Court. Nuckolls was found guilty and fined $100 plus costs.[11] Indeed, his victim Reuben Williams had suffered head trauma that rendered him partially deaf for the rest of his life. Williams's civil suit fared better in the Page County, Iowa, District Court. In May 1860 the court ordered Stephen Nuckolls, Harvey G. Bourne, Heath Nuckolls, G. W. Hail, and others to pay Williams $8,000 in damages plus $39 in expenses, a sentence that "served him right," with the hope that the verdict and damages would "prove a wholesome lesson to slaveholders in all the western territories."[12]

The editor at Iowa's *Page County Herald* hoped that the case's outcome would prevent future violence, praising the jury's strong stand against mob law. He added that the case was important because "Mr. Nuckolls, the principal defendant, is one of the most wealthy and esteemed men in the West; and aside from this one unfortunate occurrence, enjoyed the confidence and respect of all who knew him." The *Herald* reported in June 1860 that despite a grand jury awarding Williams $8,000, Nuckolls settled with him for $2,500 plus attorney's fees.[13]

The story of a settlement was in error, however, and the wheels of justice continued to turn. On August 6, 1862, Reuben S. Williams, through his attorney James Sweet, filed an action against Nuckolls and ten others to recover $5,039 plus interest and court costs due him by order of the Clarinda, Iowa, District Court after deducting $3,000 paid from the $8,000 judgment. The petition reminded the debtors that the full $8,000 judgment remained "in full force and effect."[14]

Likewise, *Garner v. Nuckolls*, in which African American Henry Garner sued Nuckolls for the horrific torture he endured during the "Civil Bend War," was settled for $600.[15] The Garner case was of particular interest as a test of Iowa's 1857 amendment to the state bill of rights allowing Blacks to testify in court. No court files are extant, but it seems likely that the court was packed with onlookers interested in seeing justice done to the slave catchers who wreaked such havoc in Civil Bend.[16]

As Nuckolls dealt with legal challenges in his usual aggressive manner, the territorial government's makeup was evolving, and not in his favor. Addison E. Sheldon's history of Nebraska states that its "people never voted for slavery," which was technically true but misleading. Efforts to prohibit the institution were delayed and overruled until right before the Civil War.[17]

Again, citing the small number of enslaved people, historians have asserted that slavery in Nebraska Territory was unimportant because local issues generated greater concern.[18] Yet the Grayson escape highlights that local, regional, and national newspapers carried a constant stream of items about slavery in Nebraska. Because of the controversy over the expansion of slavery to the territories, national editors, both proslavery and antislavery, eyed events in Kansas and Nebraska for signs of its expansion or demise, viewing the territories as laboratories in which to test whether popular sovereignty would work.

The *National Era* of Washington DC described Nebraska Territory's first inaugural ball in 1855, quoting the *Nebraska City News*, which it characterized as an "unscrupulous, unprincipled newspaper": "Now Slavery is here, in a small way—a few negroes, twenty or so, and its supporters are coming faster and faster," another example of a number that exceeds official counts. The *News* reported "some excitement" over the issue, asking whether Nebraska south of the Platte River might become a slave state.[19] To some extent, the national North-South divide was replaying in miniature in Nebraska Territory.

The citizens south of the Platte River, calling themselves South Platters, were more numerous than the population north of the river, and they resented the territorial capital's location north of the Platte at what was then called Omaha City. And as in all territories, the capital's location was of prime importance. Indeed, the controversy over where Nebraska's capital would be located is one reason historians have concluded slavery was relatively unimportant.[20] But Nebraskans were capable of caring about more than one issue at a time. As sectional tensions between North and South played out at the national level, Nebraska's North and South Platters experienced sectional differences of their own. Mirroring national debates, the problems of slavery and of "fugitive slaves" were a continuing source of friction. When Nebraska's enslaved people crossed the border toward freedom, the public discussion that ensued was as heated and inflammatory as any debate about the capital city.

The related issue of popular sovereignty also continued to be a major point of contention in the territory. In 1855 Nebraska's legislature recognized the Kansas-Nebraska Act's provision that federal law "shall have the same force and effect within the said Territory of Nebraska" and that the people were "perfectly free to form and regulate their domestic institutions in their own way."[21] When acting territorial governor Thomas Cuming addressed the legislature in 1857, he raised the specter of Kansas-style violence over slavery, while commending the Nebraska members on their rejection of the "lamentable dissensions" that plagued their "sister territory."[22]

In December 1858, while Celia and Eliza were still in hiding and Nuckolls was wreaking havoc in Iowa, Republican representative Samuel G. Daily's bill to "abolish slavery in the territory of Nebraska" wound its way through the territory's bureaucracy. The bill was referred to a special committee. The committee report dressed Daily down for introducing the bill, implying that his motive for slavery's abolition was political ambition, while stating that strife and sectionalism had "done much to embitter our social relations, and to destroy those feelings of brotherhood which should ever exist amongst the pioneers of a new country."[23] One committee member repeated that "slavery does not exist in this territory in any practical form."[24]

Again, the proslavery elements in the territorial government referred to the violence in Kansas as a reason to leave slavery unaddressed, concluding, "The page of blood which Kansas has furnished to the history of the world should have been warning to the fell hand [meaning Daily and the Republican Party] which has attempted to strike such a blow at our peace and quiet."[25] When the bill was sent to the territorial council, a motion passed 9–1 to postpone the act indefinitely.[26] In the background of the December 1858 session was the departure of territorial governor William A. Richardson on December 5. Replacing him as acting governor until a new one could be appointed was J. Sterling Morton, whose tolerance of enslavement in the territory was well established.

At the same time, an interesting twist to territorial politics took place. In 1858 South Platters entertained the idea of seceding to Kansas under its Lecompton Constitution, which permitted slavery and excluded free Blacks from residing in Kansas Territory. Robert W. Furnas, editor of Brownville's *Nebraska Advertiser*, criticized the "Kansas shriekers" who would "tie us to Kansas to settle, without doubt, the slavery question." However, after an initial, and probably rigged, vote for the Lecompton Constitution, and the U.S. Senate's approval amid great controversy, the House of Representatives rejected Kansas's bid for statehood. By the time the South Platte convention to consider annexation met, Kansas voters had gone to the polls again and had rejected the Lecompton Constitution.[27]

But this muddled situation did not deter the South Platters. The convention to consider annexation began at Brownville, Nebraska, on January 5, 1859, while Celia and Eliza were still making their way across Iowa. Many South Platte worthies attended as delegates, including Stephen F. Nuckolls, his brother Houston, and Nebraska City builder Charles F. Holly, all slaveholders, as well as representative Samuel G. Daily of Nemaha County,

Villainy and Meanness

an antislavery advocate.²⁸ Although Daily had argued against the measure, he voted yes to annexation amid some consternation. Political opponents did not fail to point out the apparent contradiction between his vocal opposition to annexation and his affirmative vote for it. He explained he was "honor bound to follow" the will of his constituents.²⁹

Ironically, Kansas rejected the South Platters' bid. Without missing a beat, Stephen Nuckolls and his brother Houston, so eager to be Kansans a few months before, ran for the Nebraska legislature and won. The Nuckolls brothers joined a strong Democratic showing that prompted the *Omaha Nebraskian* to proclaim, "Abolitionism in Nebraska Wiped Out."³⁰ Of the thirty-nine members in Nebraska's house, twenty-five were Democrats.³¹ Upon the Nuckolls brothers' victory, Stephen Nuckolls wrote in October 1859 to J. Sterling Morton, "Democracy is triumphant in Nebraska.... I wish old Ossawattamie [John] Brown had had, say, 1000 of the Abolitionists, Republicans, Opposition People's party or whatever they may be at Harpers Ferry with him from Nebraska and about 3000 from Iowa. So that J. B. could deal out justice to them himself. Then we would have no trouble hereafter in carrying Nebraska and Iowa."³²

The sobriquet "Ossawattamie" referred to Brown's unsuccessful defense of the free-state town of Osawatomie, Kansas, on August 3, 1856, in which five free-staters died, including Brown's son Frederick. Nuckolls's letter was dated only a week after John Brown shocked the nation with his attack on the federal armory at Harpers Ferry, Virginia. Proslavery Democrats seized on the event to paint the entire Republican Party with the brush of treason.

A week after Nuckolls penned his triumphant letter to Morton, the *Nebraska City News* charged that Republican leaders were responsible for Brown's actions because they had furnished Brown and his men with "money and Sharp's rifles to carry out the hellish purposes." In fact, John Brown and his attack almost filled the issue's entire second page. Under the headline "Another Republican Leader Gone," they proclaimed "John Brown of Ossawattamie" dead (although he was not executed until early December). With a nod to the story's local angle, the editorial reminded readers that some ten months before, John Brown had "passed through this very town with thirteen stolen negroes and a like number of stolen horses."³³

The Fugitive Slave Law in Nebraska Territory

A year after Celia and Eliza left, and with no success in retrieving them, Nuckolls went to court to recover the value of his lost "property" under the Fugitive Slave Law. The first hurdle was whether the territorial court would take the case. And again, the issue of whether slavery actually existed in Nebraska Territory was raised, along with the assertion that Nebraska Territory was free until a vote in the territorial legislature declared otherwise.

The justice who would decide if Celia and Eliza were legally enslaved, and thus subject to the Fugitive Slave Law, was Joseph Miller. Originally from Chillicothe, Ohio, Miller had been elected to Congress for the 1857–59 term. While a representative, he "supported the southern contention as to the Kansas-Nebraska controversy, and this so incensed his [Ohio] constituency that he was defeated for the second term." After this defeat, President James Buchanan appointed Miller to the judgeship in Nebraska.[34]

It was no surprise, then, that he ruled "that under the Constitution and laws of the United States, the owners of slaves or persons owing service in this territory, could maintain an action against parties enticing and carrying away slaves, or persons owing such services," implying that Celia and Eliza, four-year residents of Nebraska, were legally enslaved. Thus Nuckolls's suit against Ira Blanchard, George Gaston, and the other abolitionists at Tabor and Civil Bend was allowed. Slavery opponents pointed to this judicial decision as proof that Nebraska Territory functioned as slave country. Given the controversy, the lawsuit must have attracted much attention, but the *Nebraska City News* remained silent.[35]

In December 1859 Nuckolls's attorneys Oliver P. Mason and his old friend Allen A. Bradford alleged a catalog of wrongs against sixteen Iowans in a thirteen-page petition (most of which was needlessly repetitive) naming the following:

> Reuben S. Williams
> [George] Hitchcock
> Egbert [Edgar] Avery
> Wesley H. Knickerbocker
> Marcus Pierce
> Alexander Gaston

George B. Gaston
Ira D. Blanchard
Thomas Reed
John Williamson, Jr.
Edgar Hill
Edwin Hill
Lester W. Platt
Julius F. Merritt
H. B. Horton
William Lane[36]

Ira Blanchard and John Williamson had indeed helped Celia and Eliza escape. Reuben Williams was the man whom Iowa courts had granted $8,000 for Nuckolls's vicious assault on him, but whether he rendered any aid to Celia and Eliza is unknown. Notably missing from Nuckolls's list were the Garners, who had been tortured; Benjamin Ladd, who had housed Celia and Eliza on the second leg of their journey; and Origen Cummings, who had accompanied their wagon out of Tabor. This demonstrates that Nuckolls's charges were based on speculation and reputation rather than real evidence.

The petition charged that the Iowans, "well knowing the said Celia and Eliza to be the property and slaves of the said plaintiff, contrived unlawfully to injure the said plaintiff and deprive him of all his property in—said slaves Celia and Eliza." They also "did hinder and obstruct and prevent" Nuckolls from "arresting Celia and Eliza, fugitives from labor and service," as well as "knowingly abet and assist Celia and Eliza to escape." The suit further alleged that the defendants carried "Celia and Eliza to Tabor, Fremont County, Iowa . . . thence to Canada, a Province of Great Britain." Nuckolls explained that the "trouble, care, and expense," he incurred in hunting for Celia and Eliza, including "employing help," amounted to more than $6,000. Celia and Eliza were also of "great value" as property, worth, "to wit, $3,000." Because of these expenses and the women's inherent value, and adding the further harm to him from being alienated from the "benefits and profits" of Celia and Eliza's domestic and household service, he demanded $10,000 from the defendants, plus the lawsuit's costs. It may not have been a coincidence that he sued for the same amount he had been asked to pay the Iowans for his assaults.[37]

Nuckolls's petition also insisted that he was Celia and Eliza's "legal owner" and "lawfully possessed" the two women in November 1858.[38] This point may have anticipated the counterargument the Iowans would use that Nebraska had not voted on the slavery issue and was free until such a vote was taken.

In fact, in November 1858 Democratic representatives in the Nebraska legislature, Benjamin. P. Rankin and William Fleming, submitted a minority report *against* the bill to abolish slavery, stating, "Slavery does not exist in this Territory in any practical form, and *can not so exist without affirmative legislation.*" Rankin and Fleming used this "nonexistence" as proof that their opponents simply wanted to "hurl this fire-brand of strife into our peaceful Territory." It was on these grounds that they recommended postponing the bill to abolish slavery. Indeed, Nuckolls's lawsuit threw this legal theory into serious question. If slavery did not exist until the legislature positively affirmed it, then Nuckolls had no legal basis for his lawsuit. Thus Nuckolls's attorneys added that Celia and Eliza were his property "under the laws of the Constitution," as well as according to "decisions in the United States Supreme Court." The attorneys did not name the Supreme Court decisions, but top of mind must have been the 1857 *Dred Scott* decision.[39]

Although the lawsuit never reached a full trial, the defendants' answer to Nuckolls's suit denied any wrongdoing. The Iowans laid out a process argument that Celia and Eliza had not been under arrest by "any judge or commissioner" when they passed through Iowa. Thus Nuckolls could not accuse the defendants of aiding or rescuing them, since they were not under any process of law. More important, the defendants' demurrer—granting the fact that Celia and Eliza had left Nuckolls's residence—specifically stated that Celia and Eliza were "not at the time *by the laws of Nebraska Territory*, property," and therefore the plaintiff could not seek damages by law.[40] Celia and Eliza's escape had crystallized the debate that had roiled national politics since before the Compromise of 1850. With no "positive law" allowing slavery in a territory, was the territory presumed to be free? This was the question that all expected would reach the U.S. Supreme Court.

"Popular Sovereignty . . . Is a Cheat and a Delusion"

Despite the predictions of abolition's demise in Nebraska, and in the wake of abolitionist John Brown's attack on Harpers Ferry, Samuel G. Daily introduced the house bill titled An Act to Abolish and Prohibit Slavery again in December 1859. This time the vote was postponed. and a three-person committee was tasked with submitting reports—a committee composed of Dr. George L. Miller of Omaha, Chair; William H. Taylor of Nebraska City; and George W. Doane, representing Burt, Washington, and Sarpy Counties.

The Kentucky-born Taylor was the only committee member on record as antislavery among the three men. The *Nebraska City News* had attacked him the year before, hoping to weaken his credibility. The editors declared him a Missouri slaveowner, whose position as an antislavery Republican was awkward, disjointed, and out of place. But there is no evidence that Taylor owned slaves (although family members did).[41] And Taylor's speech to the legislature in December 1859 was far from disjointed; he supplied facts to counter falsehood and distortion.

Taylor referred to Celia and Eliza in his response to the continued assertion that slavery did not exist in Nebraska:

> I know of my own knowledge the Hon. Stephen F. Nuckolls had three colored persons, whom he claimed as slaves up to a very late period. Two of these persons escaped from Mr. Nuckolls, in the winter of '58 and '59 and the other, a colored man of twenty-five years of age, was sold by him . . . in the spring of 1859 and carried to some of the southern slave-holding states, as a slave. This man had been a resident of Nebraska for about three years . . . as evidence that slavery does exist and is considered to be a legal institution here I have only to cite the fact that the Hon S. F. Nuckolls before alluded to has instituted suit in the second judicial district court of this territory against certain parties residing in Iowa for the value of two colored persons—his slaves.[42]

Taylor also cited Edward A. DesLondes, Alexander Majors, and Judge Charles F. Holly, all of Nebraska City, for their ownership of slaves. In fact, since Taylor had lived in Nebraska, he knew of no federal appointee "who has not brought with him into the Territory, a Negro or Negroes," concluding, "The fact is indisputable. African slavery does practically exist in Nebraska." But the strongest fact in Taylor's arsenal was Nuckolls's lawsuit against the Iowa abolitionists, the allowance of which recognized Celia and Eliza as slaves.[43]

Stephen Nuckolls's ally, George Miller, emphasized that because of the "stealing propensities of an unprincipled set of abolitionists" in Civil Bend, the numbers had been reduced, so there were only a few slaves in Nebraska but so few it did not matter. The legislation would still be a useless waste of their valuable time.[44] Meanwhile, the *Nebraska City News*, incensed by any antislavery efforts, declared once again that "slavery does not, nor can it, practically exist here," calling out the "Black Republican small beer politicians" who only wanted to frighten people and make trouble by "abolishing a myth, slavery."[45]

Miller also stated that "no sane person" would think that Nebraska was in any danger of becoming a slave territory or slave state. Even if slavery were to become law, the "controlling laws of nature peculiar to the latitude" would prohibit its permanent continuance. He also ridiculed Taylor's report as revealing "six slaves and a half." As to the slaves in the territory, Miller also asserted that by moving these slaves from Missouri and Louisiana to Nebraska Territory, the slaves had been changed from a "worse to better condition—surrounded—by increased comforts, having before them the almost certain prospect of ultimately gaining their freedom." Indeed, the legislation would only "compel their owners to sell them [enslaved people] into a worse bondage, where these prospects would be forever blasted."[46]

George W. Doane joined Miller to weigh in against the bill on the grounds that slavery did not exist and there was "no danger of its introduction therein." Nebraska legislator Milton W. Reynolds of Otoe County, and then editor of the *Nebraska City News*, agreed, stressing that when Nebraska's "masters emigrated from Missouri to Nebraska, they [enslaved people] voluntarily and cheerfully accompanied them."[47] In his view, rather than slavery, Nebraska practiced voluntary servitude. Reynolds also made the extraordinary claim that he spoke on behalf of the enslaved:

Villainy and Meanness

> The only persons alleged to be held in a state of servitude in this territory are three or four in number at Nebraska City. These three or four beloved servants are in an infinitely better condition than a majority of the white servants of this very city in which is located the seat of government of the territory of Nebraska. Theirs is a paradise compared with nine-tenths of the white servants of the north. They fare better and go better dressed, and are treated more kindly and affectionately than the hotel servants throughout the entire northern states. In behalf of these servants I protest against the passage of this bill. Have they petitioned and prayed your honorable body to pass any such enactment? Do they desire its passage? Do you not know that it will operate most detrimentally, seriously and most prejudicially to their best interests? Driven out from their homes of quiet ease and luxury, they will be obliged to seek a bare and scanty subsistence in that cold, cheerless and already crowded charcoal district in Canada, or they will be transported to the cotton fields and rice plantations of the south.[48]

With these reports Miller, Doane, and Reynolds repeated that the bill to prohibit slavery was a waste of time.

When William H. Taylor rose to support the prohibition of slavery, he addressed all his opponents' arguments. First, to counter their assertion that slavery did not exist in Nebraska, Taylor provided ample proof that it did, including Nuckolls's lawsuit to recover damages under the Fugitive Slave Law, demonstrating that slavery was "considered a legal institution" in Nebraska Territory. Regarding the issue of the nature of enslavement in the territories, was it a positive good? Did Nebraska's enslaved people cheerfully accompany their masters? Celia and Eliza's actions answered that question through their determined flight, with the added emphasis that Nuckolls had sold an enslaved man south in the spring following the sisters' escape, and this enslaved man had been a territorial resident for several years. Finally, Taylor's opponents had minimized slavery's importance because of the small number of enslaved people in the territory. This argument was more difficult to address. Forced to admit that slavery existed, they answered that slavery did not *practically* exist. The addition of "practically" refocused the issue on the problem's magnitude. Being mocked over his concern for "six and a half slaves," Taylor framed his response on moral grounds. If slavery was wrong, it was wrong regardless of the numbers.[49]

Taylor's report reminded everyone of the picture that Celia and Eliza's flight to freedom had painted for the entire country: Two women crossing the Missouri River at night, moving through the cold and dark of winter. The mock lynching and torture of free Blacks. The sack of an entire free-state town. The picture was anything but pretty. Their departure gave the lie to the Nebraska Democrats' protestations that slavery did not, and could not, exist in Nebraska. In the end, Taylor used the knowledge of Celia and Eliza's escape to prove without a doubt that the institution of slavery was present in Nebraska, and no one countered the underlying accuracy of his report. Indeed, his detractors challenged the importance of his facts without disputing the facts themselves.

National news editors had taken note of the deliberations in Nebraska's legislature and that Celia and Eliza's act of resistance and the resulting lawsuits had placed legislators who wanted to avoid the issue in a bind. Celia and Eliza were living proof that enslaved people were in Nebraska and that their enslavement may not have been cheerful, voluntary, or benign. The territorial legislature could no longer table the debate or bury the bill in committee.

After more wrangling, which included changing the title to use the verb *prohibit* instead of *abolish*—a sop to those who still asserted that slavery did not exist in the territory—the house voted 21–17 to pass the bill (Houston Nuckolls voting nay). Nebraskans either rejoiced or lamented, depending on their view. Newspapers as far away as Alexandria, Virginia, chimed in: "The House of Representatives in the Legislature of Nebraska have passed 'an act to prohibit slavery in the Territory of Nebraska.'—the negative vote was not a vote in favor of slavery, but a vote against the passage of a most unnecessary piece of buncombe. There are no slaves in Nebraska, and none are ever expected to be there."[50]

But the debate was not over. Although the measure passed the legislature, Nebraska's territorial governor still had to sign it into law. Gov. Samuel W. Black, a Nuckolls ally and pro-Southern Democrat, had served as a territorial judge in Nebraska City before he became the governor.[51]

He vetoed the bill on January 9, 1860. Governor Black's veto represented a failure of popular sovereignty in many Nebraskans' eyes. For the newly formed Nebraska Republicans, the veto turned out to be an "opportunity to discredit the Black regime," along with the entire Democratic Party.[52]

Governor Black vetoed the bill on several grounds. He mentioned that the lands in Nebraska Territory were originally acquired through the 1803 Louisiana Purchase, at the time "slave territory." The Missouri Compromise was "now pronounced unconstitutional and void," and therefore the old Louisiana Purchase terms held sway. He concluded that enslavement should be allowed to continue during the territorial period.[53] In essence, instead of the territory being presumed free until a vote, it was slave territory.

The governor referred to Celia and Eliza, albeit indirectly, writing that some slaves in the territory "were enticed or stolen away, but no process of law was ever invoked, or could have been invoked, to have them pronounced free." He also addressed the "power in the Territorial Legislature," through popular sovereignty: "I must say 'the people' mentioned in the 14th section of the organic act, never did mean and never was intended to mean 'the Territorial Assembly.'" In other words, the territorial legislature had no control over the slavery question, and popular sovereignty meant nothing.[54]

Black's veto also took a page from President Buchanan's third annual message to Congress, delivered three weeks earlier. Buchanan had congratulated Congress on the Supreme Court's "final settlement" of the "question of slavery in the Territories" with the *Dred Scott* decision. He celebrated the right of "every citizen to take his property of any kind, including slaves, into the common Territories," in an eerie echo of the provision that Nuckolls, Holly, Hiram Bennet, and others had debated the entire night in Missouri when petitioning to open Nebraska to settlement. Buchanan's happy optimism that popular sovereignty would apply only when the territory voted on its state constitution, while leaving slavery in place during the territorial period, seems naive in hindsight.[55]

As a Buchanan appointee, Black probably would have vetoed the bill regardless. But not long after the veto, the *Nebraska City News* ran a short item about Stephen F. Nuckolls in St. Joseph, Missouri, who was "traveling in company with Governor Black of Nebraska." The account describes Nuckolls as "one of the most distinguished and wealthy and unquestionably most sagacious businessmen in the North West," demonstrating the power of political connections he enjoyed.[56]

Mills S. Reeves, a former Democrat calling himself independent, was also a representative for Otoe County in the territorial council that session. He wrote at length on the governor's 1860 veto. A proponent of popular sovereignty, Reeves took issue with Governor Black's logic on the Louisiana Purchase. It was true that the Missouri Compromise had been repealed by the Kansas-Nebraska Act, but the Organic Act contained an important provision that "nothing herein contained shall be construed to revive or put in force any law or regulation which may have existed prior to the Act of 6th of March 1820, either protecting, establishing, or abolishing slavery." He noted that if the Missouri Compromise had been unconstitutional, then slavery would be legal in Iowa too, because a state could not cancel a U.S. treaty. Reeves pointed out that even Sen. Andrew Butler of South Carolina agreed: the language in the Organic Act gave the territories of Kansas and Nebraska "a perfect carte blanche" for the people to decide the slavery question. Reeves observed, "If the right of the Territorial Legislature to exclude slavery does not exist, the boasted popular sovereignty of the Kansas-Nebraska Act is a cheat and a delusion." He predicted the impending "downfall of the old National Democratic Party, [due to] this attempted usurpation of the peoples right."[57]

In addition to other legislative matters, the sixth territorial legislature passed a bill to hold an election in March 1860 to weigh whether Nebraska should move forward toward statehood and elect delegates to a constitutional convention. Among others, the house appointed Houston Nuckolls to the committee for state organization. In the run-up to the March 1860 election, Republicans William H. Taylor and Oliver P. Mason invited prostatehood Democrat Harvey C. Blackman to a public discussion about statehood—a discussion in which Taylor posed the following question: "Mr. Blackman, do you agree with the Governor that the Territorial Legislature has no power to legislate on the subject of slavery?" Blackman dodged the question by stating that he did not think that was what Governor Black had said. Taylor pressed Blackman again and again, framing Nebraska's march to statehood along the sectional issue of slavery. He asked, "Does the Constitution recognize slavery in the territories?" Blackman answered,

"If slaves are property here, yes!" Taylor countered, "Are slaves property here?" Blackman replied, "That is a judicial question, and I do not believe in discussing legal questions in a mass meeting." When pressed to answer, he pronounced, "Whatever the constitution recognized as property when it was adopted, it recognizes as property today. And the constitution will protect the rights of the citizens here in his slaves just as it will anywhere else."[58]

Cornered, Blackman became so exasperated that he suggested Taylor and his companions try the question of whether slaves were property in Nebraska Territory in the courts, to which newspaper editor Orsamus H. Irish responded, "You know that Mr. Nuckolls has brought a suit that will test that question." Blackman finally clarified his stance, declaring that when the "Constitution in 1789 provided that private property should not be taken for public use, without just compensation, it meant a man's slave just as much as it did a man's horse," throwing his support to Nuckolls's court case to recover damages under the Fugitive Slave Law.[59]

The meeting's questions and answers illuminated the growing split between North and South Platters over the question of statehood, and slavery was the sticking point. By a vote of 2,372–2,094, a slim majority of Nebraska voters rejected the call for a constitutional convention. They were not ready.[60]

Thus the issues of whether Nebraska Territory was slave or free and whether the legislature had the power to regulate it continued to dog politicians. Commentators like Reeves and Republican editors homed in on the inconsistencies raised by Nuckolls's lawsuit. Either slavery did not exist and the territory was free or it did exist and the territory was slave.

The enslaved also continued to challenge Nebraska Territory's system. In the wake of the territorial governor's veto, in late June 1860 six more freedom seekers fled Nebraska City, this time from freighting company owner Alexander Majors, who had brought them there in 1858 from Westport, Missouri. Described as "three females of ebony complexion, one crippled ditto dark, and two boys with ivory teeth and impish faces," the *Nebraska City News* asserted that Majors's "servants" did not realize how good they had it in their life of bondage, lamenting that they "preferred nakedness and starvation in Canada to rice puddings, jell[y] cakes and slap jacks in the comfortable and luxurious mansion of our worthy citizen."⁶¹ The continued theme of the supposedly easy life that Nebraska Territory's enslaved persons enjoyed, notwithstanding their flight, was familiar to those who had already read of Celia and Eliza having had nothing but light housework to do, while Shack and Shade went hunting and fishing.⁶²

The *Nebraska City News* predictably blamed their escape on "N—— thieves," who were probably not from Nebraska City but "nasty abolitionists of Civil Bend and Tabor." In response, the *Omaha Republican* editor asked how "N—— thieves" existed when the *News* editor Milton Reynolds, as a representative in the territorial house, had just asserted in the last legislative session that slavery did not exist in Nebraska as long as there was no "positive" local law for it. With inexorable logic, the *Republican* pointed out that either the editor had been mistaken in his views then or he was mistaken now. If slavery did not exist in the territory, "We would like to enquire of the *News* how it happens that they were slaves? By what law were they held as 'servants'"?⁶³

The *News* response sidestepped the question, reiterating that Nebraska City was probably not "infested with n—— thieves," pretending the phrase was a generalization. The original piece that announced Majors's "servants" leaving clearly regarded them as enslaved, but Reynolds repeated that "where there is no law establishing slavery, we consider the institution has no legal existence." To deflect from his own inconsistency, Reynolds pointed out that the Otoe County commissioners (Republicans) had taxed "these servants or persons" as property. A month after these exchanges, a *News* headline blared, "A Negro Kidnapped by a Prominent Republican in Nebraska and Sold into Missouri to Get Money to Carry an Election." Quoting the *Rulo (NE) Guide*, the article reported that the charge was that "black Republican" J. A. Burbanks took a "boy" into Missouri who had been "kept" in Falls City a year or two, some saying he was free, others saying he was a runaway. The *News* declared, "He undoubtedly done the negro a great kindness in bettering his condition" by selling him into slavery. In a postscript, the editor wondered why "they [the Republicans] were not so benevolent when old Ossawatomie Brown run forty through their [Falls City] place."⁶⁴ Thus newspapers on both sides of the slavery debate kept a running "tab" on its place in the territory, with more to come.

Villainy and Meanness 125

Although the *News* had denied the existence of "n—— thieves" in Nebraska City, Nuckolls must have read the piece and agreed that the "nasty" abolitionist Iowans were probably to blame. He knew his lawsuit against them had upset the "nothing-to-see-here" strategy Nebraska Democrats had adopted to argue the bill was unnecessary. He must have hoped it would be worth it. There was no telling when the actual trial would take place. There were motions and delays, and the trial date was still not set. Slavery in Nebraska was in legal limbo.

In the meantime, Nuckolls had not given up on finding the two women. Unbeknownst to him, Eliza had not gone to Canada but had stopped in Chicago and changed her name to Lottie Grayson. No doubt posing as a free woman, she was in a large city where she must have hoped to blend in. How comfortable she had become there is unknown, but as time went by, she may have become complacent. And complacency was dangerous.

{ 8 }

Slave Hunting and Eliza's Chicago Rescue

In the summer of 1860 the prohibition of slavery in Nebraska had been staved off, and the Iowa cases against Stephen Nuckolls were behind him. It seemed that his legal troubles with slavery were over, although his case in Nebraska's territorial court against the "slave stealers" of Iowa was still ongoing. But he had not given up his quest to find Celia and Eliza. Although he was no longer pursuing the sisters himself, he had hired help, and his $200 reward was still in force.[1]

Nuckolls was always busy, but the fall of 1860 stands out as remarkably hectic. He was probably still smarting from the heavy fines granted to Civil Benders Reuben Williams and African American Henry Garner. He may have brooded over Garner's testimony against him in the Iowa court—that a Black person could testify against a white, and win, may have shaken him.[2]

In mid-September 1860 Henry Garner was back in the news. Jacob Hurd, an infamous slave catcher known for his depredations in Kansas, was patrolling in Iowa with two accomplices, N. B. Beck and Joel Wildey. It is unknown whether they were engaging in random patrols, hoping to catch word of a fugitive slave, or had been hired by someone for a specific purpose. Whatever the reason, the three men were in the vicinity of Tabor, Iowa—a known center for abolition. And they came across John Williamson, who had rowed Celia and Eliza across the Missouri River, in company with Henry Garner, whose testimony had condemned Nuckolls for assault. Henry's sister Maria joined the two.

The free Blacks were heading west to Council Bluffs because Williamson's wife, Eliza Garner, was ill, and the Garners wanted to help nurse their sister. The Hurd company drew abreast of them and forced them off the road. Hurd's men leaped into the African Americans' rig and overcame them, breaking Henry's cheekbone in the fight. The men took their cap-

15. Fake bank note mocking Nebraska as a "Land of Liberty."
Private collection. Used with permission.

tives south to Missouri. Once there, John Williamson somehow escaped the kidnappers, but he was picked up south of Rock Port and jailed in Oregon, Holt County, Missouri, as a suspected vagrant.³ No doubt wanting to move fast, the kidnappers went on to St. Louis with the Garners. It later came out that Wildey had raped Maria while she was in their grasp.⁴

African Americans without papers were assumed to be fugitive slaves. Williamson had been charged for being in Missouri "without a permit." According to Missouri law, Williamson would be held and his presence in jail advertised. If no one claimed him, he would be sold. Ira Blanchard and his fellow Civil Bender George Gaston arrived in Oregon and testified that Williamson was known as a freeman but admitted they "could not swear to his place of birth or that his mother was a free woman when he was born." So Williamson went back to jail, still in danger of being enslaved.⁵

News spread fast. The *Council Bluffs (IA) Non-Pareil* declared the entire episode an "atrocious deed." Council Bluffs citizens raised $75 to help rescue their townsman. Iowa representative James Craig also heard the story. He was originally from Holt County, Missouri, where Williamson was in jail. His brother Seth H. Craig was the Pottawattamie County sheriff. The Craigs called on old friends to help, and Sheriff Craig succeeded in bringing Williamson back to Council Bluffs. But he reported "no tidings" about the Garners. Blanchard and Gaston heard that Henry and Maria had been taken to St. Louis. At that point, Gaston went back to Iowa, and Blanchard continued to St. Louis alone to find the Garners.[6]

Situated on the Mississippi River, St. Louis was the largest slave-trading city in Missouri. It was famous for its slave pens, which held people who were to be auctioned either in St. Louis or farther south down the Mississippi River. The 1859 St. Louis City directory listed two slave dealers, Bernard Lynch and Corbin Thompson. Lynch posted his rules in his office, laying out his per-day fees for housing slaves and noting, "My usual care to avoid escape, or accidents, will be taken, but will not be made responsible."[7]

Abolitionist minister and theologian Galusha Anderson visited the Lynch slave pens in 1859 with some of his fellow ministers, writing that the cell they visited had a bare dirt floor and plaster walls with three wooden benches pushed up against them. A dim light shone from "one small window high up near the ceiling." Seven enslaved men and women occupied the room with no privacy. One of Anderson's colleagues remarked, "Thank God, I never had anything to do with that." Anderson replied to his compatriot not to be too sure, asking, "How have you voted?"[8]

Whether in one of Lynch's slave pens or at another site, Blanchard eventually found Henry and Maria and secured their release. Without Blanchard's determination to find them, there is little doubt Henry Garner and his sister would have been sold south. Coming so quickly on the heels of Garner's win against Nuckolls in court, it seems possible the kidnapping was a form of revenge for Henry's audacity in taking a white man to court for assault.[9]

The *Nebraska City News* carried no items about the Garner kidnapping or their rescue, but the newspapers in Missouri and Iowa were full of reports on the incidents. With so many ties between Nebraska City and Fremont County, Iowa, the omission had to be deliberate. Even the *New York Dispatch* reported on the "Exciting Times in Missouri."[10]

Would Celia or Eliza have heard about the Garners? It is difficult to say. But the Nuckolls clan may have had more than a passing interest in the Garner kidnapping, as well as in the slave catcher Jacob Hurd. After releasing the Garners, Blanchard identified Hurd, Beck, and Wildey as the kidnappers. They were arrested and jailed in St. Louis, and it was decided that the men would be returned to Iowa for trial. On October 4 Ira Blanchard and three St. Louis police officers, Officer Charles Woodruff, Deputy Marshal Ed

Brooke, and Detective William Henley, boarded the steamboat *Warsaw* to deliver the kidnappers to the Iowa authorities.[11]

At every stop, the party conveying the kidnappers to Iowa faced trouble. Tensions ran strong, and many people along the way felt Jacob Hurd should not have to go back to Iowa. The crowd was particularly aggressive in St. Joseph, Missouri, where Hurd was apparently well known. The night after leaving St. Joseph, the boat lay by at some point below Nebraska City, when one of Stephen Nuckolls's brothers came aboard to make trouble. The *Missouri Democrat* reported:

> A gentleman named Nuckels, of wealth and high standing in the community, came on board and said that two negroes of his brother had been run off by this Blanchard; that his brother once caught this negro Henry, of whom Blanchard claimed to be a guardian, put a rope around his neck, and thus hauled him once or twice up to the bough of a tree to make him confess what Blanchard had done with the slaves.... Blanchard then brought suit for $8,000 damages for the maltreatment of Henry ... the negro himself being the witness on whose whole testimony the verdict was given.[12]

The brother was almost certainly Houston Nuckolls. He had represented Richardson County in Nebraska's territorial legislature of 1859 and had the ferry rights at Yankton and St. Stephens below Nebraska City. Local historian Lewis C. Edwards reminisced about Houston, "Who among the old settlers can forget Houston Nuckols and his schemes? How he ruled the limited world in which he moved; how he carried on his real-estate transactions, much as boys would swap jack knives?" Houston's speech was designed to stir up people onboard as well as onshore, and his target that day was Ira Blanchard. Houston called Blanchard a "N—— thief," "penitentiary bird," who was "fit only for the gallows." He offered a $100 reward to anyone who would throw Blanchard "over the vessel's rail and on the gang plank."[13]

The steamboat captain took firm charge of the volatile situation. He stressed that all the passengers were "under his protection," and he would brook no violence or lawbreaking. Houston Nuckolls and his friends decided to leave the boat. But Nebraska City was the next stop, and "news of their approach had been telegraphed from Brownville . . . the country alive with excitement. . . . It would not be safe to convey the party to Nebraska City." The steamboat captain chose to dock at the Hamburg, Iowa, landing, which lay south of the town on the Missouri side of the border. Mobs gathered there as well, so it was decided to take the kidnappers back over land to St. Joseph, to be held until a safe exchange could be orchestrated.[14]

These incidents may have brought back memories of the "excitement" in Nebraska and Iowa surrounding Celia and Eliza's flight to freedom, as well as the sack of Civil Bend and the specter of vigilante violence that seemed to hover in the air. Williamson, Gaston, and Blanchard were all still facing Nuckolls's lawsuit in the District Court of Nebraska under the Fugitive Slave Law. And Houston Nuckolls had nearly caused another bout of mob violence—only the firm control of the steamboat captain averted a disaster.

In mid-November the *Missouri Democrat* announced that Sheriff Seth Craig of Pottawatomie County, Iowa, the same man who had helped John Williamson leave the Holt County jail, had transferred Hurd from St. Joseph to the jail at Council Bluffs. Around the same time, Hurd's accomplices, Wildey and Beck, were taken to Sidney, Iowa, near Civil Bend. Hurd was not in jail for long. On December 7 he escaped custody, with newspapers surmising he would return "to the scene of his former exploits in Kansas." Iowa's *Page County Herald* reported that not only had Jacob Hurd escaped from the Pottawatomie jail, but also two prisoners (unnamed, but doubtless Wildey and Beck) had broken out of the Sidney, Iowa, jail on the same night, with "assistance from the outside." The authorities suspected a coordinated escape plan.[15] Who in the area would have perpetrated such an escape? No one knew.

But the appearance of Houston Nuckolls in support of such a notorious criminal and slave catcher like Jacob Hurd raises questions. Did the Nuckolls clan, with vengeance in mind, have anything to do with the initial kidnapping? What was the nature of this intense interest in freeing Hurd? Perhaps Nuckolls wanted to get back at Blanchard for his role in Celia and Eliza's escape as well as for acting as young Henry Garner's guardian in the Iowa lawsuit. Was the notorious Jacob Hurd one of the slave catchers Nuckolls had hired to pursue Celia and Eliza? Many questions but no answers.[16]

The Eliza Case

Shortly after the Garner kidnapping and rape and the arrest of Jacob Hurd, word reached Stephen Nuckolls that Eliza (and perhaps Celia) was in Chicago. Once again, he acted to retrieve them. Perhaps having learned from his illegal searches in Civil Bend, he stopped in Springfield, Illinois, to procure a warrant under the Fugitive Slave Law. The November 5, 1860, warrant, titled "Stephen F. Nuckolls vs. Negro Girls Named Eliza and Celia," adopted the language of the Fugitive Slave Law to name the women as "fugitives from service and labor."[17] The day after Nuckolls obtained the warrant, voters went to the polls and elected Republican Abraham Lincoln president of the United States. The country was more divided than ever. The *Baltimore Sun* published the remark of Sen. Albert G. Brown of Mississippi that when "the government shall be in the hands of Abraham Lincoln, the Union will be dissolved."[18]

There was no time to lose. Nuckolls traveled to Chicago, planning to call on the full force of federal law to pursue his property rights, preferably while Buchanan was still in office. At the same time, Eliza probably continued to work and listen to all the talk of union and disunion that dominated discussions. She may have felt even safer in her new life with the antislavery Republican Party taking charge.

Why did Nuckolls choose Springfield instead of going straight to Chicago for the warrant? Despite being Lincoln's hometown, Springfield was a more sympathetic place for Stephen Nuckolls to obtain a warrant in pursuit of a "fugitive slave." The commissioner there, Stephen Corneau, had heard one fugitive slave case the year before and had sided with the enslaver, while Chicago had a reputation for harboring freedom seekers. A Springfield newspaper editorial described Chicago as a "place that had repudiated the Constitution and the Acts of Congress," where "persons from the south, in pursuit of fugitive slaves, when they learned that fugitives had reached Chicago, made no further effort."[19]

Stephen Nuckolls made the effort. Warrant in hand, he went to Chicago with characteristic energy and purpose.

When Nuckolls arrived in Chicago in the fall of 1860, African Americans made up less than 10 percent of the population. The Illinois legislature had passed an act in 1833 that granted at least partial protection to African

Americans and insisted on preventing the kidnapping of free Blacks. Moreover, Chicago had at least seven identified stations in the Underground Railroad. Whenever possible, freedom seekers were absorbed into the small Black community, which was dispersed among the white population.[20]

How Nuckolls learned of Eliza's presence in the city developed a folklore of its own. A Chicago newspaper mentioned that Eliza worked as a domestic in a Chicago brothel and had confided her circumstances and her Nebraska origins to one of the "unfortunate white females" working there. This woman may have disclosed her presence to a client, who contacted Nuckolls. The newspaper report assumed that the $200 reward was paid and taunted that in a Chicago "brothel was hatched this pure desire to save the Union."[21]

A New Orleans newspaper picked up the brothel story, adding the detail that a woman named Mary Beebe operated the house of ill repute where Eliza worked. Proslavery elements implied that Eliza was a prostitute rather than a domestic—supporting the contention that enslaved people were better off being cared for by their kind and paternal masters.[22]

Perhaps Eliza did confide in the wrong person, although it seems likely that someone, such as Chicago councilman Hiram Joy, J. Sterling Morton's father-in-law, recognized Eliza in the street and sent word back to Nebraska City. Morton's newspaper later implied that Nuckolls hesitated to pursue Eliza because she was "damaged" goods.[23] Nuckolls's actions spoke otherwise.

When Nuckolls presented his warrant to U.S. Commissioner Philip Hoyne in Chicago, Hoyne hesitated to execute it. He appointed a temporary deputy named Jake Newsome, who was eager to help Nuckolls.[24] On November 12 Nuckolls and Newsome may have gone to Eliza's residence and dragged her out, or they may have caught her in the street. All versions agree that the men tried to force Eliza, who had been going by the name "Lottie Grayson," from the street into a carriage or wagon.[25] The *Chicago Daily Tribune*'s front-page report described Eliza as a "stout and sharp girl," noting that "her services as a domestic [were] much prized. A handsome compliment to these traits is to be construed from the affectionate zeal with which her master Nuckolls sought her return."[26]

Eliza resisted and screamed "at a desperate rate."[27] A crowd gathered. An abolitionist lawyer named Chancellor L. Jenks rushed to her defense during the struggle, and "he and Jack Newsome and the slave holder were soon rolling over each other in the gutter."[28]

The mob, composed mainly of free Blacks, pressed in close, like a "dark and angry sea," screaming and cursing at Nuckolls and Newsome.[29] Nuckolls later reported he could have been killed, so great was the mob's fury. Accounts diverge on what happened next. Some reported that both Nuckolls and Eliza Grayson were arrested for disturbing the peace.[30] Others emphasized Nuckolls's narrow escape, while agreeing that Eliza was taken to the armory and only later charged with disturbing the peace. J. N. White, "a respectable merchant" who claimed to have been in Chicago with Nuckolls during the affair, provided yet another version. According to White, Sheriff Anderson took Nuckolls to the armory. Nuckolls stayed calm, saying that "though a mob in the city of Chicago might take his life," he would not be insulted. He told Anderson that if the sheriff would get a room, the two men could enter, lock the doors, and discuss the issue with pistols or knives. A Chicago councilman, no doubt Hiram Joy, apparently came to the armory and had Nuckolls released.[31]

It may be that Hiram Joy took Nuckolls "to a 'place of refuge' and supplied him with a beard and disguise so he could leave the city safely." But a local reporter asserted that Nuckolls was "saved from violence by [someone] placing a policeman's badge upon him" and taking him to the Briggs House under guard. Meanwhile, free Blacks and sympathetic whites in a "high state of excitement" crowded the streets outside the armory where Eliza was being held, intending to "prevent the woman from being taken away from the city."[32]

The official plan was to take Eliza to Springfield the next morning "for examination before Commissioner Conan [Corneau]." Had Nuckolls succeeded in taking Eliza to Springfield to identify her as his property, she would have certainly been reenslaved.[33]

But another plan was afoot. Chancellor Jenks, who had wrestled with Nuckolls and Newsome over Eliza, was not a random passerby. Jenks was a well-known Chicago attorney and real estate agent who had been indicted in 1850 for the rescue of a fugitive slave, and he remained active in Chicago's abolition movement, defending free Blacks and helping freedom seekers.[34]

Jenks went to a sympathetic judge, Calvin DeWolf, to have Eliza arrested for disturbing the peace so that Deputy Sheriff George Anderson could take custody of her. Anderson may have also asked for a warrant to arrest Stephen Nuckolls for attempted kidnapping, but DeWolf later reported that the warrant was never served. Armed with the new arrest warrant, Anderson went to the armory to have Eliza moved. The *Chicago Journal* reported that Anderson "had hardly got out of the door with his charge before she was wrenched from his grasp," adding that he "did not make a very sturdy resistance." She was taken down Adams Street "by the [Underground Railroad] agents and removed to a place of safety," presumed to be headed to Canada.[35]

Safe from the angry mob, Nuckolls demanded immediate action against the abolitionists who had interfered with his legal rights. The same night, a federal grand jury indicted Jenks, DeWolf, Anderson, and others for violating the Fugitive Slave Law.[36] Shaken and empty-handed, Nuckolls spoke with a reporter before he left town, saying he would "spend $20,000 'in following the thing up,' if necessary." The journalist noted, "He has two or three other fugitives formerly belonging to him now in this city, and says there are several more here who belong to his brother."[37]

Nuckolls's mention of other people enslaved by him and his family members living in Chicago raises questions. Was he telling the truth or exaggerating his losses? If true, who were they? Nuckolls had already sold Shack south in the spring of 1859. He had bought Raleigh from his father's estate in 1857, but Lucinda had written that Heath had taken the "boy" instead. The phrasing "several more here who belong to his brother" suggests they were Rebecca, Richard, Mary, and her child, bought by Houston Nuckolls. Houston was the only sibling who had acquired more than one enslaved person at the sale.[38]

Because slavery was still allowed in Nebraska, Houston could have taken Rebecca, Richard, Mary, and her child to the now-obsolete village of Yankton or to St. Stephens. Yankton was also on the Missouri River south of Nebraska City, opposite Holt County, Missouri.[39] Unfortunately, Richardson County's extant tax lists do not begin until 1861, so whether they were ever held there cannot be determined. No reports of these enslaved people as fugitives have come to light. What is certain is that by 1860, the Nebraska Territorial Census did not list any Blacks in Houston's household.

What about Shade? His enslaver, Lafayette Nuckolls, had gone to Texas and was killed there in February 1860. Apparently, Lafayette left Shade behind, because Shade was listed in Columbus Nuckolls's Pacific City household in the 1860 census. With his ownership now in the hands of Lafayette's widow, Shade could have left the Iowa household and traveled on his own to Chicago. There were no fugitive slave advertisements, but since Shade was in the free state of Iowa, the family may have hesitated to place one. It was one thing to claim Celia and Eliza as enslaved in Nebraska Territory but another to claim someone residing in Iowa was enslaved. Still, another possibility is that Shade, too, was sold south. Whether other members of the Grayson family were residing in Chicago may never be known.[40]

The princely sum of $20,000 that Nuckolls pledged he would spend to recover his property could have been hyperbole or journalistic license; however, it was clear that Nuckolls had already expended much larger sums of money than his initial $200 reward in his ongoing search for Celia and Eliza. In his lawsuit against the Iowa abolitionists, he claimed he had spent over $6,000 looking for them, including "employing help" to hunt them down, and that was a year before his trip to Chicago.[41]

From the beginning, Nuckolls had held out the promise of a rich reward for the return of Celia and Eliza, incentivizing professional slave hunters to keep up the pressure. He also had a wide network of business associates that he could tap. Given his unwavering resolve, it may be that he was willing to spend that much. If so, Nuckolls was going way beyond his actual damages. For him, it must have been the principle involved, coupled with the personal affront to his pride and public persona.[42]

Finding Eliza in Chicago may have felt like a victory. When Celia and Eliza had first left Nebraska City, Stephen Nuckolls obviously knew where to look: in what he called the "abolition holes" of Iowa. With family in Fremont and Mills Counties, he probably thought his odds of discovering them were high. It may have not only surprised him when they slipped through his grasp but also infuriated him. A man of energy and means, he was used to having his way. Yet these two women over whom he had exercised control since they were young girls had minds of their own, demonstrating uncommon bravery and resolve.

On a personal level, he may have wanted to cultivate the same reputation as his father, Ezra, before him—that of a benign, fatherly figure who took good care of his slaves, treating them as "servants" who were a part of the family. This sense of self may have been personally satisfying but also could have had public advantages. As he and his family were well aware, many eyes were on them as they strove to show that domestic family-style enslavement could exist in the West. They believed that abolitionists were extremists who did not understand the advantages that the "peculiar institution" might bring to the West and to the enslaved themselves. Celia and Eliza's journey to freedom challenged his reputation and that of his entire family as "good masters," while raising further questions about the extension of slavery into the territories and the nature of domestic bondage.

The Chicago affair also showcases what Nuckolls had learned from his prior experiences in Iowa. This time, he had a legal warrant to retrieve both Celia and Eliza. And there is little doubt that he would have succeeded had he been able to take Eliza to Springfield for examination.

Regardless of how many enslaved people Nuckolls and his extended family claimed in Chicago, once again Eliza's public resistance prompted comment and debate across the country. Newspapers from Baltimore to Richmond, Chicago to New Orleans, and back in Nebraska and Iowa carried items about the "great excitement" over Eliza—many of them on the front page.[43] Eliza's case attracted attention at the highest levels. After hearing about her rescue, President Buchanan thought Jenks's first name of Chancellor was a title and telegraphed Chicago's U.S. attorney that Jenks should be immediately removed from office due to his role in Eliza's escape.[44]

Buchanan's intervention was not without precedent; he had taken an interest in local flare-ups over the slavery question before. His administration had relentlessly pursued a number of Oberlin, Ohio, citizens in the case of the rescue of African American John Price—even charging citizens who were not present during the event but were known Republican agitators. Indeed, Buchanan was interested in punishing Republican activists wherever he found them. The process undoubtedly would have been repeated in Chicago in the Nuckolls case.[45]

With all this excitement, attention, and controversy, Eliza had become famous. She was such a celebrity that the *Nebraska City News* pointed out with some bitterness, "Some people are born great, others acquire greatness.... Eliza Africanus of this city, belongs to the latter class." The piece bemoaned her enticement away from the "home of luxury" and "sumptuous fare" the Nuckolls household had provided, only to live in a "free-love and freedom-loving brothel." The item further predicted that Eliza would "end a miserable existence in a low and dirty brothel" in Canada.[46]

On the political front, the *Chicago Tribune* carried an interesting editorial about Eliza's rescue, contrasting the Danites (proslavery Democrats) with the Douglasites, arguing that the Douglas Democrats were as against slave catching as the Republicans. According to the editor, Republicans and Douglas Democrats alike were asking when Nebraska had become a slave state. If free, "some of the Democrats wanted to know ... what right the fellow Nuckolls had to take the colored woman back there as a slave?" The next day, a letter to the *Chicago Tribune* editor signed J. L. B. asserted, "It is conceded on all hands that said fugitive ran away from the free Territory of Nebraska where it is not pretended there was any law for slavery."[47] Predictably, the *Nebraska City News* took Nuckolls's side, writing, "They take her from an officer of the government and send her kiting to Canada to finish her existence in a house of ill fame."[48]

Eliza's actions and her escape from recapture also prompted a newspaper item that challenged the constitutionality of Nuckolls's claims on Eliza, with a narrow interpretation of the clause in the U.S. Constitution that says, "No Person held to Service or Labour in one State, under the Laws thereof, escaping into another, shall, in Consequence of any Law or Regulation therein, be discharged from such Service or Labour, but shall be delivered up on Claim of the Party to whom such Service or Labour may be due."[49] In high dudgeon over Nuckolls's pursuit of Eliza, the writer pointed out that the "Constitution says nothing about 'persons held to service or labor in a Territory.'" The writer argued that since slavery had not been established by law in Nebraska, until the legislature voted, Nebraska should be considered free.[50]

More than one writer distinguished between states and territories. An editor for Nebraska City's competing newspaper asked, "Is a Territory a State within the meaning of the Constitution? If not, then this clause really gives no right to reclaim a fugitive from Nebraska." Furthermore, even if the constitutional clause referred to territories as well as states, the reference was to enslaved people "held to service or labor in one State, under the laws thereof."[51] Thus the key question remained: Was Eliza held as a slave in Nebraska Territory *under the laws thereof*?

Proslavery forces felt that the *Dred Scott* decision applied to Celia and Eliza's case, since Dred Scott had lived for about a year at Fort Snelling (in today's Minnesota) in a region where enslavement had been barred through the Missouri Compromise. However, army and navy officers were not considered citizens of a state where they were stationed. Clearly, Stephen Douglas's adoption of popular sovereignty as a solution to settling the slavery question in the territories left Americans on both sides of the issue even more divided and with little light to guide them. In the background of Eliza's case and the ongoing discussion surrounding her rescue and legal status, the *Chicago Tribune* was also running a regular column titled "Doings of the Secessionists," an interesting juxtaposition of the imminence of disunion while the U.S. court system continued to administer the Fugitive Slave Law.[52]

Chancellor Jenks, Judge Calvin DeWolf, and Deputy Sheriff George Anderson were indicted for helping Eliza Grayson. They appeared at court on November 20, 1860, paying bond of $3,500 each for their release until trial. A Richmond newspaper cheerfully announced the "Arrest of the Rescuers," pointing out that they were all Republicans, including "Calvin DeWolf, Republican Justice of the Peace; George Anderson, Republican Deputy Sheriff; Isaiah I I. Williams Republican Lieutenant of Police; Holland H. Harris Republican City Policeman; Chancellor Jenks, Republican practitioner of law; Daniel Webster, a negro; Benjamin Mercer, a negro; Henry Lisbes [probably Isbell] a negro." Another item added the name E. Langley to the list of those indicted.[53]

Nine people altogether were scheduled to be tried in January before Judge Thomas Drummond, with the *Chicago Daily Tribune* declaring that in the new year, "the most interesting case to be tried is that for rescuing the fugitive slave, Eliza Grayson." In an early 1861 update, the *Tribune* reported that because of "its importance," the Eliza Grayson case had been moved to the U.S. Circuit Court.[54]

Eliza's case was widely viewed as one that could reach the U.S. Supreme Court to decide the question of slavery's legality in the territories once and for all. In the wake of the 1857 *Dred Scott* decision, enslavers like Nuckolls had good reason to expect the same court would extend its decision to include Nebraska Territory and rule that Eliza's residence there did not change her legal status. An Iowa newspaper editor hoped that Nuckolls would find out "that Nebraska is a Free Territory; though should he appeal to the Federal Supreme Court, that tribunal would perhaps have no scruples in making a decision favorable to his case, as they did in that of Dred Scott."[55]

The same five slaveholders on the Supreme Court who had participated in the *Dred Scott* decision still occupied their positions in 1861, their animus toward abolitionism well known.[56] Buchanan had recently replaced Benjamin Curtis, the one justice who had written a devastating dissent to the Taney opinion in *Dred Scott*, with Maine native Nathan Clifford. Although a New Englander, Clifford was against interfering with Southern states and abolishing slavery on the federal level. In 1859 Clifford had voted to uphold the Fugitive Slave Law.[57] If anything, the court would have been even more disposed to uphold the *Dred Scott* precedent in Eliza's case and expand the decision expressly to include U.S. territories.

Nuckolls's pursuit of Eliza had other repercussions. The *Chicago Daily Tribune* observed that slave catchers had entered the city in greater numbers after her escape and that many Blacks fled Chicago in the aftermath, saying, "Such a scattering, and such clearances by U. G. R. R. [Underground Railroad] have never before been witnessed."[58]

A Real Slave Sale at the Otoe County Courthouse

Not long after Nuckolls returned from Chicago, another incident took place in Nebraska City that challenged the status quo. Despite numerous official pronouncements that slavery did not exist in Nebraska, on December 5, 1860, the local sheriff sold the enslaved couple Hercules and Martha on the steps of the Otoe County courthouse. Stephen F. Nuckolls's uncle

William B. Hail had sued their enslaver, Charles F. Holly, and was awarded damages, which Holly decided to pay through the sale. When the public auction started with Hercules on the block by himself, no one bid. Then both Martha and Hercules were offered together. Hail bought both for $300, and no one bid against him.[59]

Before the sale, a group of citizens had told Hercules they had raised enough money to buy him and set him free, but they did not have enough money to buy Martha. Perhaps they held out the hope that by remaining free, Hercules could eventually buy her freedom. Hercules refused to be separated from his wife, in essence saying that if she was sold, he would be sold with her. No matter what, they would stay together.

In addition, Hercules may have been confident that Holly's promises to him and Martha would be honored, even in the face of their imminent sale. Over several years, he and Martha had paid money to Holly to buy their freedom. When hired out to work, they were allowed to keep some of their wages, and the deal was that once they paid $1,300 total, they would be free. When Hail sued Charles Holly for debt, Hercules and Martha had already paid $1,100 and were only $200 away from emancipation. William B. Hail, the same man who had hunted down four slaves and sent three to their death in Grayson County, had told Hercules and Martha that he would honor the deal and would set them free when they paid the last $200.

Hercules and Martha may have believed Hail's promises and felt secure. Holly had hired the couple out to a man who lived on the levee. After the drama of the sale on the courthouse steps, Hercules and Martha returned to the house near the levee. But a few days later, Hail went in the early morning hours to the house where they worked. When Hercules and Martha came to the door, they spied Hail's wagon at the doorstep. Five or six men stood by the wagon, looking like a guard. Hercules and Martha may have been puzzled by this show, as most of the town still slept. What was going on?

Hail told Hercules and Martha with some urgency that he was there to protect them from the wicked abolitionists from Tabor, Iowa. The Taborites had heard of the sale and had gathered a group of fifteen to twenty men to come to Nebraska City and take them. The couple would be sent to Canada, where, Hail explained, they would suffer in cold, dark poverty. Hercules and Martha may have even heard the story published the month

Slave Hunting

before that Eliza had been toiling in a "house of ill fame" and was now in frigid Canada, living a dissolute life there as a prostitute. Hail explained he would take them to his farm for a few days, where they would be safe, and then they could return to the family that housed them.

Fond of their current employers, Hercules and Martha said their goodbyes to the family, assuring them they would be back in just a few days. With coats and clothing to keep them warm during the December cold, they climbed into the wagon. One can only imagine what a mix of surprise, dread, and betrayal struck them when the wagon headed toward the river, where they could see a boat waiting, instead of going in the direction of Hail's farm.

Whether they simply exchanged looks or whispered to one another is unknown, but both of them jumped out of the wagon. Hail and his men almost immediately caught Hercules and threw him to the ground, gagging and tying him. Meanwhile, Martha ran up the hill on the main road, screaming and shouting, rousing the entire neighborhood. When the men caught up with Martha, she continued to scream. People had begun to emerge from their homes. Martha begged the onlookers to help her. Was there not a single person who could come to their aid?

Eliza had been lucky—when she screamed and resisted in the streets of Chicago, a crowd composed mainly of free Blacks rescued her. But in Nebraska City, the stunned townspeople who gathered that morning to witness "Aunt" Martha's distress did not know what to say or do when she begged for their help. Many there probably remembered the sack of Civil Bend just two years before. And Nuckolls's $10,000 lawsuit against the Iowans under the Fugitive Slave Law was still pending at the territorial court. While the crowd stood immobile, Martha was marched down the hill, crying and pleading, to join her bound and gagged husband on the boat. Nebraska Citians learned in the days that followed that Hail had sold the pair for $500 to a man who lived fifteen or twenty miles below Nebraska City in Missouri. For all they knew, from there Hercules and Martha were sold south. The couple was not heard from again.[60]

A week later *Nebraska City News* editor Milton Reynolds guessed that "except for the little girl that nurses Col. Deslonde's babies, I believe there is not now a person called a slave in Nebraska," once again complaining that Republicans were neglecting the legislative needs of white people by "dwelling on the N——," who were "first in all their thoughts." Reynolds asserted that Black Republicans would insist on legislating for the "'poor slave' who ain't here and never will be." Reynolds also evoked the magic of geography: the climate and soil of Nebraska was at least part of the reason slavery would be impossible there. He surmised that everyone knew there would be as "much probability of alligators coming up the Platte River, as there would be that Nebraska would have slavery."[61] No response was published asking whether Hercules, Martha, Celia, Eliza, Shack, Shade, and the Majors's slaves were alligators.

Hercules and Martha had just been hauled off from a place where proslavery forces had continuously declared slavery did not exist, and their tragic story was a replay of scenes across the borderlands. After Abraham Lincoln's election in November 1860, the winds of secession blowing throughout the 1850s became a strong gale. As uncertainty about slavery and the Union's future increased, Brownville's *Nebraska Advertiser* carried a column in November 1860 stating, "[The] owners of negroes in the border states are selling their slaves south as fast as they can."[62] A Missouri editor remarked, "The agitation of the slavery question on our frontiers is having the effect of inducing the owners of slaves to sell their negroes South," citing a 17 percent decrease in the number of Blacks in Jackson County, Missouri, including the Missouri River towns of Independence, Kansas City, and Westport.[63]

The Democratic *Nebraska City News* reported on Abraham Lincoln from national and local angles, complaining that the *Omaha Republican* was "jubilant and ecstatic over the election of Abraham," while charging that Republicans had perpetrated fraud to take the elections in Nebraska. In column three on the same page, the *News* talked about E. S. Dundy receiving a certificate of election from Richardson and Pawnee Counties as a "damnable" act of corruption. In the midst of the election news, the same column carried the headline "Eliza in Limbo." Quoting the Chicago papers, the editor crowed, "Mr. Nuckolls of this city, has 'procured' his servant Eliza. The combat deepens—on ye brave!"[64] Clearly, reports of Eliza's rescue had not yet filtered west. A few days later the writers at the *Chicago Tribune* mocked the *Nebraska City News* over its joy that Eliza had been "procured," noting that she had "made up her mind that she wouldn't stay 'procured'" and guessing that Nebraska City's joy would "give place to mourning."⁶⁵

The *News* did not miss a beat after its display of premature victory. The editor responded that the "Black Republican journals with one accord are very happy over the rescue of Eliza from Mr. Nuckolls of this city, by a mob in the Republican City of Chicago." The item emphasized that actions like these were going to "push the southern people to extremes—the Union will be destroyed."⁶⁶

Yet Nebraska Republicans kept the pressure on regarding the institution of slavery in the territory. In December 1860 Nebraska's territorial legislature passed a bill to prohibit slavery, similar to the one from the year before that had been passed and vetoed.

Democrat representative Asa M. Acton of Richardson County rose to protest the vote, with the now-familiar argument that the bill was unnecessary. At age twenty-five, the Illinois-born attorney had hung up his shingle in the small town of Rulo, close to Nebraska's extreme southeast corner. The *Nebraska City News* published his formal protest in full, declaring it "worthy of perusal." Acton argued that the U.S. Supreme Court was about to weigh in on the case of the "persons lately arrested at Chicago, on charge of abetting and aiding the rescue of the slave woman Eliza." If the court decided that slavery could not be established in the territory, it would render the antislavery bill unnecessary. If not, then the legislature's bill would be unconstitutional. But the legislation would "further the cause of disunion and render the future of our common country . . . at best but hopeless, by defeating all efforts at conciliation."⁶⁷

In essence, his argument was to let the Supreme Court decide whether Eliza's case would prove the Republican contention "that the normal condition of the Territories is that of freedom, and that Slavery can never be legally established therein." But Acton's real emphasis was on the Union. Why should "the peace and prosperity of this Union," he asked, "be jeopardized—for the sake of a few negroes?" When the Civil War broke out, Acton joined the Confederate Cavalry in Missouri; he died at the Battle of Corinth in 1862.⁶⁸

For the second time in the space of a year, Eliza's plight entered into the public discourse, locally, regionally, and nationally. Eliza's resistance in Chicago prompted yet another fugitive slave case (joining the one in Nebraska Territory) and added to the ongoing discussion. A contingent of Nebraska Democrats continued to protest passage of an "unnecessary" bill as Eliza's rescue case wound its way through the courts—destined, it was believed, for the U.S. Supreme Court to settle the constitutional question. In addition to urging legislators to wait for the case to play out, Acton's protest warned about the Nebraska slavery bill's likely potential to further disunion. His arguments failed to carry, and again the territorial legislature voted to prohibit slavery in Nebraska Territory, this time by a wide margin.

Despite the bill's passage with a much larger majority than the previous year, Governor Black vetoed it on January 1, 1861. He continued to argue that until Nebraska reached statehood, the treaty for the Louisiana Purchase, where slavery was allowed, held sway. As historian Nicole Etcheson has pointed out, "Determining *when* slavery could be prohibited from a territory... was precisely another of popular sovereignty's ambiguities."[69] Predictably, the proslavery side favored waiting until statehood (probably with an eye to a grandfather clause for current resident enslavers if slavery was prohibited), while Northerners argued that territorial legislatures could decide.

Governor Black's remarks also appealed to legislators' local business interests, arguing that if Nebraska prohibited slavery, "No steamboat with a hired slave on board, can with safety, touch the shores of Nebraska." His veto's last salvo addressed the threat of disunion, asking, "Shall we add fuel to the flames of discord and feed the fires of dissolution?"[70] In essence, Black rejected the notion of popular sovereignty that Sen. Stephen Douglas had so confidently put forth as a solution to the extension of slavery.

Brownville's *Nebraska Advertiser* noted that Black's veto demonstrated that Democrats were "dodging and squirming around on the Popular Sovereignty issue at an astonishing rate."[71] Unlike 1859, however, the November 1860 election had tipped the Nebraska legislature's balance of power to the Republican side. Of thirty-eight members of the house, only eleven were Democrats. This time Governor Black's veto was overridden, and on January 5, 1861, slavery was prohibited by law in Nebraska Territory.

After his staunch defense of slavery in Nebraska Territory, Governor Black resigned his post on February 24, 1861, returning to his home state of Pennsylvania. He entered the army to lead the Sixty-Second Pennsylvania Volunteers in the Civil War and died at Gaines Mills, Virginia, in June 1862.[72]

Did popular sovereignty work in Nebraska? Citing all the other bills that Nebraska territorial legislators passed in the 1850s, many historians have argued that it did. Based solely on levels of violence, it would seem so, particularly in comparison with Kansas. However, popular sovereignty was expressly promoted as a solution to the impasse over whether Southern U.S. citizens could take slaves into new territories and specifically designed to settle the slavery question through local self-determination.[73]

Governor Black's vetoes of the antislavery bill in two legislative sessions represented a failure of popular sovereignty in many Nebraskans' eyes. Only after the election of a new Republican president who would most assuredly appoint antislavery governors, and after the secession of Southern states was well underway, did Nebraska Territory finally succeed in overriding the federal will and pass a bill to prohibit slavery. Even then, Celia and Eliza's legal status in November 1858 would have remained unsettled until Nuckolls's cases progressed through the legal system. And there could have been further constitutional challenges to Nebraska Territory's prohibition bill. But as the Civil War progressed, the cases were finally dropped. Popular sovereignty did not solve the problem it was proposed to address. Thus it failed to fulfill its primary purpose.

Where was Eliza all this time? Almost to a person, newspaper editors assumed she had been sent "kiting to Canada" after her close brush with reenslavement in Chicago. But the record is silent on her fate. The Grayson story underwent many embellishments with the passage of time, and more famous names were brought into the narrative. One account featured James Lane rowing Celia and Eliza across the Missouri, while another mentioned John Brown. A long piece that appeared in the *Nebraska City Daily News Press* in 1927 asserted that "one of Nuckolls' Negro women" (perhaps Eliza), after hiding in Tabor, went to Cincinnati "under the wing" of famous Quaker abolitionist Levi Coffin.[74]

The Civil War commenced on April 12, 1861, and the Eliza Grayson case in Chicago against DeWolf, Anderson, and the others, which Nuckolls had lodged with such fanfare, moved into the background. On December 7,

1861, the *Chicago Tribune* reported that the charges had been dropped and "the case stricken from the docket by order of the Attorney General."[75] The whereabouts and fate of Eliza remain unknown to this day.

In the end, Celia and Eliza's story captured headlines in late 1858 through 1860 with their dramatic display of courage and tenacity in the face of slim odds. They brought the existence of slavery in Nebraska Territory into sharp relief, challenging notions of the "impossibility" of slavery in the West as well as the utility of popular sovereignty as a solution to the problem of slavery's expansion. Whether they went to Canada to stay or returned to the United States to join millions of emancipated African Americans in their struggles through the Reconstruction era, they should be remembered as leaders who challenged the expansion of slavery in an era of territorial fluidity.

Epilogue

> I had crossed the line. I was *free*; but there was no one to welcome me to the land of freedom. I was a stranger in a strange land.
> —HARRIET TUBMAN

In my efforts to follow the main characters in this drama, I encountered many roadblocks. Numerous authors and historians have remarked on the difficulties of researching African Americans throughout the United States, where one can only fashion their stories from fragments of evidence dominated by a white point of view. Celia and Eliza's story began in Virginia, but it did not end there. Centered in what was then the West, they and others enslaved by the Nuckolls family were eventually scattered across the United States and perhaps Canada. It is difficult to accept their post–Civil War invisibility.

The evidence surrounding the others enslaved by Ezra Nuckolls suggests that most of them belonged to one family. The Hampton branch of the Graysons, descendants of Edith Grayson and Gilbert Hampton, can be reliably followed to the present day, while Shack, or Jackson, Grayson's branch died with him in Louisiana. I wanted to *know*, and still want to know, what happened to them all.

I was moved by Celia and Eliza's courage and determination, not fully realizing the magnitude of the risks they took until I was deep into the story. Before I began my research, I did not believe the institution of slavery could have taken hold in Nebraska. But once I started to look, I saw pockets of slavery almost everywhere. Call it small-scale or domestic, slavery was the lived reality of people who have been dismissed by historians because of their location. There was no magic of geography. Slavery existed in all kinds of places and in different forms, whether it was on a Louisiana plantation, the high plateaus of the Appalachians, or the streets of Nebraska City. And at least from 1854 to 1861 the judicial system pronounced Nebraska slave territory.

When Celia and Eliza left Nebraska City in November 1858, they could not have known what the future would hold. Because of their brief celebrity as freedom seekers, some of their story can be pieced together. But the story is incomplete. Even during Celia and Eliza's period of celebrity, details about them are few. Then they disappear, leaving lingering questions in their wake. Did they make it to Canada? Where did they live? Did they marry, have children? Most important, were they happy, sad, content, lonely, homesick? After the Civil War, did they try to find their families? When did they die?

As the sisters passed from obscurity to celebrity and back to obscurity, their trail is difficult and sometimes impossible to follow. However, given Eliza's narrow escape from capture in Chicago in November 1860, it is almost certain she headed to greater safety in Canada. It may be that other people formerly enslaved by the Nebraska Nuckolls clan followed suit. Yet even in Canada, the Graysons may not have felt secure. They may have changed their names to avoid pursuit, at least until after the war was over.

Changing names to avoid detection was common. Black abolitionist leader Harriet Tubman began her life as Araminta "Minty" Ross, adopting her new name after she escaped to freedom. Frederick Douglass started life as Frederick Augustus Washington Bailey. When he went to Baltimore, he was Stanley, and in New York, he became Frederick Johnson. Once in Massachusetts, he settled on Frederick Douglass.[1]

After the Civil War, some formerly enslaved people took the enslavers' surnames, while others chose to forge their own identities as freed people. For instance, veteran Dick Lewis Barnett explained that he served in the United States Colored Troops as Lewis Smith because his mother was Phillis Smith, but he later decided to take his father's surname. Thus it would not be surprising if Celia and Eliza changed their names.[2]

However, the 1861 Canada Census lists an Eliza Grason, a twenty-year-old American-born Black woman who was working as a washerwoman in Windsor, Ontario. Her age does not fit exactly but is close enough, given how commonly mistakes in age appear in censuses. Moreover, many former enslaved people did not know their exact ages. Only two miles across the river from Detroit, Windsor was long a destination for freedom-seeking African Americans. In fact, Windsor's 1861 census is full of American-born Blacks.[3]

Today Windsor highlights its history with a grand sculpture called the Tower of Freedom, part of a monument to the Underground Railroad. The Tower of Freedom is one half of the memorial, and the other half is in Detroit. The Windsor side includes four life-size figures depicting an arrival in Canada. One of the figures is looking back across the river whence they came, and another has his arms raised in praise. On the Detroit side, there are six freedom seekers waiting to cross.[4]

Subsequent Canada Census enumerations do not list Eliza Grayson or Grason, at least under that name. She could have married, died, or changed her name to an emancipation name. A married woman named Celia Flenoy appears on the same census page as Eliza, but she was the former Celia Toucey, who had married in Michigan in 1852.[5] Thus it is difficult to confirm the woman's identity as the Eliza Grayson formerly of Nebraska Territory.

What would life have been like for Eliza in Canada? For many years, Canadian historians celebrated their country's role as a place of safety and liberty for formerly enslaved people. Black people had long filtered into Canada to live. But after Britain formally abolished slavery in 1833, Blacks began entering the province of Upper Canada in a steady flow.[6] Some were freedom seekers, while others were free Blacks seeking an environment with less discrimination. Places like Windsor, Amherstburg, Colchester, St. Catherines, and the Elgin Settlement (Buxton), Ontario, attracted substantial Black populations.[7] When many free U.S. states began enforcing Black codes in the 1840s, even more freedom seekers headed to Canada's "promised land."[8]

Historians agree that upon passage of the 1850 Fugitive Slave Law, self-emancipated Blacks living in U.S. cities like Boston, Rochester, Buffalo, and Detroit no longer felt secure, contributing to a surge in Canada's Black population throughout the turbulent 1850s. A famous incident took place in 1853, in which abolitionists breakfasted with a party of twenty-seven or twenty-eight freedom seekers in Detroit before accompanying them to a boat headed for Windsor. Some U.S. citizens crossed to Windsor and spent the rest of the day with the refugees.[9]

Windsor also figured into the John Brown story during the winter of 1858–59, around the same time that Celia and Eliza left enslavement in Nebraska City. Brown liberated twelve slaves from Missouri and killed a plantation owner in the process. His twenty-five-hundred-mile trek resembled Celia and Eliza's route, although Brown's group did not stop in Chicago but traveled straight to Detroit before ferrying the freedom seekers to Windsor.[10]

Black people in Canada certainly enjoyed rights they could have only dreamed of in the United States. Yet they still faced prejudice as they struggled to adjust to a new place. Black leaders differed on how to approach helping the fugitives. Josiah Henson tried to collect donations to help a struggling settlement at a place called Dawn. Mary Ann Shadd, the Black editor of the *Provincial Freeman* newspaper, complained that Henson's actions had done a great deal of "injury to the colored people" by begging for them and charged that he was actually begging for himself.[11]

Shadd did not protest against temporary assistance, but she emphasized that such help should not be long-term. She and like-minded leaders disapproved of efforts that suggested Blacks could not care for themselves, because that had been one of the arguments Southern enslavers regularly used to deny freedom to enslaved people in the United States. During the five years of her newspaper's existence, she promoted "measures for such improvement as shall make them independent, self-sustaining laborers," proving "the fitness of the slaves for freedom."[12]

As leaders like Henson and Shadd fought over how best to assimilate former enslaved people into Canadian society, aid societies on both sides of the U.S.-Canada border came under attack as financial problems and inadequate leadership plagued efforts to relieve the plight of the refugees. This was the situation that Eliza and any of the others formerly enslaved by Nuckolls family members would have faced if they crossed into Canada, where Black communities were already established and ready to help. At the same time, failures to establish thriving, prosperous, and independent Black communities contributed to images of "black indigence and ineffectiveness" among Canada's white population.[13]

Celia and Eliza had many domestic skills that Nuckolls had clearly valued, given his dogged pursuit of them. But they would have been competing for jobs with European immigrants. Eliza Grason's enumeration in the 1861 Canada Census indicated that she did not live in an employer's household. She was probably hired for short-term laundry service. After this brief 1861 glimpse of a candidate for Eliza, Windsor's Eliza Grason drops from the record.[14]

Turning the Page on Slavery

Stephen Friel Nuckolls left Nebraska City in late 1862 or early 1863.[15] It may be that the divisions of the Civil War were part of the reason for his departure. His eyes had already been drawn farther west, lured by the mines in Colorado, where he had extensive business interests. His son Peter Paul Nuckolls, called Paul, was born in Nebraska City in 1862. Although Nuckolls's sympathies were almost certainly with the South, he sat the war out, first going to Colorado, then living in New Jersey and New York. He continued to own a considerable amount of property in Nebraska, Iowa, and Missouri, likely watched over by family members.[16]

The war had consequences for the Nuckollses other than causing them to constantly move around. Lucinda Bourne Nuckolls wrote to a brother in November 1864 that she and the children had left Central City, Colorado, in early October and arrived in Parkersburg, West Virginia, where Friel would join them. She had not heard from any "relatives in four years" and was most anxious for news, suggesting the Nuckolls family may not have tried too hard to get mail through to their Confederate family members, perhaps for fear of being labeled rebels. The family continued to live in changing circumstances, because Lucinda wrote from New York City the following month to report to her brother that they had moved to a private boardinghouse, which was "much better" than where they had been. By July 1865 the Nuckolls family was in New Brunswick, New Jersey, where they lived on French Street near their old friend Judge Hiram Bennet from Nebraska City.[17]

Nuckolls returned to Nebraska in 1866. At first he seemed poised to retake the reins as a local leader. He is on record supporting the adoption of the state constitution that had been submitted. The *News* reported his attendance at social gatherings and that he contributed the prize for school commencement at Talbot Hall, where his son William attended.

In July he was numbered among the honored guests at the opening of a new Nebraska City hotel, Cincinnati House.[18]

But Nuckolls may have been restless and looking for new opportunities. He may have scouted Dakota Territory before relocating to the new town of Cheyenne, Wyoming Territory. He once again opened a store, where just a few years before had been a vast, windswept prairie. Stephen Nuckolls intended to be a mover and shaker in this up-and-coming town.

By January 1868 Stephen Nuckolls was in New York City buying goods and shipping them to Cheyenne, promoting his "immense stock" of dry goods, "staple and fancy groceries, wooden and willow," hardware—in short, "any thing good and cheap." He joined the local board of trade and once again threw himself into politics, attending a meeting "for the people." In the summer he was one of the leaders at what the *Wyoming Weekly Leader* dubbed a "Democratic Pow-Wow," complete with a good deal of "bluster." But Lucinda stayed in Nebraska City for most of this time, moving to Cheyenne in June 1868. By August he was one of Laramie County's delegates to the Democratic Convention.[19]

In a brand-new town where everyone was new to the area, Stephen's fellow Democrats chose him as their candidate for Congress. The Republican-leaning *Cheyenne Leader* newspaper responded that "if the people of Wyoming send Mr. Nuckolls to Washington they will do a very foolish thing," describing Nuckolls as a person with "pockets filled with denunciations of the authorities."[20]

During his campaign, stories of Eliza's dramatic escape dogged Nuckolls, but without the antebellum power to move hearts and minds. In "Laboring Men of Wyoming!" the editors of the *Cheyenne Leader* wrote, "Bear in mind that S. F. Nuckolls, Democratic candidate for Congress is one of the men, who under the infamous Dred Scott decision endeavored to force slavery and slave labor into the free State of Nebraska, and thus crush out the free laborers of that State. . . . [B]etter send him back to Nebraska to hunt down his poor slave girl Eliza, than to set him up as the representative of the free men of Wyoming."[21]

The Democratic *Cheyenne Argus* must have protested this piece as a personal attack on Stephen Nuckolls, because the *Cheyenne Leader* later denied it had attacked his private character. The editors argued that "slave-catching" and "woman-hunting" were part of "his political character and history," adding that voters should be informed about them. In addition to appealing to working men, the *Leader* reported on a "colored men's" meeting, hoping that no man among them would "disgrace his people by casting that vote for S. F. Nuckolls."[22]

The *Leader* kept the pressure on, referring to Nuckolls as "a slave chasing master of human flesh in Nebraska City" and asking, "Do the people of Wyoming wish to insult the National Congress by now sending such a man to represent them in Washington?" Although the *Leader* answered no, the people answered yes. Nuckolls carried the election and became Wyoming Territory's representative in Congress.[23]

What Celia, Eliza, Shack, or others formerly enslaved by the Nuckolls family thought of Stephen Nuckolls's elevation to Congress can only be surmised. But white Nebraska Citians responded with glowing support regardless of political affiliation. In December 1869 Nebraska City held a Grand Testimonial Banquet in Nuckolls's honor at the Seymour House, with speeches, toasts, and bonhomie. Regaling Nuckolls as a man of "rare ambition," his friends pronounced him "first and foremost in deeds of charity." Local leaders congratulated him and one another over their many achievements in establishing the town, sharing hardship and want in those early days. Nuckolls was in fine fettle and at his charming best. Champagne flowed and tongues were loosened. He gave a "graphic description of his early experiences" in Nebraska, prompting much laughter. J. Sterling Morton, who once wrote that he was hard up if the Nuckollses were his best friends, was in enthusiastic attendance, as were many men considered Republican Radicals.[24]

When not in Washington, Stephen operated his huge store in Cheyenne. But Lucinda Nuckolls was not content in her new surroundings. In 1872 she wrote home that although they had a "good share of this worlds goods," she feared that living in such a place would "be a curse to our children the way we are raising them in this place." The weather was "coldest I eve[r] saw," and the hired help was "trifling." But it was not all misery. She added, "I am in the land where women's rights runs high and I have voted five times," adding in a private and playful note to her sister Ann, who was living with their parents, "Would you not like to see me walk up to the

Epilogue

poles and hand in my ticket?" She told Ann, however, that she would not want their parents to see her vote.[25]

What Lucinda left out was that Stephen Nuckolls was opposed to women's suffrage. As the leader of the Democrats addressing the Wyoming legislature in 1872, he stated, "I think women were made to obey men. They generally promised to obey, at any rate; and I think you had better either abolish this Female Suffrage act, or get up a new marriage ceremony to fit it."[26] But once the suffrage act passed, Nuckolls may have encouraged Lucinda to vote, thinking his wife would obey his wishes in the privacy of the ballot box.

Lucinda's sister Mary Bourne Curran visited the family in Cheyenne in April 1872. Mary agreed with Lucinda's feelings about Wyoming and wrote home with a healthy dislike of "the country where they live." Mary and her family were on their way farther west, and she added, "Lucinda was almost deranged to go with us to Oregon." Stephen Nuckolls must have been aware of his wife's sentiments about their new frontier home.[27]

Indeed, the year before, Nuckolls had vacated his position as a representative to Washington, and when Wyoming Democrats responded by putting him up for the Wyoming Territorial Council, he declined to run. Given Lucinda's unhappiness, his rationale may have been personal, but he also may have been assessing his long-term economic prospects. In August 1871 he and his business partner, John Gilman, had apparently discovered a "rich deposit of gold and silver ore" in Utah. The following summer Stephen and his family went to Utah, planning to be "absent for some time," while he attended to his mining interests there. This trip was the precursor to their next move, this time to Salt Lake City.[28]

Salt Lake City was more to Lucinda Bourne Nuckolls's liking. In May 1873 she wrote to her parents that they were living in a pleasant eight-room house with a beautiful view of the city. The climate was fine and healthy, "almost like being in old Grayson." In fact, she liked Salt Lake City better than any place they had been since they left Linden. After moving about most of her adult life, she seemed confident that they were finally settled. Stephen, as usual, entered into the life of the town, donating money to libraries and other causes. The local Republican newspaper remarked in 1874 on Stephen's benevolence and excellence in character, "untouched by bigotry or prejudice," probably a commentary on his friendship with Mormon leaders.[29]

Around 1875 Utah newspapers began to call him Colonel Nuckolls, the nonmilitary honorific bestowed on leading Southern gentlemen. "Colonel" Nuckolls continued to interest himself in Democratic politics, representing Utah at Democratic conventions in St. Louis and Philadelphia. In 1876 he supported New Yorker Samuel Jones Tilden, the Democratic candidate for president. Yet most of his time was spent on his mining interests; his political activities remained more in the background than in earlier years.[30]

Nebraska Citians continued to appreciate Nuckolls, especially his largesse. He conveyed the right-of-way on an island he owned in the Missouri River so that the city could improve the river channel to its benefit, prompting a resolution of thanks for his "liberal and graceful manner," contributing to the public good at the sacrifice of his private interest. Nuckolls replied that he had mounted the resolution on the wall of his "sanctum sanctorum," and it would be forever treasured as a memento. He claimed that no spot was dearer to him and that he would continue to make "humble sacrifices" for the "fair city."[31]

Although Lucinda thought her health was improved by the move to Salt Lake City, she died just four years later, on October 17, 1877, while Stephen was away in the Sweetwater country. Her obituary cited "general debility" as the cause of death, saying her health had been "failing for a number of years." A "most estimable lady in every respect," she had been devoted to her family. In addition to her husband, four sons survived her.[32]

Stephen F. Nuckolls died in Salt Lake City two years later, on February 14, 1879. and was buried at Mount Olivet Cemetery. His obituary honored him as Nebraska City's founder and highlighted his congressional term, describing him "one of the best known and honorable mining men in the country."[33]

Nuckolls's estate had probate proceedings in Nebraska, Missouri, Iowa, Colorado, and Utah. His will indicated that he was disappointed in his oldest son, William, known as Billy, because of Billy's drinking. He directed his executors to keep property in trust for Billy, distributing sums as needed. Upon Billy's death, the property would be equally divided among Stephen's other sons, Paul, Rupert, and Bruce Johnson Nuckolls, or their survivors.

By 1885 William Nuckolls resided in Custer County, Colorado, with his younger brother Paul, both of them single and working as miners. He lived with his younger brother Bruce in Montana in 1910. William died in Eureka, Montana, December 14, 1922.[34]

Paul's obituary explains that after receiving a "good education" at St. Mark's of Salt Lake City and the Salt Lake Collegiate Institute, he "began to grow reckless, and after knocking about the country some six years, he... met his death among strangers" in Rosita, Colorado, on December 14, 1922. Bruce also "knocked about," living in Sheridan County, Nebraska; Dillon and Jefferson, Montana; and Dover, Idaho. It appears he never married, and details of his death are unknown. Of Stephen and Lucinda's sons, only Rupert married and had children. He also moved around, serving as the vice president of the State Savings Bank of Butte, Montana. Rupert died in Salt Lake City on March 4, 1947, at age eighty-two.[35]

Did Stephen Friel Nuckolls try to find out what happened to the enslaved people that he described as part of his family and "scarcely regarded as slaves"?[36] We may never know.

Edith Hampton and the Legacy of Enslavement in Nebraska

Although Celia and Eliza disappear from the record, Edith, their likely older sister, does not. She remained in Atchison County, Missouri, enslaved by the Schooler family for the duration of the Civil War. When Ezra Nuckolls transferred Edith to his daughter Polly Nuckolls Schooler, a copy of the deed was never recorded at the courthouse, but it was signed in 1842, when Edith was twelve years old. Just as Celia and Eliza were in Stephen Nuckolls's household before their "official" 1850 transfer, Edith may have already been working for Polly before Ezra formalized the arrangement.[37]

Edith was born on January 27, 1830, so she was older than Celia and Eliza. She was listed in the 1850 Grayson County slave schedule as a twenty-year-old female in the Wrice Schooler household, with a one-month-old baby boy. The household did not include any other enslaved people, so she may have had an "abroad marriage" with a man on a nearby farm. The birth of her first child was close in time to the birth of Polly and Wrice Schooler's son Wrice, so it is possible that Edith served as a wet nurse in addition to doing other domestic work.[38]

16. Harding Hampton of Nebraska City, likely the nephew of Celia and Eliza. Courtesy of Morton-James Public Library and Nebraska City Historical Society.

It is unknown how close Edith may have been to Celia and Eliza when they lived in Missouri and Nebraska, given their heavy work schedules. In all likelihood, they met whenever the extended Nuckolls family spent time together, snatching moments from their work to catch up on the details of each other's lives. Edith was almost certainly one of the four enslaved people listed in the Schooler household in the 1854 Nebraska Territorial

Census. Another may have been her young Virginia-born son Harding. Given that Edith had another child by the next year, one of the others was probably Gilbert Hampton, who became her husband.[39]

Following the brief 1854 sojourn in Nebraska Territory, the Schoolers returned to Missouri, where Edith and her family spent the rest of the 1850s, serving the young and growing Schooler family. As John Hope Franklin and Loren Schweninger note in their definitive work on freedom seekers, women with children to care for were less likely to seek their freedom, and so she remained.[40] Given the close proximity to the Nuckolls family across the river, the Schoolers no doubt discussed all the family news among themselves. Edith must have heard about Celia and Eliza's flight to freedom. What she felt or thought during their public escape can only be imagined, but it seems likely she silently cheered them on.

After the Civil War, Missouri passed a law requiring former slaves' marriages to be "redone," since their prefreedom marriages were not considered valid. Edith's post–Civil War marriage to Gilbert Hampton appears in the courthouse records, along with the names of the children already born to the couple. On January 20, 1867, Justice of the Peace Thomas Crosby certified that he married Gilbert Hampton and "Edie" Schooler, who already had children Jane, Celia, Martha (called Mattie), and "Hardin," all of Atchison County, Missouri.[41] This record reveals that at least in 1867, Edith had adopted the surname Schooler—or the clerk gave the surname to her—to reflect her former enslavers' family name.

Although listed last, Harding Hampton was Edith's oldest child—the only one of her children born in Grayson County. There was a gap of five or six years between his birth in 1849 and Jane's in 1855. Either Edith had a baby in between, who died, or perhaps Gilbert Hampton was not Harding's father, although Harding went by the surname Hampton during his life. If the census ages for Gilbert Hampton are close to accurate, he would have been only fifteen when Harding was born, so it seems likely that Edith's first "husband" was left behind in Virginia.[42]

Not long after their 1867 marriage, Edith and Gilbert Hampton moved to Franklin, Iowa, near Hamburg, to farm. Son Harding's obituary indicates that the Schoolers told Gilbert that if he stayed with the family "until the close of the war he [Schooler] would give them an outfit with which to start farming." The 1870 census lists Harding as a laborer, while Jane, Celia (likely named for her aunt), and Martha attended school. The Hampton family now also included little Henry, age two, and a girl named Clementine, age one. Mary Albertha was their last child, born about 1870, but she does not appear in the 1870 or 1880 censuses.[43]

Around 1872 the Hamptons moved from Iowa to Nebraska City, where their post–Civil War experience offers insights into the legacy of slavery in southeastern Nebraska and the lower Missouri River Valley. What prompted the Hamptons to live among those who knew them as slaves is uncertain, but one of the attractions to Nebraska City may have been the Episcopal Church's opening of a school for "colored people," along with a small church called St. Augustine's.[44] Although no longer destined to be the "Emporium of the West," as Nuckolls had earlier promoted it, Nebraska City still provided ample employment opportunities, with steamboat service and a lively riverfront business district—all in familiar surroundings to the Hamptons. Another factor for the move could have been the presence of Heath Nuckolls in Nebraska City, a man who could vouch for them as the Hampton family navigated new lives as free people.

Whatever the reasons for the family's relocation, the Democratic *Nebraska City News* continued to publish pieces that showed that prewar notions of race and African Americans' place in society were not fading. In 1868 the *News* attacked Republican Party radicalism, noting that "colored electors" attended the meeting in support of Republican presidential and vice-presidential candidates Ulysses S. Grant and Schuyler Colfax.[45]

The *News* continued to pour scorn on the African Americans who had participated in their first vote. In October an editorial bemoaned local Blacks' involvement in the recent Republican electoral victories. African American business owners had joined in the Republican "exultation meeting." Main Street business proprietors urged all "loyal citizens" to illuminate every house and business with candles supplied for the event. Headlines included mention of "N—— Barber Shops."[46] At least seventeen African American men had voted, perhaps more, and given the numerous mentions of African American–operated barbershops, the editors of the *News* obviously identified these Black-owned businesses as hotbeds of Republican radicalism.

Judge Oliver P. Mason, one of Stephen Nuckolls's defense attorneys in the Page County, Iowa, District Court for his Civil Bend assaults, addressed a crowd that include Black citizens. Although he had been supportive of Nuckolls in the early days, Judge Mason had risen to the Nebraska Supreme Court as a staunch Union Republican. The *News* styled his speech as "the very life and soul of Radicalism in Otoe County."[47] Thus the Hamptons would have come to live in an atmosphere of support from some Nebraska Citians, mixed with bitter and racist bile on the part of others.

Gilbert Hampton first appeared in the local newspaper in 1872, offering a $100 reward for the capture of John Johnson, who had "borrowed" Hampton's mule and team and left for "parts unknown." In 1878 Gilbert Hampton was in a "shooting scrape" at a local barbershop. Apparently, he and an African American barber named Tim Thomas had a disagreement, and "Gil" came in, struck Thomas in the ribs, and "commenced firing." Hampton pleaded guilty to assault and battery and paid a $10 fine. The item's tone does not convey a sense of gravity, perhaps because Hampton and Thomas were African Americans, or perhaps because Hampton was only "shooting to scare."[48]

Gilbert Hampton died at age forty-five of asthma and heart disease in February 1880. Although he was listed in the mortality schedule as a farmer, his asthma may have been another reason for the family's move to Nebraska City, where they may have hoped for a little relief from his symptoms. The loss of Gilbert and his income may have presented a challenge both emotionally and financially, but Edith continued to work and save, employed in washing and ironing. The census lists her later that year as living with her married daughter Celia and son-in-law Charles Hicks.[49]

Edith apparently had no trouble exercising her newfound rights as the head of her family. In 1881 she filed a complaint against John W. Anderson, who was white, for slapping her child. Anderson pleaded guilty and paid a $1 fine.[50] She must not have stayed long with the Hickses, because in 1881–82, she and daughter Martha were residing at Pawnee Street between Fourth and Fifth, not far from her son Harding, who is listed at Pawnee near Fourth.[51]

Edith likely continued to perform domestic work while acting as the family matriarch. No stranger to hard work, by 1900 Edith is listed as the owner of her house at 413 Second Corso. Her granddaughter Cora, age thirteen, was living with her and attending school. Edith reported in 1900 that she had had seven children, of whom four were still living.[52]

During the Christmas season of 1905 Edith suffered a coughing fit so severe it caused a cerebral hemorrhage from which she never awoke. The local newspapers noted Edith's death. Born enslaved, she had been a "resident of Nebraska City since territorial days." She was known as the "mother of Harding Hampton, one of the best-known colored men" of Nebraska City. Although the newspapers did not report a full list of her survivors, her son Henry had died earlier in the year, so her immediate survivors must have been son Harding Hampton and daughter Celia, who now went by Cecelia Hampton or Nichols. Out of seven children, Edith had outlived five of them.[53]

A record of Edith's inner life is nonexistent, yet the contours of her experiences reveal the ongoing legacy of enslavement in the Missouri Valley. She was a woman who continued to work for others, performing tasks that she had before emancipation, but on her own terms. She carved out a new identity in freedom, reclaiming her position as a mother and grandmother, directed her own work, lived in her own house, and went to court for redress, even against whites. She did not have an easy life. She almost certainly hoped that the lives of her grandchildren would be better yet, while knowing there would be continuing obstacles in their way.

Harding Hampton, "Man of All Work—Trusted by All"

Harding Hampton was born in Grayson County, Virginia, before the second wave of Nuckolls emigration west to Missouri. His early years were spent with his parents and siblings on the Schooler farm in Missouri, as well as being hired out to Nuckolls family members in Nebraska. After emancipation, he moved with the rest of the family to Nebraska City via Iowa. He married Angeline Williams in Nebraska City at the Church of St. Augustine's on December 27, 1872.[54]

In the fall of 1873 he bought a house and lot from Maria Butler, the young widow of another African American, Alfred Butler, who had been a cook at the Galt House hotel. Heath Nuckolls had purchased the lot from his brother Stephen on October 31, 1861. The next deed for the parcel was that of Maria Butler to Harding Hampton in 1873, with no intervening grantor deed from Heath Nuckolls to Maria or Alfred Butler.[55] This situation raises the possibility that either Maria or Alfred Butler had been enslaved by the Nuckolls family.

Harding Hampton continued to perform the same kinds of jobs he had before emancipation. Called a "man of all work," he labored in various capacities. In 1880 he "lived in" and worked for Rufus F. McComas, a farmer and steamboat man. In 1888 he went on the Camp Sheridan Expedition with the Nebraska City Home Guards as a cook. He worked as a janitor for the local banks, a gardener for Mrs. Gus Mueller, and a sometime "house cleaner." The Nebraska City town council also paid him for doing the jail laundry.[56]

At the same time, he became a leader in Nebraska City's small Black community. In 1872 he was one of the men who gave a gift of appreciation to Rev. Dr. Robert W. Oliver, the white pastor who headed up the private school for African Americans. Calling it a school for the "exclusive education of colored people," Reverend Oliver described his mission there as "the civilization and Christianization of that poor and long-oppressed race."[57] That Harding signed the card, along with five other men, was almost certainly mentioned as one of the accomplishments of the educational mission.

What happened to Harding's first wife, Angeline, is unknown, but the Wyuka Cemetery records show that a Mrs. Hampton died in May 1879. In 1881 Harding Hampton married Georgia Robinson, a young woman born in Atchison County, Missouri, and who had resided with the Hamptons in Iowa. That same year Harding was one of the "colored pupils to sign a thank-you card for more school supplies." Thus Harding was still taking advantage of educational opportunities that created classrooms of old and young learning together.[58]

By December 1882 Georgia had died, leaving him with a young baby girl, Lena May, who died in May 1884 of pneumonia. Although associated with the Episcopal Church, Harding may have also attended the Mount Zion African Methodist Church in Nebraska City. A good deal of the town's Black social life revolved around this church, and he is mentioned in connection with many of that church's leaders in the Nebraska City newspapers.[59]

In March 1885 the *Nebraska City News* announced Harding's third marriage, to Mrs. Belle Tarwater. The decade must have been good to Harding, as he bought a lot from Alexander Hart in 1888 and transferred it to his wife Belle in 1889. In 1889 he also bought another property from Walter Osage. Belle was a "'great favorite' with the 'old families' of Nebraska City," noted as a cook and housekeeper who was in "great demand in Nebraska City kitchens."[60]

In 1890 Harding served as a delegate from Otoe County to a "Colored Men's Convention" held by the Afro-American League in Omaha, along with friend Barney Botts, his brother-in-law Brainard Makins, and nephew Daniel Smith, all of Nebraska City. The Nebraska League's resolutions dealt with the protection of African American suffrage in American government. Not long after the convention, Harding was one of the men appointed to approach Nebraska City's Board of Education to ask that the "colored boys" be able to attend the public schools, a petition that was not looked upon with favor by the *Syracuse (NE) Journal*, which counseled that the "colored people must be patient and bide their time."[61]

Indeed, African American education had been a public concern from the beginning of emancipation. In 1867 Nebraska's acting governor, Algernon Paddock, blocked legislation that sought to provide equal education and integrated public schools. Although he saluted the legislation's good intent, given ongoing racism, he stated that "better results might reasonably be expected in the education of both white and colored children if separate schools could be provided for each." Paddock's pronouncement presaged the 1896 Supreme Court *Plessy v. Ferguson* decision, which codified the practice nationwide.[62] In this atmosphere, it is no wonder that Harding's efforts fell on deaf ears.

The Black community in Nebraska City was never large. In 1870 the census identified 195 individuals as Black, among a total population of 6,050. The 1880 census saw a notable decline, with 174 African Americans among a population of 4,183. This decline was not a good sign for the Black community. It signals not only the departure of Black citizens, but also a decline in the formation of families that would have raised future citizens to live and work in the area. In 1890 the census returns were lost, so the number of African Americans cannot be determined, but Nebraska

City's total population that year was 11,941—the apex of Nebraska City's growth. By 1900 the census shows 145 Blacks in the town of 7,380. With fewer Blacks as a percentage of Nebraska City's population, Harding lived and worked in a town whose opportunities were diminishing for the next generation.[63]

But when Nebraska City marked its fiftieth anniversary as a town in 1904, Harding Hampton joined others, including Heath Nuckolls, as a part of the old settlers' celebration. The settlers named were all natives of Grayson County and relatives of his enslavers.[64] Did Harding join in the storytelling and recollections? As he sat there as a Nebraska City "pioneer," did he wonder what had happened to Celia, Eliza, and the other Graysons?

In 1922 Harding died at his house at 405 Fourth Corso after an illness of several months. His funeral was held at St. Mary's Episcopal Church. Harding was said to be a "man of all work—trusted by all."[65]

When Harding made out his will in 1922, he called himself a "retired laborer." The will shows that he had crafted a lifestyle in Nebraska that reached at least the lower middle class. He treated his stepchildren as his own, while remembering his nieces and nephews. He appointed his niece Cora Smith (daughter of his brother Henry) the executor of his will, and she received one of his properties. The bulk of his estate, including his house and furnishings at Fourth Corso and two life insurance policies, went to his "granddaughter," Arafura Stewart, who was his stepgranddaughter. Harding died owning at least three properties in Nebraska City and a railroad leasehold.[66]

Harding's life demonstrates another dimension to the legacy of slavery in the Missouri River Valley. In some ways, he was better off than many of his fellow free people farther south, yet he still experienced and resisted racism and encountered obstacles, obstacles that Black people faced not only in Nebraska City but also across the American West. Although he confronted significant racial barriers, Harding adapted and created a life in freedom within the limited societal framework available to him in Nebraska City. He had the right to vote, attended school, obtained property, and continued to work on behalf of his community for expanded access to education and suffrage.

Other Hampton Nieces and Nephews

The rest of Celia and Eliza's Hampton nieces and nephews had mixed experiences in Nebraska City. Henry G. Hampton, born after emancipation, was an expert tinner employed by Hugh Aird. He threw himself into the Black community's social life, singing in plantation quartets and excelling in athletic events in his "free time." Unlike his older brother, Harding, Henry had a few legal scrapes, but none so serious as to damage his reputation. At his death, the local newspapers described him as one of the "best known colored men that ever made his home in this city." He ended his days in St. Joseph, Missouri, probably having moved to the larger town for work.[67]

Not much can be gleaned about Edith's daughters, Jane and Martha, called Mattie (likely Celia and Eliza's nieces). They were listed with their parents in the 1870 Iowa census and also went to Nebraska City, where Jane worked as a laundress at the Grand Central Hotel at 118 Main Street, just four blocks from the scene of Celia and Eliza's escape.[68] Mattie appears in the *Nebraska City Directory* for 1881–82 as Martha Hampton in the same house as Edith on Pawnee Street.[69] Jane and Mattie were probably two of the three children that Edith reported as having died before the 1900 census. Edith's daughter Clementine, who appeared in only the 1870 census, probably died young in Iowa.[70]

Edith's daughter Celia Hampton married a man named Charles (Charlie) Hicks, with whom the newly widowed Edith Hampton lived in 1880. In 1884 Celia divorced Hicks as a victim of domestic abuse. A few years before the divorce, the local news carried an item about Charles "whipping his wife," opining, "The brute should be given a dose of his own prescription."[71] Celia and Charles had one daughter, named Ada, before their marriage broke apart. Celia Hampton Hicks must have moved away from Nebraska City soon after, because although Charles was mentioned in the newspaper from time to time, she was not. From 1920 to 1940 Celia adopted the surname of Nichols, perhaps as a variant of Nuckolls, and worked as a domestic in Portland, Oregon. She died in Portland on April 5, 1944.[72]

Edith's youngest daughter, Mary Albertha, called "Birdie," attended school in Nebraska City. In December 1885 she married a Black teacher from the school, Brainard Cyprion Makins.[73] The Makins family lived in

Nebraska City until about 1891, when they moved to Indian Territory in Oklahoma. By 1900 Brainerd and Birdie had five children in the household, and Brainerd was working as a painter. Birdie died not long after this census.[74]

Shack Grayson, "A Sharp and Industrious Boy"

Shack, enslaved by Stephen Nuckolls along with Celia and Eliza, was sold south in the spring after the sisters left Nebraska City for freedom. Territorial representative William H. Taylor reported that Nuckolls had sold "a colored man of twenty-five years of age" in the spring of that year, and Lucinda Bourne Nuckolls's correspondence confirms the report, saying, "Friel has sold Shack, he got twelve hundred & fifty dollars for him." In January 1868 the *Nebraska City News* announced that a letter had arrived from Shack Grayson, a "sharp and industrious boy" who "minded his own business" when he had lived in Nebraska City working as a pressman. Now the *News* declared he was a tool in the "hands of political meddlers." The *News* sneered at the "distinguished" Shack, who as a "full-blooded Congo" was said to be a member of Mississippi's Reconstruction Convention then in session.[75]

The dismissive and racist tone demonstrated that in Nebraska City, the old idea of slavery as a "positive good" was alive and well. Just as the *Nebraska City News* had commented in 1860 on Eliza ending up in a house of ill repute, rather than enjoying the comforts her master could provide, the newspaper surmised that the freedman Shack would ostensibly starve to death without his white sponsors—a victim subject to white Reconstruction leaders' bidding.

News of Shack reappeared some forty years later. In 1907 an item in the *Omaha Daily Bee* headlined "Old Nebraska Slave Prospers" cited a letter recently received in Nebraska City from Shack Grayson of Louisiana. Unfortunately, the newspaper neglected to say to whom the letter was addressed, although it may have been one of Shack's relations in the Hampton family. The item reiterated that Shack had been one of Mississippi's legislators, adding that he was "now the proprietor of a plantation in Louisiana."[76]

An African American man named Jackson (Jack) Grayson resided in West Feliciana parish, Louisiana, from 1870 to 1900. When Jackson died in 1907, his property was divided between his widow and his "absent heir," nephew Harding Hampton of Nebraska City. The naming of Harding Hampton proves that Jackson Grayson of West Feliciana was indeed Shack of Nebraska City.[77] Like so many others, Nuckolls descendant Lulu Wesner may have confused Shack and Shade when she congratulated the *Nebraska Daily News* on its anniversary edition, saying that Shade "never went with the other S. F. Nuckolls' slaves. He had money in the bank and didn't want to leave it." She went on to say that Shade went south and left Harding Hampton some money, facts that fit Shack, rather than Shade.[78]

What Nebraska Citians did not know was that Jack (formerly Shack) Grayson was a Civil War veteran. In May 1863 Shack escaped from his enslaver, Theodule Dumesnil of St. Martin Parish, Louisiana, taking a mule with him. He enlisted in the United States Colored Troops at Brashear City, Louisiana. The enlistment papers describe him as born in Virginia, with dark hair, eyes, and complexion, and record his former employment as "servant." The compiled service record makes clear that Jack, Jackson, and Shack were all names he used.[79]

He participated in the siege of Port Hudson, Louisiana, and was wounded there. After he recovered enough to return to duty, he served the remainder of his time working at the regimental hospital as both a cook and a nurse.[80]

Shade Grayson, Remaining in Shadow

More confusion surrounds Shade's fate, whose story is marked by error. After his appearance in the 1860 Iowa census with Columbus Nuckolls in Pacific City, Mills County, Iowa, he also drops from the record. According to the census, he was born about 1832 in Virginia. Coupled with a statement that he was "one of a family" enslaved by Ezra Nuckolls, he was likely a brother to Celia and Eliza Grayson.[81] Multiple accounts say Shade was also a freedom seeker, and one states that he "and two Negro girls were smuggled away by the famous Underground."[82] Had Shade escaped with Celia and Eliza, the *Nebraska City News* would have included him.

Other stories, quoting J. Sterling Morton, asserted that both Shack and Shade left "shortly after" Nuckolls returned from Chicago in 1860, implying that they, too, were fugitive slaves. Another writer for Morton's later publication called the *Conservative* related that Shade "ran off," without specifying when. It is almost certain that Morton knew what had actually happened, given his close ties in Nebraska City. Later Morton-influenced accounts contain obvious errors that may have been designed to obfuscate his role in proslavery efforts during the territorial period.[83] However, the census lists Shade as residing with Columbus Nuckolls in 1860, which was almost two years after Celia and Eliza left.

Shade's life story became even more fanciful. A much-repeated account related that after the Civil War, Shade went to South Carolina and served in the state legislature, using the surname Nuckolls. This version may have originated from a 1929 article stating that Stephen Nuckolls received a letter from Shade saying that he "had prospered and entered the turbulent political arena of South Carolina, sat in the legislature of that state and used the name of his former master"—an account that probably confused the letter Nuckolls wrote in 1872 about Shack, mixing it with Shade and changing the venue to South Carolina, where there was indeed a Black representative with a similar surname.[84]

A freedman much older than Shade named Samuel Nuckles served in South Carolina's legislature. State senator Samuel Nuckles testified in the U.S. Congress in 1872, explaining that he had been a "hard-down slave" who was "bred and born in Union County, on North Pacolet, fifteen miles above Union Village."[85] Thus Shade of Nebraska did not migrate to South Carolina and become a legislator there. His whereabouts after the 1860 census are still unknown.

Uncovering the Stories

The unknown fate of Celia, Eliza, and Shade highlights one of the most prominent legacies of enslavement in the Missouri Valley region—permanent separation from family members. No evidence has yet been found of Graysons searching for family in advertisements, although the practice was common.[86] Shack obviously wrote back to Nebraska City to reconnect with his sister Edith and her family. That Shack only mentioned his one heir, Harding, suggests he did not find anyone else.

What about the rest of the people enslaved by Ezra Nuckolls and his children? Clayton, Jane, Rebecca, Richard, Charles Raleigh, Mary, and her child never appear again. Were they sold south? Did they live in Missouri and become emancipated after the Civil War? As archivists, librarians, and historians discover and digitize more sources, it may be that more evidence about the rest of the Graysons and their descendants will come to light.

Celia and Eliza's courageous act of resistance illuminates the antislavery and proslavery debates within Nebraska Territory and at the national level. Their story also illustrates the shifting attitudes regarding the Fugitive Slave Law, abolitionism, and popular sovereignty. Their successful escape and subsequent pursuit as "fugitives from labor and service" gave the lie to the argument "There is no slavery in Nebraska."

The Graysons were brought west as involuntary migrants accompanying whites as they moved into Indigenous homelands. Most of them have dropped from the record. But those who remained in the area mingled and intermarried with Southern families and forged their identities as free Americans of color in the West. Indeed, African Americans played important and varied roles in the development of the Lower Missouri River Valley region, whether as enslaved workers, freedom seekers, abolitionists, or free citizens making their way in a post–Civil War society still dominated by whites. It is time to retrieve their stories from the fringes of history and illuminate their lives, their work, and their communities.

Appendix A

TRANSCRIPTION OF THE ENSLAVED
LISTED IN NUCKOLLS ACCOUNT BOOK

Matilda the Black woman born in the year 1804
Mariah born May 1820
Benjamin born March 1822
Beverly Born Jany 1824
Milly supposed to be Born in the year 1813
Mary Born Augt 4 1826
Benjamin [blotted] June 9. 1827 at 10 oclock pr Evening
Rebecah Born Jany 14 1828
Milly died 31st Oct 1828 at 11 oclock pr Evening
Edieth Born Jany 27. 1830
Mariah Died 15 Jany 1831 at 8 oclock pr Evening
Dorcas Born Wednesday Jany 11 1832
Henry Born Decr 2 1833 at 8 oclock pr Evening
Beverly [died?] 31 Decr 1833 at ½ past 8 oclock pr Evening
Celia Born Feby 12. 1836 at ½ past 1 oclock
Eliza Born Jany 24 1838 at 11 oclock pr Evening
Calvin Born Jany 10 1840 at 11 oclock pr Evening
Ellin Jane Born May 26. 1842 and
Died August 1842
Jane Born Octo 23 1844
Malinda Born July 9 1844
Charles Raleigh Born May 10 1848
Clayton Born 2nd July 1850
Newborn Born Nov 1 1851
Newborn Died June 20 1852
Eliza Caroline Born 2nd June 1853
Rebecca Died 14th June 1855
Rebecca (Mary's Daughter) born 5th September 1855
Eliza Caroline Died 20th November 1855
Malinda died 18th March 1856

Source: Nuckolls Family Papers, History Nebraska Archives, "From the best information we could get."

Appendix B

GRAYSON FAMILY TREE

Ezra Nuckolls's Enslaved People per Account Book and Estate Inventory

Note: Others in Nuckolls's account book for whom relationships are unknown: Milly, 1813–28; Charles Raleigh*, b. 1848; and Clayton*, b. 1850. It may be that Richard, who was called a "man" in Ezra's estate papers and was not in the account book, was Mary's partner, as he, Mary's named daughter Rebecca, and Mary's unnamed younger child were kept together for the estate sale.

* Denotes inclusion in estate inventory. Relationships are listed tentatively.

† Matilda is likely the mother of most of the children, given that she is the only woman in the account book meeting nearly all the criteria. However, Mary (1826) and Rebecca (1828–55) are mother candidates for the children born later (i.e., Malinda, Jane, Charles Raleigh, and Clayton), because Matilda was nearing the end of her childbearing years.

‡ Henry, born in 1833, died in 1857 before the estate sale.

§ Shack and Shade are not in the account book; however, census ages for the two suggest they were born ca. 1830–33, so they are placed between Rebecca and Dorcas.

‖ Paternity is uncertain.

Shack's Louisiana estate named his nephew Harding Hampton of Nebraska City.

Source: Created by Ben Kruse, History Nebraska.

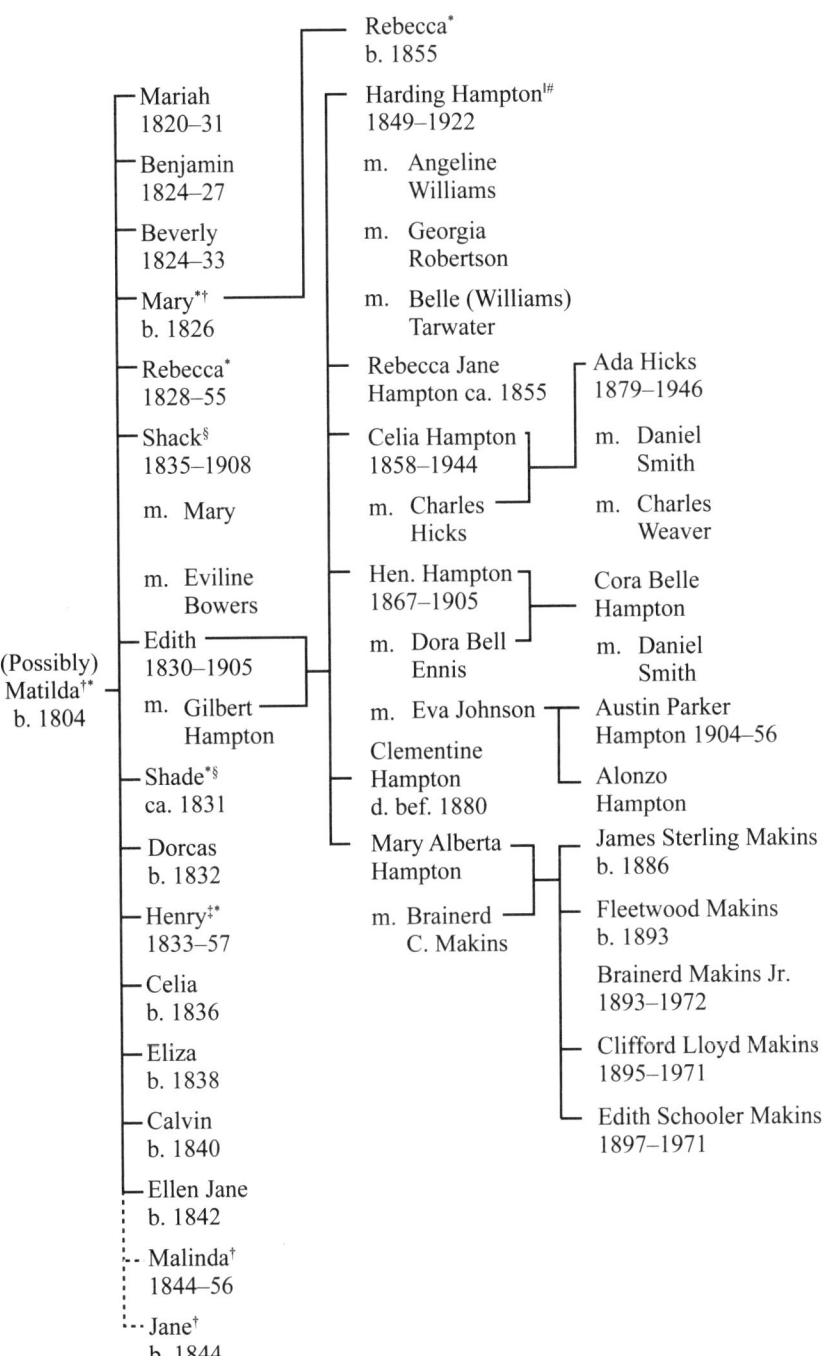

Appendix B 175

Appendix C

NUCKOLLS–BOURNE–HAIL RELATIONSHIP CHART

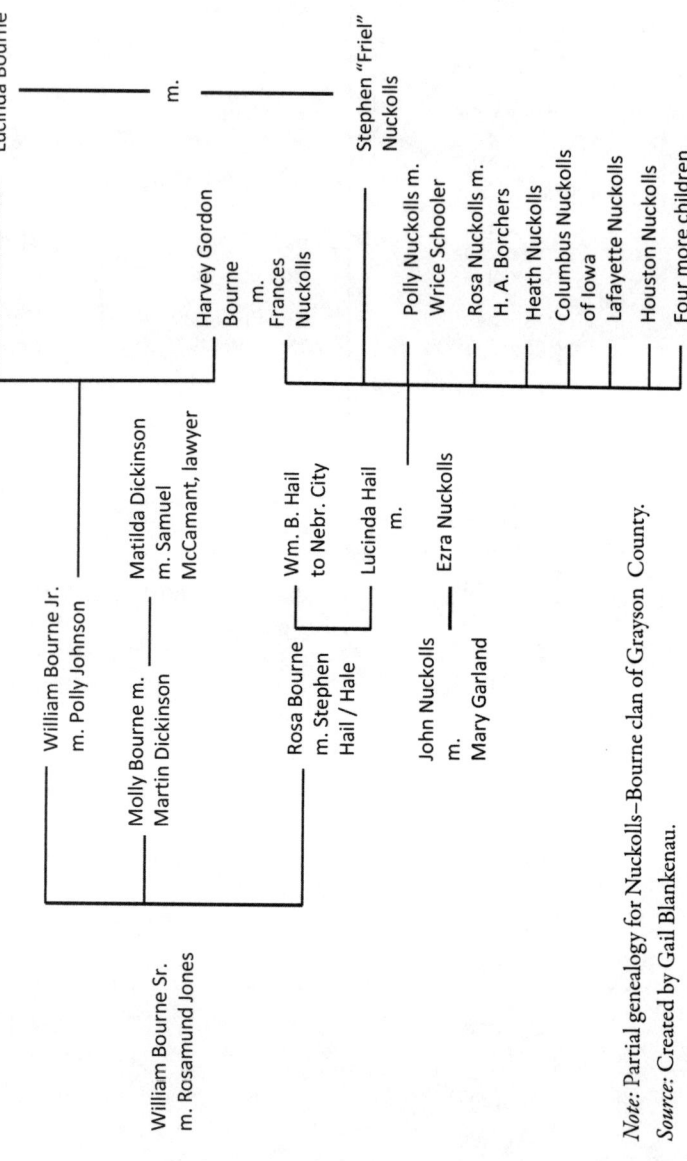

Note: Partial genealogy for Nuckolls–Bourne clan of Grayson County.
Source: Created by Gail Blankenau.

Notes

All quoted material has been reproduced as it appears in the original, including any errors in spelling, grammar, syntax, and punctuation.

Abbreviations

BDHE	*Burlington (IA) Daily Hawk-Eye*
BDSG	*Burlington (IA) Daily State Gazette*
CDT	*Chicago Daily Tribune*
CL	*Cheyenne Leader*
CT	*Chicago Tribune*
FH	*Fremont (IA) Herald*
HNA	History Nebraska Archives
NARA	National Archives and Records Administration
NCDN	*Nebraska City Daily News*
NCN	*Nebraska City News*
NCNP	*Nebraska City News Press*
NDNP	*Nebraska Daily News Press*
NFP	Nuckolls Family Papers
NSHS	Nebraska State Historical Society
ON	*Omaha Nebraskian*
OSHS	Ohio State Historical Society
PCH	*Page County (IA) Herald*
USCB	U.S. Census Bureau

Prologue

1. In addition to early Nebraska histories, Soike, *Necessary Courage*, 134–42, mentions their flight; Blackett, *Captive's Quest*, 460, also refers to their story.
2. "The Western Democracy," *CT*, November 15, 1860; "The Eliza Grayson Case," *CT*, November 16, 1860.

Introduction

1. Account book, folder 3, ser. 11, NFP; "Slavery in Nebraska," *BDHE*, January 8, 1859; *Cleveland Plain Dealer*, December 28, 1858; Todd, *Early Settlement*, Historical Department of Iowa, Des Moines, 1906; Ellen Gaston Hurlbutt letter, March 18, 1935, Ohio Memory, https://ohiomemory.org/digital/collection/siebert/id/8694; "The Excitement Continues—The Fugitives Heard From—Swamped in an Abolition Hole," *NCN*, December 4, 1858; "Weather," *FH*, November 27, 1858. Handy and Handy, *Someday*, 41, has another version of this story in which John Williamson encouraged the women to escape, but Jim Lane of Kansas provided the boat for crossing over at Old Wyoming, describing the river as running full of ice. His account, however, is not well documented. Yet another version is in Bartling, *John Henry Kagi*, a short booklet that mentions a party of men taking Celia and Eliza to Wyoming Station. J. Potter, "Fact and Folklore," 73–88, debunks Bartling's John Brown's Cave story, which puts the rest of Bartling's work in question. The territorial legislature granted a ferry license on February 23, 1855, to Josiah Burget and associates to keep the Wyoming ferry, which crossed over to Lambert's Landing by Civil Bend, Iowa. Nebraska Territory, *Laws, Joint Resolutions*, 448.

2. "Great Excitement—Escape of Negroes—$200 Reward!," *NCN*, November 27, 1858. A month later, newspapers were still printing the story, such as "Excitement on the Iowa Border," *Baltimore Liberator*, December 31, 1858, about slaves "held in Nebraska" escaping from their "pretended owner."

3. "Union Clean Gone," *Chicago Tribune*, November 16, 1860; "The Union Again Threatened," *Chicago Tribune*, November 13, 1860. Analysis of 1850 Atchison County, Missouri, Slave Schedule, District 3, p. 19, lists a total of thirty-two slaves, of which three were mulattoes. Celia and Eliza were designated as Black.

4. Census of the Second District, Nebraska Territory, 1854–56, HNA, Nebraska Territorial Census Records, subgroup 1: 1854–56, 1854–60, microfilm roll 1, USCB; "Population of the United States in 1860: Territory of Nebraska," USCB, https://www2.census.gov/library/publications/decennial/1860/population/1860a-40.pdf; *Missouri Republican*, quoted in "Slavery in Kansas and Nebraska," *Madison (IN) Dollar Weekly Courier*, June 13, 1855; *St. Louis Republican*, quoted in *New England Farmer*, June 16, 1855. Several researchers have found consistent census undercounts, including Steckel, "Quality of Census Data," 590, who noted an undercount rate of 3 percent for whites and 40 percent for Blacks in the District of Columbia in 1940; Debats, "Hide and Seek"; M. Anderson, "Sectional Crisis."

5. Bish, "Black Experience," 20. According to USCB, by 1860 Kearny and Otoe Counties reported fifteen enslaved people; the rest of the Blacks in Nebraska Territory were ostensibly free. One of the numbers is smudged and is a one

instead of a two, so the total count is actually fourteen instead of fifteen. "Population of the United States in 1860: Territory of Nebraska."

6. Census of the Second District, Nebraska Territory, 1854–56, HNA, Nebraska Territorial Census Records. The microfilm for the 1860 Nebraska Territorial Census at HNA has a one-page list of enslavers and the number of enslaved people for each one; this list does not appear in online digital collections. Judge Edward Randolph Hardin brought an enslaved man named Sam with him to Nebraska. Others in public office whose enslaved people were not counted were George H. Nixon, register at the Federal Land Office at Brownville (Nemaha County), and Edward A. DesLondes, register at the Land Office at Nebraska City. Also not mentioned was Robert M. Kirkham, who still had two enslaved persons listed in the 1860 census. HNA microfilm RG 513, Nebraska City, Otoe County, USCB, *Eighth Census of the United States, 1860*, loose paper before the regular schedule.
7. The estimate of fifteen thousand to twenty thousand freedom seekers in the 1850s is repeated in countless works without citation. One early source of the number seems to be Landon, "Negro Migration to Canada," 22, based on Canadian census numbers and anecdotal accounts in newspapers.
8. For more about Morton, see the biography by Olson, *J. Sterling Morton*. Morton was the editor of the *NCN* in 1855 and again in 1857 until Milton Reynolds took over. He returned to the editorial board in 1865. *NCN*, November 20, 1869.
9. Blackett, *Captive's Quest*, xii.
10. Maizlish, *Strife of Tongues*, 6, 45.
11. For countless examples of domestic enslavement in small numbers persisting in Northern climes, see Lehman, *Slavery*.
12. Franklin and Schweninger, *Runaway Slaves*, 25–26, discuss opportunities such as proximity to free territory, borderland areas, and travel.
13. Speer, *Life of Gen. Lane*; Connelley, *James Henry Lane*; Noble, *John Brown*.
14. For a full revision of the role of John Brown's Cave, see J. Potter, "Fact and Folklore." For the site's current state, see "Mayhew Cabin with John Brown's Cave," Mayhew Cabin Foundation, accessed April 11, 2023, https://mayhewcabin.org/.
15. "The Ball Opened Slavery," *Washington (DC) National Era*, June 28, 1855.
16. Andreas, *History of Nebraska*, "Otoe County," part 4, "Early Settlement."
17. Lehman, *Slavery*.
18. Examples are numerous. See, e.g., *NCN*, December 17, 1859, quoting Rep. George Miller.
19. Berlin, *Many Thousands Gone*, 8–10 (emphasis mine). He continues to use this analytical framework in his later works, such as *Generations of Captivity*.
20. George L. Miller, representative in the Nebraska Territorial House, in Nebraska Territory, *Council Journal, Sixth Session*, 47.

21. Dunaway, *Slavery*; Inscoe, "Race and Racism," urges scholars to study Black life in Appalachia in its own right, regardless of smaller numbers. Likewise, Kukis, "Master and Slaves," suggests that diverse areas deserve more attention.
22. Dunaway, *Slavery*; Pudup, Billings, and Waller, *Appalachia in the Making*; Kukis, "Master and Slaves."
23. Campbell, *Slave Catchers*; Burke, *On Slavery's Border*.
24. Burke, *On Slavery's Border*, 3. Burke quotes John G. Haskell, "The Passing of Slavery in Western Missouri," who describes enslavement there as "more a domestic than commercial institution," emphasizing that enslaved people and white farm families worked side by side. *On Slavery's Border*, 3.
25. Burke, *On Slavery's Border*, 94.
26. Burke, *On Slavery's Border*, 6; Epps, *Slavery on the Periphery*, 4.
27. Burke, *On Slavery's Border*, 25.
28. Burke, *On Slavery's Border*, 3.
29. Burke, *On Slavery's Border*, 1. Historians such as Diane Mutti Burke, Kristen Epps, and Wilma Dunaway also address the "small scale" of enslavement in these areas and problematic descriptions of it as more familial and thus more benign.
30. "Slavery in Nebraska," BDHE, January 8, 1859.
31. Berlin, *Many Thousands Gone*, 8.

1. Growing Up in Slavery

1. Howe, *Historical Collections of Virginia*, 284.
2. Coxe, *Ancestry of John Nuckolls*, a five-page report, undated but with good citations. Self-published and shared with Nuckolls family members.
3. Currey, *Geological Visit*, 13. Copper mines are mentioned in Fielden L. Hale to Ezra and Lucinda Nuckolls, February 15, 1856; S. McCamant to Ezra Nuckolls, February 16, 1856; Jeremiah Jennings to Ezra Nuckolls, March 4, 1856; Ira B. Coltrane to Ezra Nuckolls, April 20, 1856; Fielden L. Hale to Ezra and Lucinda Nuckolls, May 26, December 4, 1856, February 13, 1857, folders 2–4, box 1, ser. 1, NFP. See also Samuel Dickey and Charles Rufus Boyd, *Map of Grayson County, Virginia*, 1897, Library of Congress, https://www.loc.gov/item/2012589206.
4. Virginia Select Marriages, Ancestry.com. Official records use Hail and Hale interchangeably. The branch that migrated to Missouri and Nebraska began to use Hail more consistently, while many staying in Virginia used Hale. Most of the private letters in NFP use Hail.
5. B. Nuckolls, *Pioneer Settlers*, 66. I contacted descendants of Benjamin Floyd Nuckolls, and none were aware of the current location of Mary Garland's prayer book.
6. Louisa County, Virginia, tax list, 1787, FamilySearch.org.

7. Louisa County, Virginia, Deed Book J, 172–73, Charles Garland to William Dickinson in trust for the children of John and Mary (Garland) Nuckolls, dated February 14, 1801, FamilySearch.org. The deed conveyed to the couple's children two tracts of land and an African American boy named Isaac, as well as the "reversion" of two other African Americans: a woman named Lacey, who was in the possession of Robert Garland and continued to live with Robert during Charles's life, and a boy named Ralph, who was in the possession of Rhodes Nuckolls until January 1803. William Dickinson, the trustee, was to hold this property until the "first" child either married or reached age twenty-one. Although the clerk's deed clearly reads "first," he must have meant to write "last," since the oldest, David Nuckolls, was over twenty-one at the time the deed was written. The language regarding reaching the age of twenty-one makes sense only under the usual terms in deeds of this kind, which generally waited until the last child was of age.
8. Louisa County, Virginia, Deed Book K:111–12, John Nuckolls to Charles Yancy, David Bullock, and William Callis, trustees of Mary Nuckolls, September 10, 1805, FamilySearch.org.
9. Louisa County, Virginia, Deed Book K:224–25, FamilySearch.org. Ned's age of thirty-six was given in a subsequent deed, Deed Book K:326, August 12, 1806, FamilySearch.org. He may be the Black person over sixteen in John Nuckolls's 1787 tax list.
10. Indeed, enslaved people often changed hands to settle debts. Researcher Wil Mahan lists 614 deeds involving enslaved people of Randolph County NC at http://www.slavedeeds.org/slavedeeds.html. Although not all deeds are clear, at least 21 involve sales to satisfy debt, and 40 used enslaved people as collateral to secure a deed. The famous Georgetown sale of 272 slaves helped the university emerge from debts. In research I performed for William G. Thomas for his book *A Question of Freedom*, John Hepburn of Maryland secured his debts in a deed of trust to Samuel Hamilton of Washington DC, involving several enslaved people, some of whom were eventually sold. For a thorough discussion of slave sales and mortgages, see Caldwell, "Financial Frontier."
11. Will of James Nuckolls, Louisa County, Virginia, Will Book 5:349, Louisa County Historical Society, Louisa VA.
12. See Dunaway, *Slavery*, 9, for plantation sizes and classification.
13. Grayson County tax list, 1824, transcription by Jeffrey C. Weaver, July 1, 1998, https://www.newrivernotes.com/grayson-personal-property-tax-list-1824/; will of James Nuckolls. For discussions of plantation classification by the number of enslaved, see Berlin, *Many Thousands Gone*, whose categorization has been adopted by most historians, including Wilma Dunaway.
14. Jones-Rogers, *They Were Her Property*, 699.

15. White, *Ar'n't I a Woman*, 201.
16. Account book, box 2, ser. 2, NFP, with Nuckolls family births and deaths; enslaved people's births and deaths; and receipts. Once the importation of enslaved people was abolished in 1808, natural increase became the main driver of demographic growth. For a comparative history of the growth rate of slavery in the United States relative to societies in the Caribbean and South America, see Tadman, "Demographic Cost of Sugar."
17. Account book, NFP; Hening, "What Persons Are Tithable," 454–55; John Barrett Robb, "Interpreting the Annual Virginia Tax Lists from 1782 On, and Their Basis in Law," http://www.johnbrobb.com/Content/VA/VA-Taxes-Law&Interpretation.pdf; Grayson County tax list, 1828, Ezra Nuckolls, Grayson County Historical Society, Independence VA. The Nuckolls list names six enslaved children under sixteen in 1828 (ages newborn to eight), so the number of enslaved people may have been closer to nine.
18. Turnmire, "'Worthy to Be Classed.'" Norman, *Portion of My Life*, 45, speaks of "Mr. Ezra Nuckolls, a very wealthy citizen of Grayson County, Virginia." See also Grayson County, Virginia, property tax lists, Grayson County Clerk, Independence VA.
19. Court documents are full of cases in which a daughter was given an enslaved person without a deed. See Curtis, *Digest of the Decisions*, 2:467–69; Jones-Rogers, *They Were Her Property*, 629. An example is "Pre-Nuptial Agreement—Mary Chew and John Hepburn, 1739," https://archives.lib.umd.edu/repositories/2/archival_objects/286348, demonstrating how a woman could receive a large dowry of enslaved people, whom her husband could "control" but only she and her children would inherit. In Lucinda Hail's case, there are no extant deeds or agreements documenting whether such a transfer took place. Her father's 1854 estate listed eight enslaved people. Stephen Hail Will, Grayson County Will Book 3:253, 254, 270–77, 389, 390.
20. Nuckolls collection, account book, NFP. The "slave" births are in chronological order, except for Milly, born in 1811 but sandwiched between births in 1824 and 1826, so she may not have been part of the main family. However, the likelihood of sibling relationships is reasonable for most entries. The entry for Celia's birth does not state whether the time was 1:30 a.m. or p.m.
21. "Slavery in Nebraska," BDHE, January 8, 1859. The article includes an editorial correcting errors in prior reporting, with added information about the "Nuckolls slave affair" and the origins of the enslaved people as having belonged to S. F. Nuckolls's parents, as well as other commentary. It has Celia's and Eliza's origins as being from one family, while *Cleveland Plain Dealer*, December 28, 1858, said they were part of "a family of Negro slaves." Coupled with the account book pattern of births spaced two years apart, the logical conclusion is that they were sisters.

22. Ezra Nuckolls to Ephraim and Mrs. Gentry, November 1855, Ancestry.com. A copy of the letter was given to Jim Nuckolls by Shirley Gordon. It is believed she obtained the letter from Judge Colin Campbell, who is related to the Gentry family from Grayson County. See also Ezra Nuckolls, line 24, 553, Grayson County, Virginia, Non-Population Schedule for Agriculture, USCB, *Seventh Census of the United States, 1850*; Nuckolls, *Pioneer Settlers*, 89; Worsham, "Survey of Historic Architecture."
23. B. Nuckolls, *Pioneer Settlers*, 24, 19. This source spells her name Rosamund, but other sources have Rosamond. I used the latter spelling throughout the book for consistency.
24. B. Nuckolls, *Pioneer Settlers*, 24, 19. The tradition held that this language was in his will. But William Bourne's will in Grayson County Will Book, 1:483, does not contain this language. Thus the statements about Granny Beck and Aimy must be considered family lore. Aimy went to live with Lucinda Bourne Nuckolls's aunt, Mary "Polly" (Bourne) Dickenson, who also "owned" Aimy's daughter Mourning. (Per William Bourne's 1835 will, Aimy was to go to Polly Dickenson after his death.) After Mary Dickenson died in 1860, Aimy went to the Elk Creek home of Francis Hale, who "owned" another of Aimy's daughters, Winny.
25. Sarah Francis (Woods) Burke in Federal Writers' Project, *Slave Narratives*, 12, 15–17, file no. 340021.
26. Dunaway, *Slavery*, 241.
27. Burke in Federal Writers' Project, *Slave Narratives*, 12, 15–17.
28. "Aunt Hannah Moore," in Still, *Underground Rail Road*, 547.
29. C. Moore, "Free in Thought," discusses childhood experiences among the enslaved. See also Dunaway, *Slavery*, 245.
30. Schwartz, *Born in Bondage*, 108. See also Burke, *On Slavery's Border*, 82.
31. Schwartz, *Born in Bondage*, 110.
32. Schwartz, *Born in Bondage*, 124. See also C. Moore, "Free in Thought," which discusses childhood experiences among the enslaved; Dunaway, *Slavery*, 245.
33. Crooks, *Life of Rev. Crooks*, 33. Crooks began the antislavery Methodist movement in Grayson County, with local Isaac Moore as the presiding elder (34–40).
34. McFayden, "Destroyer in Our Midst," 28. See also Philip Stone, "How the Methodist Church Split in the 1840s," *Wofford College Archives* (blog), January 30, 2021, http://blogs.wofford.edu/from_the_archives/2013/01/30/how-the-methodist-church-split-in-the-1840s/.
35. C. Johnson, "American Missionary Association," 14–26.
36. For the most comprehensive treatment of Bacon's ministry and trial, see McFayden, "Destroyer in Our Midst." Bacon is also mentioned in Herrold, *Rise of Aggressive Abolitionism*.

37. Virginia, Act of March 14, 1848, Ch. X, § 24, 1847–48 Va. Acts 113, 117.
38. "The Destroyer in Our Midst," *Abingdon (VA) Democrat*, quoted in *Richmond Enquirer*, April 27, 1849. See also 1850 Federal Census, Grayson County, Virginia, Slave Schedule, District 19, entry for Stephen Hale, 4–5. For a different view of the trial from an economic point of view, see Hall, *Mountains on the Market*, 77.
39. Now known as the Old Grayson County Courthouse in Old Town, the 1834 building served the county until 1851–52, when a new courthouse in Independence was completed. Ten years earlier the Virginia General Assembly had divided Grayson County, creating Carroll County to the east. The courthouse then perched on the eastern edge of Grayson County, so a more central location was chosen in Independence. National Register of Historic Places Registration Form, Virginia Department of Historic Resources, https://www.dhr.virginia.gov/historic-registers/038-0004/. The courthouse has a classic central main entry into the stair hall. Ezra Nuckolls's brother-in-law, Mastin Hail, bought the old courthouse, selling it in 1871 when it became a hotel.
40. For more on the Southern tradition of court days, see Shephard, "This Being Court Day," 459–70; McDonald, *Life in Old Virginia*; Rubenstein, "A History of the County Court in Virginia." Bonner, *Milledgeville*, 80, noted that "great crowds" attended court proceedings. The state of Virginia held a convention in the early 1900s to address the tradition of court days and lessen their impact.
41. Adam Crooks, "A Wesleyan Minister in Bonds," *Anti-Slavery Bugle*, July 6, 1849. This part of the story relies on Bacon's fellow Methodist missionary to the South, Rev. Adam Crooks, who attended the proceedings and wrote about them in this article. Bacon's attorney, Andrew Steele Fulton, had served in the Virginia House of Delegates.
42. Crooks, "Wesleyan Minister in Bonds."
43. Bill of Indictment, September 1849, "Commonwealth of Virginia versus Abolitionism," *The Uncommonwealth* (blog), Library of Virginia, January 30, 2013, https://uncommonwealth.virginiamemory.com/blog/2013/01/30/commonwealth-of-virginia-versus-abolitionism/.
44. Crooks, "Wesleyan Minister in Bonds."
45. "Visit to Grayson, VA.: Jarvis C. Bacon's Trial," *True Wesleyan*, October 20, 1849.
46. "Worthy of the Dark Ages," *Pennsylvania Freeman*, November 22, 1848.
47. Bacon v. Commonwealth, Supreme Court of Virginia, 48 Va. 602, 1850; "Visit to Grayson, VA"; "Destroyer in Our Midst," *Abingdon (VA) Democrat*; *Pennsylvania Freeman*, October 25 and November 22, 1849; "Rev. Jarvis C Bacon," *Rochester (NY) North Star*, November 9, 1849; Grattan, *Reports of Cases*, 7:602–12, 606.

48. B. Nuckolls, *Pioneer Settlers*, 13. The extant testimony appears in Grayson County Order Book, 1844–51, 581–84, Wytheville Community College, Wytheville VA, Mary B. Kegley Collection, Kegley Library Vertical Files, Blacks—Part 1. None of the slave catchers in the case owned enslaved people themselves, supporting historians' thesis that low-level enslavement was more widely accepted in Appalachia than previously assumed. Nuckolls, *Pioneer Settlers*, mentions a bulldog, but William B. Hail's court testimony makes no mention of it—the bulldog was probably an embellishment.
49. Grayson County Order Book, 1844–51, 581–84.
50. B. Nuckolls, *Pioneer Settlers*, 12. "Tragedy in Grayson," *Southern Press* (Washington DC), September 9, 1851, gives a full account, including the arrest of Simon in Wythe County, although some details do not match William Hail's testimony; "Affairs in Grayson County," *Cooper's Clarksburg (WV) Register*, gives details of Cornutt's torture, as well as the interference with the lawsuit, quoting both the *Lynchburg Virginian* and the *Staunton (VA) Spectator*. John "Clemments" was the first burial in Wyuka Cemetery, Nebraska City, memorial ID 17166471, Find a Grave, https://www.findagrave.com; he died January 1, 1855. Although some accounts say Lewis and Simon were captured in Bland County, the 1850 federal census shows Jack Lambert indeed residing on a small farm in Wythe County, District 69, 317b.
51. *Wytheville (VA) Republican*, quoted in Stowe, *Key to Uncle Tom's*, 189–90; "Lynch Law," *Richmond Times*, reprinted in *American Telegraph* (Washington DC), September 29, 1851; "News of the Day," *Alexandria (VA) Gazette*, September 27, 1851; *Green Mountain (VT) Freeman*, October 23, 1851.
52. *North Carolina Daily Standard*, October 1, 1851; *Kalida (OH) Venture*, October 10, 1851.
53. Fields and Hughes, *Grayson County*, 83.
54. The extant testimony, list of justices, and charges appear in Grayson County Order Book 1844–51, 581–84.
55. "Important Meeting in Grayson County, Virginia," *Lynchburg Virginian*, October 6, 1851. Ezra Nuckolls and Stephen Hale were appointed to the Grayson County committee. See also B. Nuckolls, *Pioneer Settlers*, 13–15, with an account corroborated by Alfred G. Bartlett, "an eye witness and actor in this distressing piece of history" (15), including details that cannot be verified.
56. Goodridge Wilson, Southwest Corner, *Pulaski (VA) Southwest Times*, March 29, 1936, describes the celebratory atmosphere with recollections from at least one witness. B. Nuckolls, *Pioneer Settlers*, 14, also places the execution in Independence, while Fields and Hughes, *Grayson County*, 83, indicates that the execution was at Hardin Cox's farm, where the men were also buried. Fields and Hughes's book lacks sources and citations, so the execution probably took place

in Independence. However, the men's burial may have been at Cox's farm. Ezra Nuckolls, along with Jeremiah Jennings, Heath Nuckolls, Orville Anderson, and George Reeves, opened a store in 1850 in the "new seat" at Independence, a complex that included a storehouse, a house, and necessary buildings for keeping a tavern. Original case no. 242, LVA Chancery Records, https://www.lva.virginia.gov/chancery/case_detail.asp?CFN=077-1860-021, dissolution of partnership, 1854 (when Ezra Nuckolls was preparing to move west).

57. Wilson, Southwest Corner.
58. Ezra Nuckolls v. Polly Clements, et al., Library of Virginia Chancery Records.
59. Grayson County, Virginia, Deed Book 10:216; "The Grayson County Meeting," *Pennsylvania Freeman*, June 3, 1852.
60. "Affairs in Grayson County," *Staunton (VA) Spectator*, May 5, 1852.
61. *Salem (NC) People's Press*, quoted in Hall, *Mountains on the Market*, 78.
62. "Affairs in Grayson County."
63. "Grayson County Meeting."
64. Wilson, Southwest Corner.

2. *Adjusting to New Lives*

1. Silliman, "'Up This Great River,'" 34.
2. Miller, *Dear Old Roanoke*. Founded in 1842, the Virginia Institute was chartered in 1845 as the Virginia Collegiate Institute. After Nuckolls's attendance there, in 1847, the founders decided to move the school to Salem, Virginia, with its better transportation and accessibility. In 1853 the fledgling college became Roanoke College, as it is known today. Nuckolls said he attended Roanoke College, although it was not called by that name when he attended. "Letter of S. F. Nuckolls," NSHS, *Transactions and Reports*, 1:32–37, http://digitalcommons.unl.edu/nebhisttrans/55.
3. "Letter of S. F. Nuckolls." Nuckolls identifies Hog Thief Bend as the later Civil Bend; however, Ewing, "Place Names," identifies the place only as a noted locality above "the Narrows" in timberland, the name reflecting pioneer humor.
4. Morton and Watkins, *Illustrated History of Nebraska*, 1:284.
5. Stapel, *Biographical History*; newspaper clipping, December 29, 1983, Atchison County History scrapbook, Rock Port Public Library, Rock Port MO. See Combs, "Slavery in the Platte Region," 15, for a survey of enslavement in the former Platte Purchase of northwest Missouri. The first county seat was at Linden in 1846, but when county boundaries changed, Linden was no longer centrally located, so the county seat was moved to Rock Port in 1856. Alexander Bradford served as the clerk of the circuit court of Atchison County in 1845–51, went to Iowa and served as a judge of the Sixth Judicial District in 1852–55, and served in the Nebraska Territorial Legislature in 1856, 1857, and 1860. He moved

to Colorado in 1860 and eventually served in Congress as a representative from that state. *History of the Arkansas Valley*.

6. Stephen F. Nuckolls to Lucinda "Bourn," Grayson County Marriage Register 1:54, Virginia Select Marriages. A deed that was never recorded in Grayson County, but remained in private hands, showed that the arrangement transferring Celia and Eliza to Stephen F. Nuckolls was formalized July 28, 1850 (account book, NFP), although both girls were already with him in Missouri, according to the 1850 Missouri census. Also in the census was a fifteen-year-old male who was almost certainly Shack. Stephen F. Nuckolls household, dwelling 288, family 290, Atchison County, Missouri, p. 153, USCB, *Seventh Census of the United States, 1850*. "The negroes belonged to a family, formerly owned by Mr. N's parents in Missouri. One of the same family is now living with Capt. L. Nuckolls at Pacific City, Iowa." *BDHE*, January 8, 1859. NFP does not include a deed for or mention of Shack, but numerous records show he was a fixture in Stephen Nuckolls's household. No individual 1850s tax lists are extant in the Atchison County courthouse.

7. "Steaming up the Missouri," 18.

8. Lingenfelter, *History of Fremont County*, 593–95; Babcock, "Steamboat Travel," 56.

9. "Steaming up the Missouri," 19.

10. *History of Holt and Atchison*, 626, devotes a section to the importance of bees.

11. *Kanesville (IA) Frontier Guardian*, June 27, 1849. Kanesville later became Council Bluffs, Iowa.

12. S. F. Nuckolls household, Atchison County, Missouri, USCB, *Seventh Census of the United States, 1850*.

13. Rosamond was still in her parents' household in Grayson County for the 1850 Census. USCB, 1850 U.S. Census for Grayson County VA, District 19, p. 179. She married August Borchers in 1851, so the courtship could not have been long.

14. *History of Holt and Atchison*, 872; C. Nuckolls, *Roses*; George Borchers to Mary Jane Todd in Platte County, Missouri, daughter of enslaver Maj. William Todd, Missouri Marriage Records, 1805–2002.

15. *Kanesville (IA) Frontier Guardian*, June 13, 1851, carried an advertisement for Nuckolls, Borchers, and Bourne, with an announcement to the people of Fremont, Mills, and Pottawattamie Counties that they had a new store in Fremont County and were in receipt of about "fifty tons of goods, consisting of everything usually kept in stores."

16. 1850 Atchison County, Missouri, Slave Schedule; USCB, *Compendium of the 1850 U.S. Census*, part 6, https://www2.census.gov/library/publications/decennial/1850/1850c/1850c-09.pdf. The Seventh Census for Missouri, with tables of statistics, counted only thirty enslaved people, plus seven "free col-

ored" in the county, with ages that would indicate one family. USCB, https://www2.census.gov/library/publications/decennial/1850/1850a/1850a-40.pdf.
17. Analysis of 1850 Atchison County, Missouri, Slave Schedule, District 3, p. 19.
18. USCB, "Statistics of Missouri," 1850 U.S. Census, https://www2.census.gov/library/publications/decennial/1850/1850a/1850a-40.pdf.
19. Norman, *Portion of My Life*, 49.
20. "Abolition Outrage," BDSG, December 18, 1858.
21. *Liberty (MO) Tribune*, March 25, 1859.
22. Aunt Sarah Waggoner of Savannah, Missouri, in Federal Writers' Project, *Slave Narratives*, 10 (stamped). For more on slave narratives, their utility, and limitations, see Escott, *Slavery Remembered*. For critiques, see, e.g., Casimir-Paz, "Footprints of the Fugitive"; Spindel, "Assessing Memory"; Crawford, "Quantified Memory."
23. Waggoner in Federal Writers' Project, *Slave Narratives*, 10.
24. Waggoner in Federal Writers' Project, *Slave Narratives*, 10. Many newspapers used the n-word during the 1850s. The n-word was in common use in the 1850s, but this book elides the word as n—— to avoid using this term.
25. Sarah Shaw Graves of Nodaway County, Missouri, in Federal Writers' Project, *Slave Narratives*, 10, 131.
26. Sarah Shaw Graves in Federal Writers' Project, *Slave Narratives*, 10, 131–32.
27. S. F. Nuckolls, "Missouri Agricultural Schedules," Missouri Secretary of State, Atchison County, 1850, https://www.sos.mo.gov/cmsimages/Archives/Census/Ag_1850/Ag_1850_Atchison.pdf.
28. C. Moore, "Free in Thought"; Lehman, *Slavery*, loc. 2364 of 3482, Kindle. Moore bases much of her analysis on the writings of Mary Lincoln's seamstress, Keckley, *Behind the Scenes*, and Jacobs, *Incidents*, to tease out the difficulties of growing up female and enslaved.
29. FH, November 15, 1858, and July 20, 1860. The latter calls Stephen Nuckolls the "principal proprietor" of Hamburg.
30. *Savannah (MO) Sentinel*, August 28, 1852.
31. Lucinda Bourne Nuckolls to her parents from Monroe House, St. Louis, September 28, 1854, Brett Conover (Bourne descendant) private collection.
32. H. G. Bourne of Sidney, Iowa, to Stephen and Alexander Bourne, Grayson County, Virginia, March 4, 1854, Brett Conover private collection. Harvey Gordon Bourne was Lucinda Bourne Nuckolls's brother, and he married Stephen's sister Frances H. Nuckolls, making their children double first cousins. Ezra Nuckolls had transferred another Grayson slave named Dorcas to the couple. After the couple settled in the free state of Iowa, it is unknown what happened to Dorcas.
33. E. H. Cowles, "Otoe County in Early Days," NSHS, *Transactions and Reports*, 1:37–42, https://digitalcommons.unl.edu/nebhisttrans/38.

34. Obituary of Heath Nuckolls, *Nebraska State Journal*, April 19, 1907; Ira B. Coltrane to Ezra Nuckolls, April 20, 1856. Heath Nuckolls's obituary in the *Lincoln Daily Star*, April 18, 1907, adds that when he came in 1854, he was with his uncle William B. Hail. Harvey Bourne was already writing back to Grayson County from Iowa in 1854, and Wrice Schooler had rented farm ground in Atchison County before Ezra's November 1855 arrival.
35. Maizlish, "The Nine-Month Debate and the Crisis of 1850," in *Strife of Tongues*, 13–24, furnishes an excellent summary.
36. Maizlish, *Strife of Tongues*, 15.
37. Maizlish, *Strife of Tongues*, 15; Holt, *Fate of Their Country*, 67–82; Hamilton, *Prologue to Conflict*, 141–42, 159–61. See also Blackett, *Captive's Quest*, which not only looks at "fugitive slaves" but also has an in-depth discussion of the Fugitive Slave Law of 1850.
38. Maizlish, *Strife of Tongues*.
39. An Act to Amend, and Supplementary to, the Act Entitled "An Act Respecting Fugitives from Justice, and Persons Escaping from the Service of Their Masters," Pub. L. No. 31-60, 9 Stat. 462 (1850).
40. Act to Amend.
41. *Wilmington (NC) Journal*, December 20, 1850, Georgia Convention.
42. *Charleston (SC) Mercury*, n.d., in *Nashville True Whig*, quoted in Blackett, "Resistance to Slavery," 311.
43. Giddings, *Speeches in Congress*, 442–43; Saler, *Settler's Empire*, 3, 10. See also Lamar, *Far Southwest*, introduction; Lamar, *Dakota Territory*, 1–26.
44. For a thorough discussion of the Missouri Crisis, see Hammond, *Slavery, Freedom, and Expansion*; Pasley and Hammond, *Fire Bell*.
45. Etcheson, *Bleeding Kansas*, 9–26. For more on the Nebraska bill and how it developed, see Malavasic, *F Street Mess*.
46. Thatcher, *Library of Original Sources*, 145.

3. Kansas and Nebraska Territories

1. Edson P. Rich, "Slavery in Nebraska," NSHS, *Transactions and Reports*, 2:95, http://digitalcommons.unl.edu/nebhisttrans/19.
2. Hammond, *Slavery, Freedom, and Expansion*, 117. The debate over slavery in Indiana and Illinois followed the same pattern regarding property as in Kansas and Nebraska, albeit with different results.
3. E. H. Cowles, "Otoe County in Early Days," NSHS, *Transactions and Reports*, 1:37, https://digitalcommons.unl.edu/nebhisttrans/38. Cowles's sister married Allen Alexander Bradford. Some sources, like this one, have the initials E. H. Cowles, but the early settler and Nebraska territorial leader was Charles H. Cowles, often written as C. H. Cowles.

4. Perley, *Repeal*, 165.
5. Perley, *Repeal*, 165.
6. The Preemption Act of 1841 permitted squatters already living on federal land to claim up to 160 acres after a residence of fourteen months. http://www.minnesotalegalhistoryproject.org/assets/Microsoft%20Word%20-%20Preemption%20Act%20of%201841.pdf.
7. James Gatewood to Nuckolls and Co., Glenwood, Iowa, clothing for Indian Chiefs, $113.15, and James Gatewood, Indian Agent, to S. F. Nuckolls for six pair suspenders for the use of the Otoe Indians, $2.40, U.S. Congress, House Document 84, item 8, February 6, 1854, and item 14, p. 26, February 7, 1854.
8. Cowles, "Otoe County," 1:38. Cowles explained that the papers that documented all this had perished in a fire, so these accounts were from his memory.
9. Wishart, *Unspeakable Sadness*, 109–11.
10. Quoted in Rawley, *Race and Politics*, 36.
11. Census of the Second District, Nebraska Territory, 1854–56, HNA, Nebraska Territorial Census Records. For the early establishment and incorporation of the town, see History of Nebraska City, https://nebraskacityne.gov/history-of-nebraska-city/.
12. Morton and Watkins, *Illustrated History of Nebraska*, 1:163, seem to confirm the story without naming Nuckolls. Francis Burt's son, Dr. Armistead Burt of New Mexico, wrote to the editors that his sick father reached Nebraska City and lodged in its only house, then hired "a two-horse wagon from the only citizen of the city," who was probably Stephen Nuckolls, given that he was the town proprietor. C. Nuckolls, *Roses*, 156, states it was Nuckolls without naming a source.
13. Morton and Watkins, *Illustrated History of Nebraska*, 1:160–64, 162; Poeschl, "Housing Nebraska's Governors," 260, citing unidentified newspaper in Watkins, *Publications*, 257.
14. Morton and Watkins, *Illustrated History of Nebraska*, 1:163–64.
15. Soike, *Busy in the Cause*, 10; Shambaugh, *Messages and Proclamations*, 2:14.
16. Douglas, *Speech*, 13.
17. D. Potter, *Impending Crisis*, 340–41. Lehman, *Slavery*, introduction, also discusses continued tolerance of enslavement among soldiers, federal appointees, and some private citizens in officially free territories, despite the Northwest Ordinance.
18. "Slavery in Kansas and Nebraska," *NCN*, quoted in *Biddeford (ME) Union and Eastern Journal*, June 15, 1855. The article was picked up by other newspapers across the country.
19. "Slavery in Kansas and Nebraska."
20. "Will Slavery Go into Nebraska?," *Springfield (IL) Journal*, quoted in the *Terre Haute (IN) Wabash Courier*, April 8, 1854.

21. *Biddeford (ME) Union and Eastern Journal*, May 24, 1854.
22. Bennet, "First Territorial Legislature," 88–89.
23. Sheldon, *Nebraska Blue Book*, 498–99.
24. "Abuse of Power," *Bellevue Nebraska Palladium*, January 3, 1855.
25. "Troubles in Nebraska," NCN, reprinted in *National Intelligencer* (Washington DC), November 17, 1855, and *Milledgeville (GA) Southern Recorder*, November 27, 1855.
26. Nebraska Legislators, Past and Present, NebraskAccess. Cowles later became a Republican, but he was Nuckolls's friend and associate in the early years of settlement.
27. Morton and Watkins, *Illustrated History of Nebraska*, 1:217. Because of this disregard of the law, Lafayette Nuckolls has the distinction of being the youngest member of a legislative assembly. Bennet, "First Territorial Legislature," 88–89. For more on Judge Fenner Ferguson, see Forbes, "Fenner Ferguson."
28. Bennet, "First Territorial Legislature," 88–89. "Morton's History, Chapter VII," *Syracuse Democrat*, March 7, 1907, laid out the members of the first legislature and territorial council, as well as the controversies between the North and South Platters.
29. "The N—— Party," ON, November 7, 1855; John H. Kagi, "Nebraska and Slavery," *New York Post*, July 22, 1856.
30. "The Ball Opened: Great Excitement in Nebraska City," *Washington (DC) National Era*, June 28, 1855.
31. Nuermberger, "Letters from Pioneer Nebraska."
32. "Letter of S. F. Nuckolls," NSHS, *Transactions and Reports*, 1:34.
33. *Nebraska Palladium*, December 6, 1855, quoted in Morton and Watkins, *Illustrated History of Nebraska*, 1:175.
34. Ezra Nuckolls to Ephraim and Mrs. Gentry, November 1855; Norman, *Portion of My Life*, 46. Norman's account relates that there were eight wagons, four carriages, and extra horses. C. Nuckolls, *Roses*, states that they moved in 1853, but this is in error. Norman was one of the unattached men who traveled with the group and worked for Stephen Nuckolls upon his arrival in Missouri.
35. Ezra Nuckolls to Ephraim and Mrs. Gentry, November 1855.
36. Ezra Nuckolls to Ephraim and Mrs. Gentry, November 1855; Norman, *Portion of My Life*, 49, who uses the term "Far West." Sonora is no longer in existence.
37. Account book, folder 1, box 2, ser. 2, NFP. When Ezra Nuckolls died, those who were still alive were listed in the estate inventory. The account book is incomplete and probably does not include any enslaved people still living but left behind in Virginia. Shade, not listed in the account book, was likely a brother to Celia, Eliza, and Shack. When Celia and Eliza left bondage, the *Pacific City Herald*, quoted in "Slavery in Nebraska," BDHE, January 8, 1859, stated, "One

of the same family is now living with Capt. L. Nuckolls in Pacific City, Iowa." Shade is listed with Columbus Nuckolls of Pacific City in the 1860 census.

38. Atchison County Historical Society, *Gone, but Not Forgotten*.
39. C. Nuckolls, *Roses*; Augustus Borchers, 1852 Iowa State Census, index, Sidney Township; Columbus Nuckolls household, family 33, 1856 Iowa State Census, Mills County, p. 384 (stamped).
40. Schooler returned to Atchison County to live. *History of Holt and Atchison*, 709.
41. 1856 Nebraska Territorial Census, RG 513, microfilm roll 1, item 3. "Heath Nuckolls Dead," newspaper clipping, NFP, folder 4, ser. 4, is an obituary that was probably written by Lulu Nuckolls Wesner, Heath Nuckolls's daughter. It states that Heath, along with others from Grayson County, came to Nebraska with five slaves: Shade and Shack, two girls, and Harding Hampton. It is known that Harding Hampton came with Wrice and Polly Schooler and that Shack was in Stephen Nuckolls's household, while Shade remained in Ezra Nuckolls's possession until Ezra's death.
42. NFP, folder 3, ser. 11. The list of enslaved people in the Nuckolls accounts only had a male named Calvin close to the age of the fifteen-year-old male in S. F. Nuckolls's 1850 slave schedule in Atchison County, Missouri. 1850 Federal Census, Slave Schedules, Atchison County, Missouri, District 3, lines 28–32. Calvin was born only two years after Eliza.
43. NFP, folder 3, ser. 11; Edwards, *History of Richardson County*, 597. The Schoolers' move back to Missouri in 1855 probably disappointed Celia and Eliza, as they took Edith, who was almost certainly Celia and Eliza's older sister, along with her family. Ezra Nuckolls had transferred Edith, later known as Aunt Edie Hampton, to Stephen's older sister, Polly Nuckolls Schooler, years before. Account book, NFP.
44. Account book, NFP, folder 1, box 2, series 2. For Houston's whereabouts, see Edwards, *History of Richardson County*, 597. Houston and Heath do not appear in the 1855 or 1856 Nebraska Census.
45. Epps, *Slavery on the Periphery*, chap. 2, explores increased enslaved mobility in the Missouri region; however, Burke, *On Slavery's Border*, 134, highlights that in smallholdings, "slave women were kept on the farm by the relentless demands of their work."
46. Epps, *Slavery on the Periphery*, 16.
47. NCN, quoted in "Slavery in Kansas and Nebraska," *Biddeford (ME) Union and Eastern Journal*, June 15, 1855. The same piece ran in *Leavenworth (KS) Weekly Herald*, June 9, 1855, and *Atlanta Weekly Intelligencer and Cherokee Weekly Advocate*, June 22, 1855.

4. Life in Nebraska City

1. J. W. Pearman, "Recollections of an Old Settler," *NCN*, February 22, 1873, describes who helped put in the main road; soldier William W. Ingraham to brother Ned, January 22, 1848 (Fort Kearney), HNA, RG 5237; "A Landmark Gone," *NCN*, June 18, 1897.
2. Lucinda Bourne Nuckolls to her brother and sister, August 11, 1855, HNA; Ellis and Ginsburg, "Studying the Landscapes," 8–9, describes the slave experience at Belmont Mansion in Wilmington; "Programme," *NCN*, June 24, 1859, records a Sunday School program held in "Mr. Nuckolls' Grove, immediately in the rear of Judge Kinney."
3. "Where Found," *NCN*, May 19, 1860; Ellis and Ginsburg, "Studying the Landscapes," 8–9; Berlin, *Many Thousands Gone*, loc. 749, Kindle (like rural slaves, urban slaves "lived in back rooms, lofts, closets," and even in "alley shacks"). Later accounts confused the three-story bank building (also brick) with Nuckolls's private residence. Andreas, *History of Nebraska*, "Otoe County," part 4, "A Judicial Joke," correctly located the "S. F. Nuckolls' residence" at the corner of Fifth and Main Streets but implied this was also the bank building. Yet it also stated the building was still standing in 1888. Contemporary newspapers, such as "Great Fire at Nebraska City! Immense Destruction of Property: Loss over $100,000," *Council Bluffs (IA) Non-Pareil*, May 10, 1860, reported that the bank building was destroyed in the 1860 fire. Andreas, *History of Nebraska*, "Otoe County," part 4, "A Judicial Joke," reported a potential change of residence ca. 1856. Pearman, "Recollections," *NCN*, February 22, 1873, described many firsts, including the first well dug for S. F. Nuckolls at lot 12, block 5, "where the transfer company is now located," and stated that the Nebraska Transfer Company was in the "first brick house which was built for S. F. Nuckolls." Ellen Kinney Ware, "Nebraska City in 1858," HNA, RG 2839.AM, MS 619, reel 1, noted that she saw the Platte Valley Bank after passing "a two-storey brick house where S. F. Nuckolls lived, the founder of the bank." The most reliable source for their location in 1858 is Heath Nuckolls, *NCN*, June 18, 1897, recalling that they lived in the military hospital until their house at the corner of Fifth Street and Central Avenue (now Main Street) was finished.
4. Pearman, "Recollections."
5. Pearman, "Recollections."
6. S. F. Nuckolls of Linden, Missouri, to Major John Dougherty, Liberty, Missouri, August 28, 1854, HNA, John Dougherty Collection, RG 3902.AM, MS 478, reel 1, microfilm at Missouri State Historical Society.
7. Pearman, "Recollections"; "News of the Day," *Alexandria (VA) Gazette*, June 24, 1856; "Hon. William B. Hail," in *Portrait and Biographical Album*, 1:492.

8. Clark Irwin, territorial settler, NSHS, *Transactions and Reports*, 3:195; Martin W. Riden to Mrs. M. E. Harden, January 1, 1855, in Nuermberger, "Letters from Pioneer Nebraska," 34.
9. *Squatter Sovereign* (Atchison KS), March 6, 1855, by S. F. Nuckolls, agent for the proprietors.
10. "Letters from the Far West," *Daily Scioto (OH) Gazette*, September 13, 1855.
11. E.g., Ellen Kinney Ware, "The Old Town on the River" and "Nebraska City in 1858," HNA, Hall-Kinney Collection, 1821–1902. RG 2839.AM, MS 619, reel 1.
12. "Morton, Thomas," History Nebraska, accessed June 19, 2023, https://history.nebraska.gov/publications/morton-thomas. Printer-editor Thomas Morton, with J. Sterling Morton (not related), numbered the newspaper from the preceding *Nebraska Palladium*, "making the paper the successor to the first newspaper published in Nebraska Territory." Thomas Morton purchased the newspaper in 1855, with J. Sterling Morton (having been hired by Nuckolls) as editor. J. Sterling Morton also served as editor from April 15, 1856, to August 26, 1857, when Milton W. Reynolds took over. At the time of Celia and Eliza's journey, Reynolds was the editor.
13. "Letter of S. F. Nuckolls," NSHS, *Transactions and Reports*, 1:34. Olson, *J. Sterling Morton*, 51, repeats Nuckolls's story, saying that Shack "was reported to have become a colored carpetbagger, and to have gone to Mississippi where he was last heard of as taking part in the deliberations of a Reconstruction Convention." The surname Grayson was probably derived from their county of birth. Foner, *Freedom's Lawmakers*, does not have an entry for a man fitting Shack's description.
14. Andreas, *History of Nebraska*, "Otoe County," part 7, "The Press."
15. "Morton Writes Publisher: Founder of Arbor Day and Early Editor of the News, Recount to Thomas Morton, the Publisher 35 Years of Paper's Existence," NDNP, November 14, 1929.
16. Day, *Mortons of Arbor Lodge*; "The N—— Party," ON, November 7, 1855. Day mentions Shack Grayson helping at the Morton farm, without citing a specific source, but she did most of her research at the NSHS.
17. Aunt Hannah Allen, George Bollinger, Betty Brown, Lula Chamber, and others in Federal Writers' Project, *Slave Narratives*, 10. These interviews mention enslaved women's common day-to-day activities. For details on antebellum laundry and enslavers, see Arnesen, *Encyclopedia of U.S. Labor*, 1:777–79.
18. Tolbert, "Murder in Franklin," 209; Paterson, "Slavery, Slaves, and Cash"; Ellis and Ginsburg, *Slavery in the City*, in particular, Ellis and Ginsburg, "Introduction," and Faulkner, "Slavery in Knoxville." Thompson, *Clinton, Louisiana*, points out that "community studies, especially of the South, deal with counties or small geographic regions within a state." Although the book is not about

small-town slavery alone, Thompson notes that in Clinton, "slaves found it difficult to create their own distinct society."
19. Nahum Harwood diary entry of August 8, 1856, in Morton and Watkins, *Illustrated History of Nebraska*, 2:385.
20. Sanford, *Mollie*, 12, 15.
21. Ware, "Old Town on the River" and "Nebraska City in 1858." The language in her reminiscence indicates that the two-story brick residence was on the corner of Fifth and Main Streets.
22. Ware, "Old Town on the River" and "Nebraska City in 1858."
23. Lucinda Bourne Nuckolls to her brother, July 21, 1859, Conover Collection.
24. Tolbert, "Murder in Franklin," 204–17; "Abolition Outrage," BDSG, December 18, 1858; NCN, February 10, 1883, December 6, 1918; "Little Journeys to Nearby Towns," *Omaha Bee*, December 1, 1918; NCN, November 14, 1929, June 25, 1948, December 23, 1954, August 8, 1956; NCNP, September 7, 1975.
25. Burke, *On Slavery's Border*, 144–45.
26. "Baptist Church Is First in Nebraska," NCDN, May 24, 1931, from "original records in the possession of its officers." Lucinda Bourne Nuckolls is not mentioned in any official history, and early newspaper issues reported on national, state, and local political and business news.
27. Frances Nuckolls Bourne to Lucinda's parents (her parents-in-law) William M. and Mary (Johnson) Bourne, September 23, 1856.
28. Troup, *Once upon a Time*, 66, contains a list of women at the first inaugural ball.
29. Lucinda Bourne Nuckolls to her brother and sister, April 12, 1858; to brother Billy (William Bourne), July 21, 1858, Brett Conover private collection.
30. Lucinda Bourne Nuckolls to her parents, August 24, 1857, Brett Conover private collection.
31. Pearman, "Recollections," remembered, "The first old-fashioned hoe-down was danced at the residence of William B. Hail in the old Government hospital," adding "Laura Hail, Celia Hail, Phi and Tabby Hail, Susan and Anna Pearman, and two Misses Kennedy and Mary Pell were the ladies present." Pearman was unlikely to forget Stephen and Lucinda Nuckolls, and their relative William B. Hail was present when these recollections were shared.
32. Edward R. Harden to his mother, January 2, 1856, in Nuermberger, "Letters from Pioneer Nebraska," 39.
33. Lucinda Bourne Nuckolls to William and Richmond Bourne, November 1857, Brett Conover private collection. "Hurd" boys are herd boys, who tended cattle. Having a large number of people living in the household was apparently normal, as the 1860 census reports twelve people in Stephen Nuckolls's household, nine in addition to his immediate family.

34. Lucinda Bourne Nuckolls to William and Richmond Bourne, November 1857, Brett Conover private collection.
35. Douglass, *Narrative of the Life*, 19.
36. Jacobs, *Incidents*, 35.
37. For a more thorough discussion of the patterns of enslaved people's attitudes of suspicion and hidden feelings, see Escott, *Slavery Remembered*.
38. *NCN*, July 14, 1855, reprinted in *Bedford (NY) White River Standard*, August 9, 1855. The *NCN* issues for the time period are no longer extant.
39. "Nebraska City Slave Sale," *Fairfield (IA) Ledger*, August 16, 1855. Stories about the Nebraska slave sale also appeared in the *Tioga County (PA) Wellsboro Agitator*; *Ebensburg (PA) Democrat and Sentinel*, August 15, 1855; *Squatter Sovereign* (Atchison KS); *Gettysburg (PA) Adams Sentinel*, August 13, 1855 (which gave the date of the original piece in *NCN* as July 14, 1855).
40. "Slavery in Nebraska," *New York Daily Times*, July 27, 1855. The unnamed writer signed with his address and the date he wrote his response: No. 293 Broadway, July 24. The 1857 New York City Directory reveals that a lawyer named John S. Patterson lived at that address. John S. Patterson, lawyer, 293 Broadway, H 40, W. 85th, New York City Directory, 1857, in "U.S. City Directories, 1822–1995," 646, Ancestry.com.
41. "Slavery in Nebraska," *New York Daily Times*. Stephen Nuckolls's uncle, William B. Hail, was elected to the first territorial assembly, having arrived in Nebraska Territory in 1854–55. Census returns do not indicate he ever kept slaves in Nebraska, nor does he appear in the 1850 slave schedules for Grayson County, Virginia, as an owner. Perhaps he had hired enslaved men and women from Atchison County, Missouri.
42. "Nebraska City Slave Sale."
43. "Slavery in Nebraska," *Squatter Sovereign* (Atchison KS), August 7, 1855.
44. "Slavery in Nebraska," *New York Daily Times*.
45. "Slavery in South Platte, Nebraska: The Two Extremes—Conservatism—Negroes Sold at Nebraska City!," *NCN*, July 21, 1855, reprinted in *New York Herald*, August 6, 1855.
46. "Slavery in Nebraska," *BDHE and Telegraph*, August 22, 1855.
47. "Slavery in South Platte," *New York Herald*.
48. *Chicago Free Press*, quoted in "Slavery in Nebraska," *Delphi (IN) Weekly Times*, September 12, 1855.
49. "Slavery in South Platte," *New York Herald*.
50. *NCN*, "One Hundred Laborers and Mechanics Wanted at Nebraska City," reprinted in *Boston Daily Advertiser*, September 22, 1855. Unfortunately, the Atchison County courthouse no longer has 1850s tax lists to help determine how many enslaved people may have been present in the county in 1855.

51. Lewis v. Nuckolls, 26 Mo. 278. Supreme Court of Missouri, January term, 1858, HeinOnline, accessed December 7, 2021; Andreas, *History of Nebraska*, "Otoe County," part 4, "Nebraska City"; H. Johnson, *Johnson's History of Nebraska*, 481; "Brownville Man Recalls Early Ferry Missouri River Ferry Boats," *Lincoln (NE) Star*, October 16, 1932. Heath and Stephen Nuckolls applied for and received a charter from the Missouri legislature in 1855 to establish a ferry in Holt County, although they eventually lost their rights through nonuse.

52. Account book, NFP.

53. Franklin and Schweninger, *Runaway Slaves*, 248, find that the majority of "slave owners, whether middling farmers to the great planters considered themselves kind . . . humane masters."

54. Sophia P. Mitchell to Ezra and Lucinda Nuckolls, March 21, 1856, folder 2, box 1, ser. 1; James Anderson from Grayson County Court House to Ezra Nuckolls, February 5, 1857, folder 5, box 1, ser. 1. Andrew Robinson had a Black male age sixty-nine and another age fifty-five, both of whom fit the age of "Old Mose," Jeremiah Jennings's oldest male was only age thirty-five. 1860 Slave Schedules, Grayson County, Virginia, 3–4, USCB, *Eighth Census of the United States, 1860*. The schedule column that reported the number of slave houses had only one for Andrew Robinson but three for Jeremiah Jennings.

55. There is no deed in the Grayson County, Virginia, deed index under Ezra Nuckolls for any property transfer involving Old Mose or any other enslaved people, except a quit-claim in Grayson County Deed Book 12:25, September 6, 1855, from Ezra and Lucinda (Hail) Nuckolls to her brother Curran Hail, giving up Lucinda's interest in her father's estate, including slaves Winney, Ballard, Wilson, and Fanny.

56. Fielden L. Hale to Ezra and Lucinda Nuckolls, May 26, 1856, Hillsville VA, NFP, box 45. Another letter related that "F. L. Hale . . . sold Harry and Charlotte to J. F. Kenney for $125 each . . . will likely sell Isom to John Early for $1000." Thus Harry and Charlotte must have indeed been older and did not want to move west.

57. Berlin, *Generations of Captivity*.

58. Ezra Nuckolls, "slaveowner," Slave Schedules, p. 2, District 19, lines 32–41, USCB, *Seventh Census of the United States, 1850*, men ages fifty-four and fifty; Andrew Robinson, "slaveowner," Slave Schedules, Grayson County, USCB, *Eighth Census of the United States, 1860*, men ages sixty-nine and fifty-five; James Anderson from Grayson County Court House to Ezra Nuckolls, February 5, 1857, folder 5, box 1, ser. 1, NFP. See also 1865 Census Returns, U.S. Freedmen's Bureau Records of Field Offices, 1863–78.

59. Martin Hail of Leesburg, Cherokee County, Alabama, to Ezra and Lucinda Nuckolls, November 8, 1855, folder 1, box 1, ser. 1, NFP.

60. Martin Hail to Ezra and Lucinda Nuckolls, November 8, 1855; Martin Hail of Leesburg, Cherokee County, Alabama, to Ezra and Lucinda Nuckolls, February 23, 1856, folder 2, box 1, ser. 1, NFP.
61. Fielden L. Hale of Hillsville, Carroll Co, Virginia, to Ezra and Lucinda Nuckolls, February 15, 1856, folder 2, box 1, ser. 1, NFP. Carroll County was formed from Grayson County in 1842. Fielden never did join his relatives out west.
62. Sophia P. Mitchell of Grayson County, Virginia, to Ezra and Lucinda Nuckolls, March 21, 1856, folder 2, box 1, ser. 1, NFP. Winney here is almost certainly the Winnie Nuckolls listed in the 1870 census as a domestic, age fifty-two, living in the household of Mastin Hale and in the 1865 census of Black people formerly owned by Eli Hale. She is the only Black person in the 1870 Grayson County, Virginia, census with the Nuckolls surname. Winney may also be the woman mentioned in the *Pioneer Settlers of Grayson County* as one of Granny Beck's granddaughters, through the William Bourne house servant Aimy.
63. Edward R. Harden to his mother, January 2, 1856, in Nuermberger, "Letters from Pioneer Nebraska," 38–39; "An Early-Day Judge Here Found Frontier Town Lively," NDNP, July 28, 1946. The two Federal Writers' Project interviews cited in chapter 2 for Missouri both mentioned hiring out.
64. Heath Nuckolls to Ezra Nuckolls, January 1857, folder 5, box 1, ser. 1, NFP. Many accounts, including NCNP, December 23, 1954, and NDNP, July 4, 1954, assumed Stephen Friel Nuckolls owned Shade, but this was an error.
65. Burke, *On Slavery's Border*, 110.
66. Nuckolls's estimate of Shack's labor value is from "The N—— Party."
67. Hail, "Settlers' First Christmas." Susan Pearman Hail attended the dance with her brother, and that is where she met Stephen Nuckolls's cousin Curran Hail, who later became her husband. Susan reported that Mrs. Friel Nuckolls prepared the supper, without mentioning Celia or Eliza. There were eleven who danced, and it is unclear whether Mrs. Nuckolls joined them when done with the meal. See also Pearman, "Recollections."
68. Stephen F. Nuckolls, line 32, p. 414, Otoe County, Nebraska, Non-Population Schedule, USCB, *Eighth Census of the United States, 1860*. After six years of residence in Nebraska City, Stephen's listing in the agricultural schedule showed only one hundred acres improved, with forty thousand unimproved.
69. Atchison County Court, April term, 1856, p. 313, Rock Port, Missouri, records the sale that took place on February 18, 1856. William Mann had eleven enslaved people in the 1850 Atchison County Slave Schedule. He bought five more in 1856. By 1860 he had moved to Savannah in neighboring Andrew County. However, he was no longer listed as a "slaveowner" in the federal slave schedules.
70. Blockson, *Underground Railroad*, 89.

5. Politics Running High

1. John Kagi, "Nebraska and Slavery," *New York Post*, July 22, 1856. Kagi lived on and off with his sister and brother-in-law in their cabin near Nebraska City. He joined John Brown in Kansas and died in Brown's attack at Harpers Ferry.
2. Kagi, "Nebraska and Slavery."
3. Meese, "Origins of the Feud"; Auchampaugh, "Political Techniques"; Karp, "People's Revolution"; Urniss, "Devolved Democracy"; D. Potter, *Impending Crisis*, 261. For a thorough discussion, see D. Potter, *Impending Crisis*, 225–65.
4. Hughes and Stubbs, *Player and a Gentleman*, 264; Ira B. Coltrane to Ezra Nuckolls, April 20, 1856, NFP; S. McCamant to Ezra Nuckolls, November 28, 1856, NFP, ser. 1, box 1, folder 4.
5. "Presidential Election," *Bellevue (NE) Gazette*, November 26, 1856; "Takes It Cool," *Brownville Nebraska Advertiser*, November 22, 1856, citing NCN; D. Potter, *Impending Crisis*, 287. Potter also states *Dred Scott* was "trivial" because there were no slaves in Nebraska (*Impending Crisis*, 190). This book challenges that view. There were slaves in Nebraska.
6. D. Potter, *Impending Crisis*.
7. D. Potter, *Impending Crisis*, 287; see also 287–90. In February 1860 Nebraska Democrats were still divided over the Buchanan camp's annulment of popular sovereignty. At their convention, Milton Reeves declared that if the party's position was that popular sovereignty was a "soft delusion," then Reeves would not "be a fit representative of the party." Many others refused to be nominated to represent the party under the circumstances. Nuckolls also declined to run but did not state the reason. *Nebraska City People's Press*, February 21, 1860.
8. George L. Miller, *Conservative*, May 29, 1902, 2.
9. Hiram Bennett to J. Sterling Morton, July 4, 1856, HNA, Morton Collection, RG 1013.AM, reel 2.
10. Miller, *Conservative*, May 29, 1902, 2.
11. Blake, "Government and Banking."
12. "A Few Facts about Arbor Day and Its Founder, J. Sterling Morton," *NCNP*, April 17, 1972; Columbus Nuckolls, Glenwood, Iowa, to J. Sterling Morton, Esq., Nebraska City, January 1858, HNA, Morton Collection, RG 1013.AM, reel 2; Morton to Lum Nuckolls, January 21, 1858, citing Olson's biography, *NCN*, May 10, 1973.
13. S. F. Nuckolls to the Hon. J. Sterling Morton, October 4, 1858, HNA, Morton Collection, RG 1013.AM, reel 2, says he paid one of Morton's drafts but Morton needed to send a remittance, given the scarcity of money.
14. Majors, *Seventy Years on the Frontier*; "City Was Busy Place during Early Freighting Days," *NCNP*, November 21, 1956, bicentennial ed.
15. *Daily Illinois State Register* (Springfield), November 1857.

16. Newspaper clippings, folder 2, box 1, ser. 3, NFP. See also "Nuckolls House," *Nebraska Advertiser* (Brownville), May 6, 1858; *NCN*, June 5, 19, 1858; *NCN*, May 15, 1860. The Nuckolls House hotel was completely destroyed by the Nebraska City fire in 1860, while his personal residence survived. "Great Fire at Nebraska City! Immense Destruction of Property," *Council Bluffs Nonpareil*, May 19, 1860, describes the fire that consumed most of Nebraska City. Also destroyed were several downtown buildings Stephen owned, including the "Bank Buildings" that housed the Platte Valley Bank, as well as the Hawke and Nuckolls dry goods store and other businesses.

17. John H. Kagi, "Nebraska and Slavery," *New York Post*, July 22, 1856, including a conversation overheard by Kagi. The gentleman was not named but was a prominent proprietor of Nebraska City—a description that best fits Nuckolls.

18. Traveler's account in *FH*, quoted in *NCN*, June 19, 1858; advertisements in *FH*, November 6, 1858, 3.

19. Sanford, *Mollie*, 69.

20. Joshua Garside, *Nebraska Farmer*, October 1859. *NCN*, May 19, 1860, also mentioned the "splendid private residences."

21. Stephen F. Nuckolls to Ezra Nuckolls, November 10, 1856; W. B. Hail to Ezra Nuckolls, January 28, 1857, NFP; Lucinda Bourne Nuckolls to parents, June 28, 1854, November 2, 1857; Lucinda Bourne Nuckolls to Richmond Bourne, September 4, 1858, Brett Conover private collection; Burke, *On Slavery's Border*, 155. These letters are a few examples of those containing discussions of health and day-to-day duties. See also Burke, *On Slavery's Border*, for common practice.

22. Burke, *On Slavery's Border*, 59.

23. Burke, *On Slavery's Border*, 10. See also Epps, *Slavery on the Periphery*, 21–23.

24. *ON*, April 21, 1858. Who all the characters were in Doesticks's satire is unknown, but "K." was Stephen Nuckolls's neighbor, Judge John F. Kinney. He is identifiable from a reference to his sojourn in Utah. Kinney was listed in Nebraska City's 1858 tax assessment with two free Blacks in his household, but their legal status has not been verified. Otoe County, Nebraska, Treasurer, 1858 Tax List/Census, 2, Nebraska City, HNA, Otoe County Records, RG 210. On May 29, 1855, a writer for the *Washington (DC) Daily Union* mistakenly surmised that Doesticks was J. Sterling Morton.

25. Twain, *Life on the Mississippi*, 33.

26. Sanford, *Mollie*, 10.

27. James Bradley, "Brief Account of an Emancipated Slave Written by Himself," *Oasis*, June 1834, http://www.oberlin.edu/external/EOG/LaneDebates/BradleyLetter.html. The *Oasis* was an antislavery newspaper.

28. See, e.g., Still, *Still's Underground Rail Road Records*, 196–98; Foner, *Gateway to Freedom*, 16; Blackett, *Captive's Quest*, 137.

29. For a full exploration of abolitionism in Iowa, see Soike, *Necessary Courage*.
30. Otoe County, Nebraska, Treasurer, 1858 Tax List/Census, 2, listed free Blacks, although some of them may have been living under enslavement.
31. Andreas, *History of Nebraska*, "Otoe County," part 1, "Winter of 1856."
32. Heath Nuckolls, Rock Port, Missouri to S. F. Nuckolls, June 2, 1857, folder 5, box 1, ser. 1, NFP.
33. Lucinda Bourne Nuckolls, Nebraska City, to her parents, August 24, 1857, Brett Conover private collection.
34. Estate of Ezra Nuckolls, 1857, probate packet no. 1956, Atchison County Probate Court.
35. Heath Nuckolls to Ezra Nuckolls, January 1857, folder 5, box 1, ser. 1, NFP.
36. Heath Nuckolls to Ezra Nuckolls, January 1857.
37. Harvey G. "Bowen" household, Fremont County, Iowa, Sidney, p. 919, USCB, *Eighth Census of the United States, 1860*. By 1860 both Sena and Elizabeth, called Betty, were living in Sidney, Iowa, with their sister Frances and her husband, Harvey Bourne.
38. Atchison County Probate Court, Estate of Ezra Nuckolls, Probate Packet #1956, Rock Port, Missouri, October 24, 1857.
39. Lucinda Bourne Nuckolls to her parents, November 2, 1875, Brett Conover private collection. Clayton and Jane were the enslaved people taken to "Ioway." C. Nuckolls, *Roses*, states that Clayton was Shade, but the Ezra Nuckolls estate sale bill shows they were two different men.
40. Estate of Ezra Nuckolls.
41. Grayson County attracted national attention for extralegal violence. See, e.g., *Wytheville (VA) Republican*, quoted in Stowe, *Key to Uncle Tom's*, 189–90; "Lynch Law," *Richmond Times* (reprinted in many other newspapers when these events became national news).
42. "A Man Shot and Killed!," *Nebraska Advertiser* (Brownville), September 10, 1857.
43. Andreas, *History of Nebraska*, "Nemaha County," part 5, "Pioneer Incidents"; "Nebraska Correspondence," *Rockport (MO) Banner*, December 15, 1857, reprinted under different titles in many other newspapers, as well as in J. Brown et al., "Nebraska Territory," 93. The African American who shot Myers was reportedly being tried in Nebraska City's U.S. District Court. See also M. M. Brown, "Brownville Story," 1–141 (for the Myers story, 22–25).
44. "Slavery in Kansas and Nebraska," *NCN*, reprinted in *Leavenworth (KS) Weekly Herald*, June 9, 1855; *Biddeford (ME) Union and Eastern Journal*, June 15, 1855. The article was picked up by many newspapers across the country.
45. "Slavery Not Abolished in Nebraska: Slavery Still Here. The N——s Coming!," *NCN*, November 20, 1858.
46. Franklin and Schweninger, *Runaway Slaves*, 26; see also 26–28.

6. Fugitive Slave Excitement

1. Ackley, "Across the Plains," 191–92; *NCN*, June 19, 1858 (travelers encountered a "horse and buggy [?]ed in mud and water and [?] paddling for shore. This is very likely to be the base in crossing the Bottom at this season of the year"). See also Todd, *Early Settlement*, 99, 139.
2. H. Williams, "Old Wyoming"; "Mormon Historian Visits Old Wyoming Landing Site," *NDNP*, July 20, 1934, Wyoming Vertical File, misc. holdings, ID# 57929, Genealogy Section, Morton James Public Library, Nebraska City.
3. H. Williams, "Old Wyoming."
4. Schneiders, *Unruly River*; Morgans, *John Todd*. Newspapers accounts include "Man Drowned," *Wyoming (NE) Post*, May 29, 1858. The river was not frozen over until early December, when the Civil Bender report in *FH*, December 11, 1858, described S. F. Nuckolls and his men laying boards across the frozen river to cross.
5. "Most Remarkable Woman of This Age," *Boston Commonwealth*, July 17, 1863; *Freeman's Record*, March 1865; Blockson, *Underground Railroad*, 120–21.
6. "The Excitement Continues: The Fugitives Heard From—Swamped in an Abolition Hole," *NCN*, December 4, 1858, reported that a skiff had been borrowed to transport them across. *Nebraska Advertiser* (Brownville), November 25, 1858 (the night of Celia and Eliza's escape), noted that the river was closed at Brownville due to floating ice "becoming gorged below here some distance," although the river itself was not frozen over. *Council Bluffs Nonpareil*, December 4, 1858, mentioned that the river had been closed for two weeks at Council Bluffs, while it was clear at St. Joseph, Missouri, on November 30.
7. "Letter of S. F. Nuckolls," NSHS, *Transactions and Reports*, 1:32–37, http://digitalcommons.unl.edu/nebhisttrans/55; Schneiders, *Unruly River*; Morgans, *John Todd*. Much of Civil Bend is now underwater, but the old Blanchard Cemetery occupies the high ground near present-day Percival, Iowa. For more on Oberlin College and its central role in the abolitionist movement, see Brandt, *Town That Started*.
8. Morgans, *John Todd*, 99–101.
9. Siebert, *Underground Railroad*, 98; Morgans, *John Todd*, 53–54. For more on Blanchard, see Morgans, *John Todd*, 97–100.
10. Handy and Handy, *Someday*, 44; Orman Paddock (great-grandson of Ira Blanchard) to the curator of John Brown's Cave, *NCN*, September 12, 1960. The house is no longer standing, but the Blanchard Cemetery is in Percival, Iowa, on the Iowa Freedom Trail. See also "Cemetery, Farm Linked to Underground Railroad," *NCNP*, October 4, 2004, interviewing Max Bebout, whose family bought the Blanchard property and who remembered going to the basement "where they kept the slaves," regretting that he razed the abandoned home.

11. Todd, *Early Settlement*, 139–40.
12. "Great Excitement—Escape of Negroes—$200 Reward!," *NCN*, November 27, 1858.
13. "Lulu N. Wesner, Descendant of the Nuckolls' Clan," *NCDN*, November 22, 1929. Lulu Wesner confused Shade with Shack in her account, however, saying that the same person left Harding Hampton money, which records show was Shack, not Shade. Confusion between Shack and Shade was common. Some accounts related that Shack and Shade also self-emancipated, but there is no evidence of this. See, e.g., "Old Nebraska Slave Prospers," *Omaha Bee*, February 16, 1907; "Slave Auctions Held in City in Early Days," *NCNP*, December 23, 1954; "Kick Column," *NCNP*, January 22, 1953; "Story of John Brown's Cave Found in Old Paper," *NCNP*, June 1, 1937. Shack was sold south, as reported in 1859 by Lucinda Bourne Nuckolls. His fate is explored in the epilogue to this book.
14. Lucinda Bourne Nuckolls to brother, July 21, 1859, Brett Conover private collection.
15. Elvira Gaston Platt, "Nebraska Negro Catchers in Iowa," *BDHE*, January 21, 1859, written January 7. How accurate Platt was regarding the conversation between Stephen Nuckolls and Ira Blanchard is unknown, but she and her husband were close friends with Dr. Blanchard and probably heard the details from him.
16. Platt, "Nebraska Negro Catchers."
17. *St. Joseph Gazette*, quoted in *NCN*, December 25, 1858.
18. Most of the account from Platt, "Nebraska Negro Catchers"; timeline drawn from another version written closer to the event (on December 7) by a "Civil Bender," *FH*, December 11, 1858. Other sources are Joseph Garner estate, Fremont County Iowa Probate Record 2, 55, Appointment of Administrator, Ira D. Blanchard, August 3, 1858; Iowa State Census, 1856, Benton Township, Fremont County, Iowa, p. 846, Joseph Garner household. Details of Henry Garner's mock lynching is from *St. Louis Daily Missouri Democrat*, October 16, 1860, which includes a quote uttered by Houston Nuckolls about his brother hauling Henry up the bough of a tree once or twice. Julius F. Merritt's letter to his brother also mentioned the mock "linching." In Houston's account, Henry confessed that Blanchard rowed them across the river. I chose to use Elvira Gaston Platt's version (also mentioned by John Todd), in which John Williamson brought Celia and Eliza across, in light of Nuckolls's lawsuit against Blanchard and others, including John Williamson, to recover damages.
19. Platt, "Nebraska Negro Catchers." Although Platt does not supply a first name for Dr. Smith, he may have been John W. Smith. The 1860 census names him as a farmer instead of a doctor, but he was one of the oldest citizens in Benton Township, Fremont County.
20. Platt, "Nebraska Negro Catchers." Lingenfelter, *History of Fremont County*, 519, alleges that a Jack Nuckolls delivered the blow to Reuben Williams, saying, "We

are indebted to Judge Sears for the particulars last given." Todd, *Early Settlement*, also identified Williams's assailant as Mr. Nuckolls. What all accounts agree on was that Williams never recovered fully from the injury, suffering from deafness for the rest of his life. Some accounts (e.g., Handy and Handy, *Someday*, as well as NCNP, July 17, 1985) mistakenly list Reuben Williams as a free Black, but he was a white resident of Civil Bend.

21. Julius F. Merritt to Rev. William W. Merritt, December 5, 1858, Merritt Papers, typescript copy in Iowa Freedom Collection. According to Merritt's letter, he obtained a warrant for the mob's crimes the same night he was assaulted. He started for Sidney to get the sheriff and an attorney. The temperature was as low as twenty-two below zero that night. The letter's recipient, Merritt's brother William, later wrote *History of the County of Montgomery*, with a section on the Underground Railroad, explaining that "fugitives" would be hidden during the day and journey at night. He admitted that in Iowa, "many of her good people lent substantial assistance to the slaves and the writer of this book, though technically a lawbreaker, harbored and helped on their way many of those needing assistance" (75).

22. Sturgis Williams (nephew and heir of Reuben Williams) to Wilbur Siebert, October 27, 1894, Wilbur H. Siebert Collection, OSHS, wrote, "Could you afford the time and space I would tell you how they got away and how Mr. N. followed across the State and how the pursuers were in the same house with the pursued, etc."

23. A Civil Bender, "Correspondence," FH, December 11, 1858 (written December 7), provides a timeline and description of the events soon after they happened; Elvira Gaston Platt, "Reminiscences," delivered to the Quarter Centennial Congregational Church of Tabor, 1877, Tabor Historical Society, Tabor IA; Platt, "Nebraska Negro Catchers." Samuel Paul was called "Mr. Paul" in her account; there is but one man with the surname Paul in the 1860 census, Samuel, an Irish-born laborer. Bartling, *John Henry Kagi*, 12, whose account has been criticized as self-serving and lacking "historicity" by Nebraska historian James E. Potter in "Fact and Folklore," states that the "first posse" was composed of seventeen men, including S. F. Nuckolls, William B. Hail, Grant Hail, Robert Mason, George Vickroy, Fountain Pearman, and W. C. Wyatt. Stephen's brother Heath Nuckolls also accompanied them. Bartling further names the two men who were kept behind as prisoners: William B. Hail (Stephen's uncle) and Grant Hail. Bartling calls them "hostages," rather than prisoners under guard, and states that the next day the fifteen from the day before went back to Civil Bend, with sixty more men in tow, and that they freed the hostages where they were kept in a schoolhouse "surrounded by a band of abolitionists." He does not mention the violence except that "a brother of S. F. Nuckolls, becom-

ing angry, struck Williams." He terms the Civil Benders' reaction as "some attempted resistance." Platt's "Reminiscences" seems to refer to the freeing of the prisoners, so that part of Bartling's account may be partially corroborated. J. F. Merritt to brother, December 5, 1858, describes eight men who were left to face the court, guarded by 100 armed men of "their party," at a local schoolhouse, since there was no jail.

24. Todd, *Early Settlement*, 142. See also Civil Bender, "Correspondence." It is thought that Elvira Gaston Platt supplied this unsigned account, in addition to her correspondence signed "EGP" that appeared in "Nebraska Negro Catchers in Iowa," BDHE, January 21, 1859. However, the accounts do differ, and the Civil Bender's identity is still in question.
25. Todd, *Early Settlement*; Ellen Gaston Hurlbutt letter, "The Underground Railroad in Tabor and Vicinity," March 18, 1935, quoting liberally from Todd, *Early Settlement*.
26. "The Excitement Continues—The Fugitives Heard From—Swamped in an Abolition Hole," NCN, December 4, 1858.
27. "Williams Case," *Conservative*, 4 (1900): 14.
28. Harrison Hannah to Harvey D. Rice, July 27, 1896, Harrison Hannah's Miscellaneous Collection, Kansas State Historical Society, quoted in Epps, *On Slavery's Periphery*, 128.
29. "To the Editor by E. R.," FH, January 8, 1859.
30. "Excitement Continues," NCN.
31. Civil Bender, "Correspondence."
32. Civil Bender, "Correspondence." Elvira Gaston Platt, "Nebraska Negro Catchers in Iowa," BDHE, January 21, 1859, differed with the Civil Bender account on whether a legal warrant to search was issued, asserting that after a few days, "they also got out a bogus search warrant, and backed up by its apparently legal face, entered and searched houses they had not otherwise chosen to go to."
33. Todd, *Early Settlement*, 140. Abolitionist Origen Cummings joined his family when they removed to Oberlin, Ohio, in the 1830s, later joining the Iowa effort to establish Tabor, Iowa, as another abolitionist center like Oberlin. His sister married fellow Taborite and Civil Bender George Gaston. Todd, *Early Settlement*, 140; Mooar, *Cummings Memorial*, 280. A competing version was forwarded later by Ellen Gaston Hurlbutt, who reported that her father, James K. Gaston, veiled Celia and Eliza and took them away from Tabor in a buggy.
34. Frazee, "Iowa Fugitive Slave Case." See also Soike, "Iowa's Anti-Slavery Movement," 49. James had taken part in the expedition in 1819–20 to the Rocky Mountains under Maj. Stephen Long and published a history of the expedition. Although a man of learning and culture, he was considered eccentric because of his abolitionist views.

35. Frazee, "Iowa Fugitive Slave Case," 134.
36. Campbell, *Slave Catchers*. Campbell broke with prior historians, who emphasized Northern protection laws and abolitionist efforts to prevent the capture of enslaved people, by concluding that overall, the law functioned. He found that most state officials tried to uphold the law, however reluctantly. An earlier Iowa case, Ruel Daggs v. Elihu Frazier, et al. (1850), decided against those who aided a freedom seeker, based on the 1793 Fugitive Slave Law.
37. *NCN*, December 4, 1858.
38. *NCN*, December 25, 1858. This item suggests there were a number of enslaved people remaining in the town to be "run off."
39. John Todd, secretary, "Self-Defense Meeting" minutes, Tabor Historical Society collections, copy provided by Kathy Douglass, secretary, Tabor Historical Society.
40. *NCN*, December 4, 1858. A "Cuffey" was a term for an African American, somewhat like Sambo, and was often used as an enslaved man's proper name.
41. *FH*, December 11, 1858.
42. *FH*, December 11, 1858.
43. *Compendium of History*, 110, gives these names.
44. Connor, "Antislavery Movement"; *Compendium of History*, 110.
45. Letter of Mrs. E. G. Platt, Ohio Memory, citing MSS 116AV, box 45, Wilbur H. Siebert Collection, OSHS; John McDougall interview, *Dewitt (IA) Observer*, January 24, 1883, Iowa Freedom Trail Collection, State Historical Society of Iowa, Des Moines.
46. Amos Bixby to Leonard L. Parker, from Boulder CO, May 16, 1887, State Historical Society of Iowa, Parker Papers, MS 44, box 1. Bixby wrote that Captain Clark met the professional slave hunter at Sugar Grove IA. Bixby did not name the Quaker neighborhood, but the McDougall interview mentioned the Pee Dee Quaker settlement (east of Springdale) as Celia and Eliza's stop before the Smith farm in Clinton County.
47. "Abolition Outrage," *BDSG*, December 18, 1858. Although the piece said the "family of negro slaves" had been reared with "Mrs. Nuckolls' father," it may have meant *Mr.* Nuckolls's father, since we can document that Ezra Nuckolls transferred Celia and Eliza to Stephen Nuckolls. "Slavery in Nebraska," *Pacific City (IA) Herald*, quoted in *BDIIE*, January 8, 1859, corrects errors in a prior issue of the *Burlington Hawk-Eye*, and states the freedom seekers had belonged to Mr. Nuckolls's parents. Columbus Nuckolls lived in Pacific City.
48. "Awful Abolition Outrage—Violation of the Dred Scott Decision—The Union Again in Danger!," *Burlington (IA) Weekly Hawk-Eye*, December 21, 1858. For a biography of Col. William Thompson, see Stuart, *Iowa Colonels and Regiments*,

559–64. Despite his sympathies and portrayal of "benign" enslavement in 1858, Thompson served in the First Iowa Cavalry for the Union.

49. "Slavery in Nebraska," *BDHE*, January 8, 1859. The enslaved person with L. Nuckolls in Iowa was Shade, given his presence in the 1860 census there. "Abolition Outrage," *BDSG*, described them as a part of "a family of negro slaves, consisting of both males and females."

50. "Run Off," *FH*, December 4, 1858; Berlin, *Many Thousands Gone*, loc. 3564, Kindle; *Compendium of History*, 110.

51. Franklin and Schweninger, *Runaway Slaves*, 274; see also 274–79.

52. Connor, "Antislavery Movement."

53. William Lee Smith family history, quoted in Mary Lou Hinrichsen, "Underground Railroad Program Set," *Clinton (IA) Herald*, last updated July 30, 2014, http://www.clintonherald.com/news/lifestyles/underground-railroad-program-set/article_ab0d818b-4dbd-5ff5-8cb3-77758e88b6db.html.

54. McDougall interview.

55. McDougall interview.

56. Stowe, *Uncle Tom's Cabin*. The Horace Anthony House is included in the Underground Railroad.

57. "Mississippi River Frozen Solid," Missouri Historical Society, Flickr, December 1, 2009, https://www.flickr.com/photos/mohistory/4150865708, with comment by thetallguy747 about crossing the river on foot with the ice singing and reverberating at different pitches.

58. McDougall interview.

7. Villainy and Meanness

1. "Another Speck of War," *Janesville (WI) Morning Gazette*, December 24, 1858; "Fugitive Slave Excitement in Western Iowa," *Greenfield (MA) Gazette*, January 10, 1859; "Fugitive Slave Excitement at Nebraska," *Nottingham (UK) Journal*, January 14, 1859; "Nebraska Negro Catchers in Iowa," *Richmond Daily Dispatch*, March 18, 1859; and many more newspapers nationwide.

2. J. Brown et al., "Nebraska Territory," 110.

3. *Waverly (NE) Republican*, December 28, 1858.

4. Fehrenbacher, *Dred Scott Case*, 130. This work is magisterial in its scope and analysis.

5. Analyses of the *Dred Scott* decision are too numerous to list, but in addition to Fehrenbacher, see Wiecek, "Slavery and Abolition"; Lehman, *Slavery*, particularly in view of Dred Scott's residence not only in the free state of Illinois but also in what became Minnesota.

6. See, e.g., *New York Tribune*, January 28, 1859; *Nashville (TN) Daily Union and American*, December 29, 1858; *Lynchburg Daily Virginian*, December 30, 1858;

Daily Pittsburgh Gazette, December 30, 1858; *Ohio Plain Dealer*, December 29, 1850; FH, December 4, 1858; *Waverly (NE) Republican*, December 28, 1858.

7. HNA, Nebraska Territorial Courts, RG 58, SG 3, Second District, ser. 1, Dockets, 1858–67, December term (starting December 7, 1858, and lasting a week); criminal case no. 21, Nebraska Territory v. S. F. Nuckolls, Wm. B. Hail, Hiram P. Bennet, William Bennet, John O. B. Dunning, Stephen F. Hail, and Curran C. Hail, indictment for riot. Otoe County District Court, Territorial Court Records, Nebraska City. Record Book A:402, December 10, 1858, Territory v. S. F. Nuckolls, et al. The jury was composed of Thomas I. Goddin, Edward Adams, Jonathan Raley, Thomas Helvey, Lewis Lewis, Joseph Moffitt, Nathan Redfield, Edgar Clayton, O. N. Updegrove, John McFarland, George W. Sroat, and J. F. C Welsh. J. Sterling Morton named other members of the first posse: Robert Mason, George Vickroy, Fountain Pearman, and W. C. Wyatt. *Conservative* 3, no. 10 (1900): 10.

8. NCN, December 11, 1858. The NARA Kansas City archivists searched for this case, with no results.

9. NCN, December 18, 1858.

10. Lucinda Bourne Nuckolls to her parents, July 20, 1859; Lucinda Bourne Nuckolls to Richmond Bourne, February 21, 1860, Brett Conover private collection.

11. "State v. Nuckolls," PCH, September 23, 1859, Iowa Freedom Collection, Des Moines. Also, in State v. W. B. Hail and State v. G. [Granville] Hail, each was fined $50 and costs.

12. "Court in Fremont County," PCH, September 23, 1859; "Served Him Right," *Janesville (WI) Gazette*, July 9, 1860. Lingenfelter, *History of Fremont County*, 519, alleges that a Jack Nuckolls delivered the blow, noting, "We are indebted to Judge Sears for the particulars last given." Todd, *Early Settlement*, also identified the assailant as Mr. Nuckolls. All accounts agree that Williams never recovered fully from the injury, suffering from deafness for the rest of his life. Some accounts (e.g., Handy and Handy, *Someday*) mistakenly list Reuben Williams as a free Black, but he was a white resident of Civil Bend.

13. "Heavy Damages," PCH, June 1, 1860; "Compromised," PCH, June 22, 1860; "Error," PCH, June 29, 1860 (item should say "attorney's fees" instead of "juror's fees").

14. Otoe County District Court, August 1862, case no. 935; Reuben S. Williams, Plaintiff v. S. F. Nuckolls, Heath Nuckolls, John W. Pearman, George W. Sroat, Granville Hail (Nuckolls's cousin), Harvey G. Bourne, David Biggerstaff, S. G. McCoy, Richard Miller, Frank McMahan, and A. J. Lenning.

15. Page County District Court Dockets, May term, 1860, R. S. Williams v. S. F. Nuckolls et al., E. H. Sears, judge; PCH, quoted in *Muscatine (IA) Weekly Journal*, June 15, 1860; "Compromised," PCH. Sheldon, *History and Stories*, 102, cites

a payment of $10,000, which might represent the total of various cases. The $8,000 fine would be $269,000 in 2022 dollars.

16. John Todd, "The Irrepressible Conflict," *Oberlin Evangelist*, February 29, 1860, gives another full account of the sack of Civil Bend, saying that Nuckolls "was found guilty through the testimony of colored persons." *Missouri Democrat*, October 16, 1860, quotes Nuckolls's brother as to "the negro himself being the witness on whose testimony the verdict was given."
17. Sheldon, *History and Stories*, 100.
18. For a discussion of slavery and territorial politics, see Olson, Naugle, and Montag, *History of Nebraska*, 73–85 (p. 141 states erroneously that there were only four slaves in the 1854 census). Potts, "Nebraska Territory," emphasizes local squabbles over patronage as more important than slavery. These works mirror Andreas, *History of Nebraska*, and Sheldon, *History and Stories*, in their discussions of slavery.
19. *NCN*, quoted in "The Ball Opened Slavery," *Washington (DC) National Era*, June 28, 1855.
20. Olson, Naugle, and Montag, *History of Nebraska*, 73–85; Potts, "Nebraska Territory"; Andreas, *History of Nebraska*; Sheldon, *History and Stories*.
21. An Act to Organize the Territories of Nebraska and Kansas, in Nebraska Territory, *Laws, Joint Resolutions*, 24–25.
22. Nebraska Territory, *Journal of the House, Fourth Session*, 14. Although Nuckolls did not serve in this year, his uncle William B. Hail was one of Otoe County's representatives.
23. Nebraska Territory, *House Journal, Fifth Session*, 199.
24. Rankin, "Minority Report," in Nebraska Territory, *House Journal, Fifth Session*, 223.
25. Rankin, "Minority Report," 224.
26. Nebraska Territory, *Council Journal, Fifth Session*, 271, transmittal of H.B. No. 131, A Bill for an Act to Abolish Slavery in the Territory of Nebraska, to the council. Houston Nuckolls applied to operate the ferry at Yankton and at St. Stephens (both in Richardson County) in the same session, 166.
27. "Proposed Annexation of South Platte Valley to Kansas," *Nebraska Advertiser* (Brownville), March 18, 1858; D. Potter, *Impending Crisis*, 297–327.
28. *Nebraska Advertiser* (Brownville), January 6, 1859, 2, carried a thorough report on the proceedings. Column 3 began with the subheading "The People Have Spoken, the Vote Unanimous for Annexation!!"
29. "Another Fabrication—A Base Lie!," *Nebraska Advertiser* (Brownville), September 29, 1859.
30. "Abolitionism in Nebraska Wiped Out," *ON*, October 15, 1859, quoted in Edson Rich, "Slavery in Nebraska," NSHS, *Transactions and Reports*, 2:101.

31. Nebraska Territory, *House Journal, Sixth Session*, 5. The journal records the credentials and seating of the members of the Sixth Session, beginning in December 1859 in Omaha City. Among them were Houston Nuckolls from Richardson County and Stephen F. Nuckolls along with five other legislators from Otoe County. The legislature had only thirty-nine members. Only Douglas County sent as many representatives as Otoe at this time. Lancaster and Cass Counties combined contributed six legislators.
32. Stephen F. Nuckolls to J. Sterling Morton, October 22, 1859, HNA, Morton Collection.
33. *NCN*, October 29, 1859.
34. Editor of the *Chillicothe (OH) News-Advertiser*, quoted in Morton and Watkins, *Illustrated History of Nebraska*, 1:706.
35. *Nebraska Advertiser* (Brownville), November 15, 1860; Otoe County Nebraska, District Court, Territorial Court Records, general index packet no. 569, original case no. 424, December term, 1859; Judges Docket, 1860, p. 106, 11th day of the December term, Case 220, HNA, Territorial Courts, RG 58. This would seem to be a continuation of suit no. 424, December term, 1859, Nuckolls v. Blanchard, et al. There was no formal proceeding dropping charges in the dockets, and no mention of the case appears after 1861, when the legislature prohibited slavery in Nebraska Territory.
36. Otoe County Nebraska, District Court, Territorial Court Records, general index packet no. 569, original case no. 424, December term, 1859.
37. Otoe County Nebraska, District Court, Territorial Court Records, general index packet no. 569, original case no. 424, December term, 1859. Some territorial court files are in NARA, Kansas City, where no further records on these cases were found. Sheldon, *History of Nebraska*, 102, stated that Nuckolls sued "sixteen Iowa people." *Conservative* 3, no. 10 (1900): 10, reported that Nuckolls sued fifteen people for $10,000 in damages and costs. Bartling, *John Henry Kagi*, named the pursuers, in addition to Stephen Nuckolls, as William B. Hail, Grant Hail, Robert Mason, George Vickroy, Fountain Pearman, and W. C. Wyatt. However, Bartling's account is riddled with errors and exaggeration because he had obtained land where the legendary cave was and planned to open it as a tourist attraction. Reuben Williams's petition to recover the balance of the $8,000 judgment named, in addition to S. F. Nuckolls, Heath Nuckolls, John W. Pearman, George W. Sroat, Granville Hail, Harvey G. Bourne, David Biggerstaff, J. G. McCoy, Richard Miller, Frank McMahan, and A. J. Lenning; this was the group that had assaulted Williams. Perhaps the others were also involved in the sack of Civil Bend but not at Williams's house.
38. Otoe County Nebraska, District Court, Territorial Court Records, general index packet no. 569, original case no. 424, December term, 1859.

39. Nebraska Territory, *House Journal, Sixth Session*, 223–24 (emphasis mine); Otoe County Nebraska, District Court, Territorial Court Records, general index packet no. 569, original case no. 424, December term, 1859; "Slavery Not Abolished in Nebraska!," *NCN*, November 20, 1858.
40. Otoe County Nebraska, District Court, Territorial Court Records, general index packet no. 569 (b) (emphasis mine).
41. "Fusion Fizzle—Black Republican Ticket," *NCN*, July 31, 1858. The 1850 census lists Kentucky-born Taylor as a farmer in Marion County, Missouri, but not as a "slaveowner." It does show a Black family in the household of his father, attorney James Taylor. USCB, 1850 U.S. Census for Mercer County KY, Herrodsburg, Dist. 2, 721–22. William H. Taylor returned to Missouri to fight for the Union during the Civil War. He died in 1865 at age thirty-eight in his native town of Herrodsburg.
42. Nebraska Territory, *House Journal, Sixth Session*, 44. Taylor added that Mr. A. Majors kept "slaves" in Nebraska City, as did Judge C. [Charles] F. Holly. Other enslavers in public office were George H. Nixon, register at the Federal Land Office at Brownville, and Louisianan Edward A. DesLondes, register at the Land Office at Nebraska City. Also not mentioned was Robert M. Kirkham, who still had two enslaved persons listed in the 1860 census. HNA, microfilm RG 513, Otoe County, Nebraska City, USCB, *Eighth Census of the United States, 1860*, loose paper before the regular schedule.
43. Nebraska Territory, *House Journal, Sixth Session*, 44–45.
44. Nebraska Territory, *House Journal, Sixth Session*, 47. George L. Miller, who served as associate editor of volumes 1 and 2 of the *Illustrated History of Nebraska*, is quoted as saying that Stephen F. Nuckolls was "one of the strongest and ablest men of business the South Platte country has ever known" (1:217).
45. *NCN*, December 17, 1859.
46. Nebraska Territory, *House Journal, Sixth Session*, 46–47.
47. *ON*, December 24, 1859; Morton and Watkins, *Illustrated History of Nebraska*, 2:55. *NCN*, November 20, 1869, reports that Milton W. Reynolds was the editor from 1857 to 1861, when August F. Harvey took the helm. J. Sterling Morton returned to the editorship in 1865.
48. Nebraska Territory, *House Journal, Sixth Session*, 46–47.
49. Nebraska Territory, *House Journal, Sixth Session*, 44, 45–46.
50. Nebraska Territory, *House Journal, Sixth Session*, 100–101; "News of the Day," *Alexandria (VA) Gazette*, December 30, 1859.
51. "Gov. Samuel W. Black," NSHS, *Transactions and Reports*, 1:68, a biography written by his daughter.
52. Potts, "Nebraska Territory," 222.
53. Black, *Veto Messages*, 13.

54. Black, *Veto Messages*, 13, 14.
55. Richardson, *Compilation*, "Third Annual Message"
56. *St. Joseph Gazette*, quoted in *NCN*, March 10, 1860.
57. "Speech of the Hon. M. S. Reeves on the Governor's Veto Message," *NCN*, January 28, 1860. According to the *History of Jackson County*, 712–13, Mills Stephenson Reeves was born in Brown County, Ohio, and lived in Indiana, Missouri, and Iowa before settling in Nebraska City. He was an early mayor of Nebraska City, as well as a justice of the peace, and served in the territorial legislature for three years. He returned to Indiana in 1870.
58. "Remarks of Mr. Blackman in Reply to Messrs. Mason and Taylor, on Saturday, February 25, 1860," *NCN*, March 3, 1860. Oliver P. Mason later served on the Nebraska Supreme Court.
59. "Remarks of Mr. Blackman," *NCN*.
60. Shearer, *Uniting States*, 738.
61. *NCN*, June 30, 1860, quoted in *Conservative* 3, no. 10 (1900): 10. The 1860 Nebraska Territorial Census shows Majors had a "mulatto" woman, age forty; a Black woman, forty; a "mulatto" woman, twenty; a "mulatto" male, fourteen; a "mulatto" male, twelve; and a Black "girl," fourteen. Jelly cakes were a dessert of the era.
62. "Abolition Outrage," *BDSG*, December 18, 1858.
63. "Ho for Freedom," *NCN*, June 30, 1860, "Ho for Freedom," *Omaha Republican*, response reprinted in *NCN*, July 21, 1860. The *NCN* reprinted the *Omaha Republican* broadside that had been published the week before (no longer extant) criticizing Reynolds above its printed retort with a focus on the phrase of "N—— thieves."
64. "Ho for Freedom," *Omaha Republican*, response reprinted in *NCN*, July 21, 1860; *Rulo (NE) Guide*, quoted in "A Negro Kidnapped by a Prominent Republican in Nebraska and Sold into Missouri to Get Money to Carry an Election," *NCN*, July 28, 1860. It is unknown whether the "boy" was indeed a very young man or fully grown, as the sobriquet was regularly used for adult Black males.

8. Slave Hunting

1. Second Territorial District Court (Otoe County District Court), Nebraska City, case no. 569, December term, 1859, Nuckolls v. Reuben S. Williams, et al. His petition mentions the sums of money Nuckolls had expended to search for Celia and Eliza, including "hiring help."
2. Only dockets remain at Fremont County for the cases against Nuckolls. However, Tabor pastor John Todd wrote in the *Oberlin Evangelist*, February 29, 1860, that Nuckolls "was found guilty through the testimony of colored persons," with more charges to be tried.

3. "Kidnapping in Pottawattamie County," *PCH*, October 5, 1860; "Three Negroes Kidnapped near Council Bluffs and Run into Missouri—Great Excitement," *BDHE*, October 3, 1860; *Sidney (IA) Argus*, June 12, 1952.
4. "The Police Trip to Iowa with Three Alleged Kidnappers," *Daily Missouri Democrat*, October 16, 1860, mentions Maria "complaining that Wildey had violated her on the journey."
5. "Three Negroes Kidnapped"; *History of Holt and Atchison*, 538. The latter erroneously uses the last name of Williams instead of Williamson but gives other details correctly, including Dr. Blanchard and Mr. Gaston of Fremont County as the witnesses. See also "The Story of Sidney and Fremont County, the History, the People and Many Interesting Events," *Sydney (IA) Argus Herald*, June 12 and 19, 1952, citing the *History of Holt*.
6. "Kidnapping in Pottawattamie County," *Council Bluffs (IA) Non-Pareil*, quoted in *PCH*, October 5, 1860; Todd, *Early Settlement*, 152–53.
7. *St. Louis Directory, 1859*, 615; Trexler, "Slavery in Missouri," 49.
8. M. Anderson, *Story of a Border City*, 184. See also Trexler, "Slavery in Missouri," 49.
9. Todd, *Early Settlement*, 152–53.
10. "Exciting Times in Missouri," *New York Dispatch*, October 27, 1860; "More Kidnappers Arrested," *Weekly St. Louis Evening News*, November 26, 1860.
11. "Departure of the Kidnappers," *Daily Missouri Republican*, October 5, 1860; "Police Expedition," *St. Louis Daily Democrat*, October 12, 1860; "Police Trip to Iowa with Three Alleged Kidnappers," *St. Louis Daily Democrat*, October 16, 1860. The main events of the trip were drawn from the October 16 account.
12. "Police Trip to Iowa"; "Exciting Times in Missouri"; "More Kidnappers Arrested."
13. Edwards, *History of Richardson County*, 198–99; "Police Trip to Iowa."
14. "Police Trip to Iowa."
15. *Daily Missouri Democrat*, November 15, December 7, 1860; *PCH*, December 7, 1860.
16. Morgans, *John Todd*, 100, also wondered whether "Williamson and the Garners were kidnapped because of the role they played in helping [fugitive slaves] . . . and their role in suing S. F. Nuckolls."
17. United States Commissioner's Docket: S. A. Corneau, February 1860–May 1880, ser. 1, box, 4, folder 27, Adams-Snyder Papers, Abraham Lincoln Presidential Library. *CDT*, November 13, 1860, reported that they had seen the warrant "made out—by U.S. Commissioner Corneau of Springfield." See also *Chicago Journal*, quoted in *New Orleans Crescent*, November 19, 1860; Bradwell, *Chicago Legal News*, 420. Just as Eliza's name came first in Lucinda Nuckolls's letter home, so it did in this warrant.

18. *Baltimore Sun*, November 10, 1860.
19. *Springfield Illinois State Register*, August 3, 1857, quoted in Blackett, *Captive's Quest*, 162.
20. Reed, "Early African American Settlement," 211–65. The 1860 census showed 955 Black residents in Chicago, representing only 0.87 percent of the total population. However, this number represented an increase of 195 percent from 1850.
21. According to "Union Clean Gone," CDT, November 16, 1860, "Eliza took service at housework in an infamous establishment on South Clark Street." "The Union Again Threatened," CDT, November 16, 1860, reported that she was at an "establishment where ebony and ivory are staples on South Clark Street."
22. *Chicago Journal*, quoted in *New Orleans Daily Crescent*, November 19, 1860, stated that Eliza was a servant "with one Mary Beebe, who keeps a house of ill fame at No. 315 South Clarke Street."
23. She was "damaged, so that perhaps he was not over keen to have his own way in the matter, save for the principle of the thing." *Conservative* 3, no. 10 (1900): 10.
24. "Union Again Threatened."
25. *Chicago Journal*, quoted in *New Orleans Daily Crescent*, November 19, 1860. The newspapers mention that a girl named Mattie was also in the house and that a revolver was drawn.
26. "Union Clean Gone: More of the Eliza Grayson Case, Sambo the Modern Martius Curtius, Jake Newsome and Other Union Savers," CDT, November 16, 1860.
27. *Antislavery Bugle* (New-Lisbon OH), December 1, 1860. She was described as "ginger-hued" in CDT, November 13, 1860.
28. Bradwell, *Chicago Legal News*, 420. A more recent article about Eliza's rescue uses many of the same sources. See Dennis Rodkin, "When a Chicago Street Mob Rescued a Fugitive from Slavery," *Chicago Magazine*, June 24, 2019, http://www.chicagomag.com/Chicago-Magazine/June-July-2019/When-a-Chicago-Street-Mob-Rescued-a-Fugitive-From-Slavery/.
29. CT, quoted in "Several Statements of the Affair," *Nebraska City People's Press*, November 21, 1860.
30. E.g., *Illinois Staats-Zeitung*, December 13, 1899.
31. C. Nuckolls, *Roses*, 194; "Slave Auctions Held in the Early Days," NCNP, December 23, 1954; *St. Joseph Gazette*, quoted in "Several Statements of the Affair"; *Conservative* 3, no. 10 (1900): 10; "Nebraska Had Her Slaves," *Nebraska City Daily Press*, November 14, 1929.
32. *Conservative* 3, no. 10 (1900): 10; *Chicago Journal*, quoted in *New Orleans Daily Crescent*, November 19, 1860. Other works, including Bish, "Black Experience," have claimed erroneously that Nuckolls did not pursue her.

33. *Weekly Ottumwa (IA) Courier*, November 15, 1860; Blackett, *Captive's Quest*, 159–60. "Conan" was Corneau, the commissioner who issued the fugitive slave warrant. He had been Lincoln's neighbor in Springfield. See Burlingame, *Abraham Lincoln*, 1:206, 811.
34. *CT*, December 18, 1850. Jenks moved to quash his indictment for aiding a fugitive slave.
35. *Biographical Dictionary*, 353; "Great Fugitive Slave Excitement: A Colored Girl Rescued," November 13, 1860, *Chicago Daily Evening Journal*.
36. Bradwell, *Chicago Legal News*, 420. The prosecutor of Eliza's case eventually entered *a nolle prosequi* on the "order of the Attorney General"—dropping the case—in December 1861. D. Webster, Isaiah H. Williams, E. Langley, H. H. Harris, and H. Lisbes were also named defendants. *CT*, December 7, 1861. *Montrose (PA) Democrat*, November 29, 1860, reported that nine people total were indicted in the Eliza Grayson case.
37. *Chicago Democrat*, November 14, 1860, quoted in *Nebraska City People's Press*, November 21, 1860, Iowa Freedom Trail Collection, ISHS, Des Moines.
38. Edwards, *History of Richardson County*, 245, 597, places Houston Nuckolls in the new town of Yankton in 1857. The 1860 census lists Houston Nuckolls household, dwelling 323, family 312, Richardson County, Nebraska, St. Stephen, p. 38, USCB, *Eighth Census of the United States, 1860*. Houston Nuckolls, age twenty-two, was a speculator worth $30,000, with personal property valued at $1,000. Tax lists at HNA for Richardson County start in 1861.
39. An Act to Vacate the Townsite of Yankton, Approved February 10, 1866, in Edwards, *History of Richardson County*, 153.
40. HNA, microfilm RG 513, Otoe County, Nebraska City, USCB, *Eighth Census of the United States, 1860*, loose paper before the regular schedule. Slaves are listed at the beginning of the census, unpaginated, and Nuckolls is no longer listed as a "slaveowner." C. Nuckolls household, dwelling 78, family 55, Mills County, Iowa, P. O. Pacific City, p. 8, USCB, *Eighth Census of the United States, 1860*. Lafe bought Shade in October 1857 from his father's estate sale. "Death of Lafayette Nuckolls," *NCN*, March 24, 1860, reported that he had been in business with his brother Columbus in Pacific City, Iowa. His personal business failed, and he went to Texas for his health, where he died on February 26, 1860.
41. Second Territorial District Court (Otoe County District Court), Nebraska City, case no. 569, December term, 1859, Nuckolls v. Reuben S. Williams, George Hitchcock, Egbert Avery, Wesley W. Knickerbocker, Marcus Pierce, Alexander Gaston, George B. Gaston, Ira D. Blanchard, Thomas Reed, John Williamson, Edgar Hill, Edwin Hill, Lester W. Platt, Julius F. Merritt, H. B. Horton, and William Lane.

42. For more about enslavers and the methods and costs of retrieval, see Franklin and Schweninger, *Runaway Slaves*, 263–300. See also Dunbar, *Never Caught*, about George Washington's determined, long-term pursuit of Ona Judge. As a man of wealth and prestige, he had the power and means to keep up the pressure, as did Nuckolls.
43. E.g., *Baltimore Daily Exchange*, November 14, 1860; BDHE, November 16, 1860; *Raleigh (NC) Spirit of the Age*, November 21, 1860; *Minnesota Staats-Zeitung*, November 24, 1860; *Cincinnati Daily Press*, November 15, 1860; *New Orleans Daily Crescent*, November 19, 1860.
44. Sheppard and Hurd, *History of Northwestern University*, 488.
45. Brandt, *Town That Started*, 117.
46. "The Eliza Case," NCN, November 24, 1860.
47. "The Western Democracy," CT, November 15, 1860; "The Eliza Grayson Case," CT, November 16, 1860.
48. "The Eliza Case," NCN, November 24, 1860.
49. U.S. Const. art. IV, § 2, cl. 3.
50. "Northern Nullification: The Union Not Worth a Straw!," *Council Bluffs (IA) Weekly Nonpareil*, November 24, 1860.
51. "Fugitives from Territories," *Nebraska City People's Press*, November 21, 1860.
52. For instance, CT, November 19, 1860, reported on fifteen witnesses in Eliza's case on the same page as items on the secession movement and doings.
53. "The Eliza Grayson Case," CT, December 7, 1861; CT, quoted in "The Chicago Rescuers: Arrest of the Rescuers," *Richmond Daily Dispatch*, November 24, 1860.
54. CDT, November 21, 1860; "United States Courts," CDT, December 27, 1860; "The Eliza Grayson Case," CT, February 14, 1861.
55. Fehrenbacher, *Dred Scott Case*; *Muscatine (IA) Weekly Journal*, December 23, 1859.
56. *New York Tribune*, March 7, 1857. The U.S. Supreme Court in 1858–60 included Chief Justice Roger B. Taney, J. McClean, J. M. Wayne, J. Catron, P. R. V. Daniel, S. Nelson, R. C. Grier, J. A. Campbell, and Nathan Clifford. Clifford was the only justice not present for the *Dred Scott* case of 1857.
57. Ableman v. Booth, 62 U.S. (21 How.) 506 (1859), upholding the imprisonment of abolitionist newspaper editor Sherman Booth of Wisconsin and the constitutionality of the 1850 Fugitive Slave Law.
58. "Union Clean Gone," CDT; Goodspeed and Healy, *History of Cook County*, 1:417. CT, December 7, 1861, reported that the attorney general ordered the case dropped. For those involved, Eliza's rescue was a badge of honor. Calvin DeWolf's biography in *Biographical Dictionary* highlights his participation in the incident. See also Sheppard and Hurd, *History of Northwestern University*, 488; Bradwell, *Chicago Legal News*, 420.

59. *NCN*, November 24, 1860; Lucy Bowen of Nebraska City to Aunt Hannah Penniman, of Samsonville, New York, January 24, 1861, HNA, Seacrest Nebraska Settlement Collection, RG 5497, folder 6. The Bowen letter furnishes the details of the sale of Hercules and Martha.
60. Lucy Bowen to Aunt Hannah Penniman, January 24, 1861, furnished the details of Hercules and Martha's situation and attempted escape, as well as Hercules's wish to stay with his wife.
61. "Nebraska and the N——," *NCN*, December 15, 1860.
62. *Nebraska Advertiser* (Brownville), November 22, 1860.
63. "Slavery in Missouri," *St. Joseph (MO) Weekly Free Democrat*, August 27, 1859.
64. "The Fraud in Richardson County" and "Eliza in Limbo," *NCN*, November 17, 1860.
65. *CT*, November 22, 1860.
66. "Felicitous," *NCN*, November 24, 1860.
67. "The Protest against the Passage of the Slavery Bill," *Nebraska Advertiser* (Brownville), December 29, 1860; *NCN*, December 29, 1860.
68. "Protest against the Passage"; Compiled Service Records of Confederate Soldiers Who Served in Organizations from the State of Missouri, NARA RG 109, Roll 1, Missouri, Lt. Asa M. Acton, Attorney, Missouri Cavalry.
69. Etcheson, "Great Principle," 22.
70. Black, *Veto Messages*, 8.
71. "The People," *Nebraska Advertiser* (Brownville), August 23, 1860. This interpretation runs counter to historian Nicole Etcheson's argument in "Where Popular Sovereignty Worked." As Potts argues in "Nebraska Territory," Governor Black's veto was an "opportunity to discredit the Black regime" along with the Democratic Party (222).
72. "Gov. Samuel W. Black," NSHS, *Transactions and Reports*, 1:94.
73. Historians arguing that popular sovereignty worked in Nebraska include Etcheson, "Where Popular Sovereignty Worked"; Blake, "Government and Banking," 425–35; Potts, "Nebraska Territory"; and J. Potter, *Standing Firmly*.
74. "The Eliza Case," *NCN*, November 24, 1860; "Slavery Days in Nebraska," *Omaha Daily Bee*, January 15, 1888; "Scene of Anti-Slave Riots: The Case of 'Eliza,' Steve Nuckolls' Negro, Matter of History," "Little Journeys to Nearby Towns," *Omaha Sunday Bee*, December 1, 1918; *NDNP*, October 23, 1927; C. Nuckolls, *Roses*, 193–94. The same issue of *NDNP* describes a problem with a Negro "indentured to Dr. Day" of Tabor, perhaps confusing Dr. Day with Dr. Ira Blanchard and the Black youth with Henry Garner.
75. "Union Clean Gone," *CDT*; Goodspeed and Healy, *History of Cook County*, 1:417.

Epilogue

Epigraph: Bradford, *Scenes in the Life*, 20.

1. K. Larson, *Bound*, 10–11; Douglass, *Narrative of the Life*, 111–13. For more on formerly enslaved people's surname changes and choices, see Regosin and Shaffer, *Voices of Emancipation*.
2. "Changing Names," Facing History and Ourselves, May 12, 2020, https://www.facinghistory.org/reconstruction-era/changing-names; Civil War Pension File of Lewis Smith (alias Dick Lewis Barnett), Co. B, 77th U.S. Colored Infantry, and Co. D, 10th U.S. Colored Heavy Artillery, NARA, Records of the Department of Veterans Affairs, RG 15.
3. 1861 Census of Canada, Canada West, Essex County, Enumeration District 2, Town of Windsor, p. 29 (stamped), line 23, Eliza Grason; Bill Dollarhide, "Census Mistakes," Genealogy Blog, last modified April 13, 2012, https://www.genealogyblog.com/?p=18199. The 1861 Canada Census asked for religious denomination, and Eliza at this time may have been attending the Church of England, which in the United States would be the Episcopal Church. The "Scene of Anti-Slave Riots," *NCNP*, October 23, 1927, relates that Eliza "eventually went to Cincinnati and lived there for many years," with no apparent source. I classify this as a legend along with the story that Shade went to South Carolina and became a legislator there.
4. "Tower of Freedom," City of Windsor, Ontario, Canada, accessed May 4, 2023, https://www.citywindsor.ca/residents/Culture/Monuments/Pages/Tower-of-Freedom-.aspx.
5. 1861 Census of Canada, Canada West, Essex County, Enumeration District 1, Town of Windsor, p. 29, line 11, Cylia Flenoy in Washington Flenoy household; *Michigan, Compiled Marriages for Select Counties*, 1851–75, index. George W. Flunoy to Celia Toucey, Wayne County, December 7, 1852, rules out that this Cecilia living near Eliza Grason was Celia Grayson.
6. Zorn, "Arkansas Fugitive Incident," 139–40.
7. Silverman, *Unwelcome Guests*, 15.
8. Winks, *Blacks in Canada*. For the fugitive slave experience in Canada, see Landon, "Negro Migration to Canada," 22–36; Landon, "Social Conditions"; Hepburn, "Following the North Star," 91–126. For a revisionist view, see Silverman, "Unwelcome Guests," 454–55.
9. Siebert, "Underground Railroad in Michigan," 14–15.
10. Siebert, *Underground Railroad*, 108, 162–65.
11. "Exposed at Last," *Provincial Freeman*, May 2, 1857.
12. "Exposed at Last"; "Fugitive Slaves in Canada," *Provincial Freeman*, March 25, 1854. The March 25, 1854, issue reported the arrest and rescue of fugitive Joshua Glover in Racine, Wisconsin.

13. For a thorough discussion of debates among Black leaders, as well as competition for labor from large numbers of Irish immigrants, see Silverman, *Unwelcome Guests*, 70–80.
14. There is one mention of Eliza going to Cincinnati "under the wing" of Levi Coffin instead of Canada and living there after the war, in "Scene of Anti-Slave Riots," *NDNP*, October 23, 1927; however, this account has no byline and contains many errors. The source of this detail has not been traced.
15. Otoe County District Court, Territorial Court Records for Second Judicial District, case no. 935, October term, 1862, no. 12, Reuben S. Williams v. Stephen F. Nuckolls, Heath Nuckolls, John W. Pearman, George W. Sroat, Granville H. Hail, Harvey G. Bourn, David Biggerstaff, J. F. McCoy, Richard Miller, Frank McMahan, and A. J. Lemming. Sheriff Granville Hail served a summons for this case to Nuckolls in Nebraska City in August 1862 but reported leaving the summons at his "usual residence" rather than handing it to him in person. *Biographical Directory of Congress* indicates Nuckolls moved to Colorado Territory in 1860; however, when he and his family actually moved is unclear.
16. *Biographical Directory of Congress*, 1624; *NDNP*, July 29, 1934. The 1870 census lists the birth of son Peter Paul Nuckolls in Samuel [*sic*] F. Nuckolls household, Laramie County, Wyoming, City of Cheyenne, dwelling 99, family 76, USCB, *Ninth Census of the United States, 1870*. The 1885 Colorado State Census lists a miner with his brother in the William E. Nuckolls household, Custer County, Colorado, dwelling 16, family 16, p. 2, microfilm.
17. Lucinda Bourne Nuckolls to "Dear Brother," November 16, 1864, Brett Conover private collection; Lucinda Bourne Nuckolls to "Dear Brother," December 28, 1864; Frances Nuckolls Bourne to her parents-in-law, July 2, 1865.
18. *NCN*, July 20 and 27, 1867. Nuckolls was still present in Nebraska City as late as October 1867, when he attended a city council meeting. *NCN*, October 5, 1867.
19. *CL*, October 29, 1867; *Daily Rocky Mountain Star*, January 28, 1868; "Board of Trade," *Daily Rocky Mountain Star*, May 8, 1868; "Mass Meeting," *Cheyenne (WY) Leader*, October 2, 1868; "Democratic Pow-Wow," *Wyoming Weekly Leader*, July 10, 1869; "Democratic Delegates," *CL*, August 11, 1869. S. F. Nuckolls advertising appears in *Daily Rocky Mountain Star*, June 18, 1868. Lucinda wrote to her parents on May 4, 1869, that they had moved from Nebraska City "last June."
20. "Unwitted Admission," *CL*, August 24, 1869.
21. "Laboring Men of Wyoming!," *CL*, August 24, 1869.
22. "Democratic Pow-Wow"; "Democratic Delegates"; "Unwitted Admission"; *CL*, August 25, 1869.
23. "To Our Friends," *CL*, August 28, 1869; "Territorial Delegates Qualified," *New York Herald*, December 7, 1859.

24. "Grand Testimonial Banquet to Hon. S. F. Nuckolls, Member of Congress," *NCN*, December 4, 1869. Dr. Renner, a "radical German," gave the first long and glowing toast to Nuckolls.
25. Lucinda Bourne Nuckolls in Cheyenne, Wyoming, to her parents, February 8, 1872, Brett Conover private collection.
26. *North Missouri Register* (Kirksville), April 11, 1872.
27. *Biographical Directory of Congress*, 1624; T. Larson, *History of Wyoming*; Malinda Curren, San Francisco, to sister Mary Ann Reeves, April 4, 1872, Brett Conover private collection.
28. "A Rich Strike," *Cheyenne Daily Leader*, August 29, 1871; *Cheyenne Daily Leader*, July 9, 1872; *Biographical Directory of Congress*, 1624; T. Larson, *History of Wyoming*. By December 1872 Stephen had sold his stock to a fellow merchant named Nagle, the family's move to Utah complete. *CL*, December 12, 1872.
29. Lucinda Bourne Nuckolls to her parents, May 28, 1873; "Munificent Gift," *Salt Lake Herald-Republican*, July 8, 1874.
30. Searches on the Utah Digital Newspapers website with the date range of 1870 to 1880 turn up mentions of "Colonel" Nuckolls starting in 1875. For his attendance at the Democratic conventions, see *Salt Lake Tribune*, March 28, 1876; *Salt Lake Herald-Republican*, July 4, 1876; *Salt Lake Herald-Republican*, July 7, 1876; *Salt Lake Herald-Republican*, November 11, 1876 (representing both Utah and Wyoming).
31. "Right of Way, Testimonial to S. F. Nuckolls," *NCN*, August 12, 1876; *NCN*, October 7, 1876.
32. "Death of Mrs. S. F. Nuckolls," *Cheyenne (WY) Weekly Leader*, October 25, 1877.
33. "Death of S. F. Nuckolls," *Deseret (UT) News*, February 15, 1879.
34. Stephen F. Nuckolls Will and Estate (1881), HNA, Otoe County, Nebraska, Probate Court, A-189 04, RG 210; Stephen F. Nuckolls, Will Book 33:498, Atchison County, Missouri (referencing Territory of Utah probate), Atchison County Probate Court; Fremont County, Iowa, Will Record 1:134, Iowa Wills and Probate Records, 1758–1997; Territory of Utah, Salt Lake City, S. F. Nuckolls Probate Case 636, Utah Wills and Probate Records, 1800–1985; Stephen Friel Nuckolls, memorial ID 159284, Mount Olivet Cemetery, Salt Lake City, Find a Grave, https://www.findagrave.com; 1885 Colorado State Census, NARA, Records of the Bureau of the Census, 1790–2007, RG 29, ser. M158, roll 3; USCB, 1910 U.S. Census for Jefferson County MT, p. 122 (stamped), family 241, Bruce and William Nuckolls; William Nuckolls, "Montana, U.S. State Deaths, 1907–2018," Ancestry.com. I was unable to locate William Nuckolls in the 1880 census.
35. On Paul: *Salt Lake Evening Democrat*, March 29, 1887; *Salt Lake Tribune*,

March 5, 1947. On Bruce: USCB, 1900 U.S. Census for Sheridan WY, p. 3, Bruce Nuckolls, farm laborer, boarder; Bruce Nuckolls, sheep herder, Dillon (MT) City Directory (1906), 177, "U.S. City Directories, 1822–1995," Ancestry.com; 1910 U.S. Census for Jefferson County MT, p. 6a, Bruce J. Nuckolls, miner; 1920 U.S. Census for Dover, Bonner County, ID, p. 4b, Ben [sic] Nuckolls, laborer. He was single in all censuses.

On Rupert: "Montana County Marriage Records, 1865–1993," Ancestry.com; Rupert Nuckolls to Georgia Johnson, November 10, 1886, in Beaverhead County MT, index from FamilySearch Library microfilm 001905607. He resided in Dillon, Beaverhead County MT, for births of three children ("U.S. Passport Applications 1795–1925," Ancestry.com). On Frances Nuckolls Kelley: "Utah, Death and Military Death Certificates, 1904–61," Ancestry.com. On Stephen Friel Nuckolls: Utah state file no. 57-18-2520. On Virginia Elizabeth Nuckolls: "Montana County Marriages, 1865–1987," marriage certificate 3601, Virginia Elizabeth Nuckolls, Ancestry.com. See also, "Rupert B. Nuckolls," obituary, *Salt Lake Tribune*, March 5, 1947.

36. "Slavery in Nebraska," BDHE, January 8, 1859.
37. Account book, folder 1, box 2, ser. 2, NFP.
38. Jones-Rogers, *They Were Her Property*, 101–33, discusses the common practice of enslaved women serving as wet nurses to free up female enslavers' time.
39. W. R. Schooler household, p. 4, Census of the Second District, Nebraska Territory, 1854–56, HNA, Nebraska Territorial Census Records.
40. Franklin and Schweninger, *Runaway Slaves*. See also White, *Ar'n't I a Woman*, 69–71.
41. Atchison County Marriages, 2, p. 46 (stamped), p. 70 (written).
42. Gilbert Hampton household, dwelling 33, family 33, Fremont County, Iowa, Franklin township, P. O. Hamburg, p. 448 (stamped), USCB, *Ninth Census of the United States, 1870*; Samuel Tate household, 118 Main Street, family 124, Otoe County, Nebraska City, p. 287, USCB, *Tenth Census of the United States, 1880* (according to this census, Jane Hampton was working in a hotel run by Samuel Tate doing laundry); Rufus McComas household, Otoe County, Nebraska, Four-Mile Precinct, p. 14, USCB, *Tenth Census of the United States, 1880* (the census lists Harding as a "man of all work" for McComas, who was a steam boatman and farmer).
43. Gilbert Hampton household, USCB, *Ninth Census*; *Nebraska Daily Press*, August 29, 1922. Although Edith was still of childbearing age for Henry's and Clementine's births, the gap in age between the older children and the youngest suggests that either Edith suffered a miscarriage or two or Gilbert was hired away during that period. Mary Albertha was Gilbert and Edith's youngest child,

age seventeen in 1885 at her marriage in Nebraska City and age thirty in the 1900 census. "Nebraska Marriage Records, 1855–1908," Ancestry.com; 1900 Census of Indian Territory, Choctaw Nation, Albertha Makins, p. 3.

44. "A hundred and fifty colored men, women, and children met at St. Augustine's church Christmas night and had a grand, good time.... This church and the school connected with it is doing a great work for our colored citizens." NCN, December 28, 1872. Harding Hampton signed a testimonial along with four other men on behalf of the congregation, donating a stand to the church.

45. "The Radical," NCN, August 8, 1868.

46. "Exultation Meeting! Speeches by McCracken, Mason, McCracken and Mason, N—— Barber Shops Resplendent: More Talk from McCracken and Mason! The N—— Barber Shops, Lindsey Hotel and Beer Saloons Ablaze! The Brass Band Out! etc., the Whole Concluded with the Laughable Farce of Let's Have Peace," *Nebraska City Weekly News*, October 17, 1868.

47. "Exultation Meeting!"

48. NCN, August 31, 1872; "Shooting to Scare: A Lively Time in a Barber Shop but No One Was Hurt," NCN, September 28, 1878; Tim Thomas household (barber), 163 Larimy St., family 171, Otoe County, Nebraska City, p. 290, USCB, *Tenth Census of the United States, 1880*.

49. Gilbert Hampton death, Otoe County, Nebraska, p. 1, U.S. Federal Census Mortality Schedules, 1850–85, USCB, *Tenth Census of the United States, 1880*; Charles Hicks household, 164 California Street, family 173, Otoe County, Nebraska City, p. 290 (stamped), USCB, *Tenth Census of the United States, 1880*. Gilbert Hampton was listed in the mortality schedule as a forty-five-year-old farmer, born in Virginia, with both parents born in Virginia.

50. NCN, March 19, 1881.

51. *Nebraska City and Otoe County Directory*.

52. Edith Hampton household, 413 Second Corso, family 27, Otoe County, Nebraska City, p. 71 (stamped), USCB, *Twelfth Census of the United States, 1900*. Edith's mother is listed as born in Virginia, father unknown. Listed in error as Edith's daughter, Cora Hampton was her granddaughter, the daughter of Edith's son Henry G. Hampton. On the same page at 405 Third Corso, family 31, was Edith's son Harding Hampton.

53. NCN, December 29, 1905; "Forty-Five Years Ago" column, NCNP, December 29, 1950, adds that Edith was a slave and a resident since territorial days. Only Harding was mentioned in Edith's obituary. Her surviving daughter, Celia, divorced Charles Hicks in 1884 and moved to Portland OR, where she worked as a maid, going alternately by the names Cecelia Hampton and Cecelia Nichols.

54. Marriage of Harding Hampton, born in Grayson County, Virginia, to Angeline Williams, born in Missouri, December 27, 1872. Otoe County Marriages, C:352

(License and Return), Nebraska, Marriage Records, 1855–1908. St. Augustine's was Protestant Episcopal. See *Tenth Annual Council*; NCN, December 28, 1872. This was a mission church and school created to serve Nebraska City's African Americans. Harry Patton, one of the marriage witnesses, also signed the memorial on Christmas night. The Episcopal Diocesan Archive reports that no church records are extant (emails from Jo Behrens, September 4 and 6, 2021).

55. Otoe County Register of Deeds, Nebraska City, Deed Book F:295–96, Maria Butler to Harding Hampton, October 22, 1873. The chain of title for the parcel is derived from an examination of the numerical index for that lot description. Otoe County Register of Deeds furnished the current address for the parcel. Alfred Butler is listed in the 1870 *Nebraska City Directory* as living at S. Sioux between Eighth and Ninth; he worked as a cook at the Galt House. The directory did not include a racial designation. The 1870 census listed Alfred Butler as age fifty and Black; his wife, Maria, as age thirty, born in Missouri, and Native American; and their son as "M" for mulatto. When their son Alfred (under his stepfather's surname of Lawrence) married a white woman, Ida Brown, in Iowa in 1905, he was called a "colored African," whose parents were Alfred and Maria with no last names, suggesting they were both formerly enslaved. Iowa U.S. Marriage Records, 1880–1945.

56. USCB, 1880 U.S. Census for Four-Mile Precinct, Otoe County, Nebraska, p. 14, household of Rufus F. McComas, dwelling 115, family 120; NCN, September 7, 1888; "Harding Hampton," NCN, September 1, 1922; "Reporter's Notebook," NCNP, June 29, 1969; NCN, February 18, 1887; NCN, September 7, 1888; NCN, January 4, 1889.

57. R. W. Oliver, letter in the *Churchman* 41 (1880): 51, soliciting funds for the school's continuation. For more on Dr. Oliver and the segregated school in Nebraska City, see Behrens, "Missteps."

58. Wyuka Cemetery, Burials/Plots, Surname H, accessed May 4, 2023, http://negenweb.net/NEOtoe/wyuka/wyuka_h.htm; Marriage of Harding Hampton, born in Grayson County, Virginia, son of Gilbert Hampton and "Eda" Schooler, to Georgia "Robison," daughter of Easter, born in Atchison County, Missouri, Nebraska Marriage Records, 1855–1908; *Churchman* 41 (1880); NCN, October 22, 1881 (both his marriage and his appearance as a pupil are in this issue).

59. NCN, December 29, 1882; NCN, May 17, 1884. The girl's name is derived from Wyuka Cemetery, Burials/Plots, Surname H. *Journal of the Annual Convention, Episcopal Church, Diocese of Nebraska, Ninth Council, 1876* (Omaha NE: Daily Herald Book, 1876), 38, describes the consecration of the Mount Zion African Methodist Church in 1876.

60. NCN, March 27, 1885; Otoe County Register of Deeds, Deed Book 24:108, Hart to Hampton; Deed Book 24:553, Harding Hampton to Belle V. Hampton;

Deed Book 25:379, Osage to Hampton; "Belle Hampton Is Dead," *Nebraska City Daily Press*, September 9, 1919.

61. *Omaha (NE) Daily Bee*, May 1, 1890; *Syracuse (NE) Journal*, May 30, 1890.
62. *NCN*, March 2, 1867.
63. USCB statistics; the total for African American residents was derived from searches for anyone in Nebraska City whose race was Black in 1870–1900 at Ancestry.com.
64. "One Half a Century," *NCN*, November 11, 1904.
65. "Harding Hampton," *NCN*; "Harding Hampton Dead: Well Known Colored Man Passed Away Yesterday Morning," *Nebraska Daily Press*, August 29, 1922; "Former Slave Dies at Nebraska City," *Beatrice (NE) Daily Press*, August 30, 1922. The Beatrice newspaper stated that instead of a farming "outfit," Schooler gave the Hamptons a farm, but there is no evidence to support this.
66. Otoe County Register of Deeds, Book 66:372–74. His will also named his nephew Austin Hampton and his niece Edith Makins, who received his silverware.
67. Andreas, *History of Nebraska*, "Otoe County," part 9, "Biographical Sketches," death notice for Henry Hampton, *NCN*, October 24, 1905; *NCN*, November 2, 1878; "Church Dedication," *NCN*, December 5, 1885; *NCN*, July 5, 1894; *NCN*, August 21, 1891; *NCN*, July 28, 1893; *NCN*, September 1, 1893; *NCN*, May 5, 1899; *NCDN*, February 8, 1894; *NCN*, July 8, 1898; *NCN*, July 18, 1890.
68. Samuel Tate household, 118 Main Street, family 124, Otoe County, Nebraska City, p. 287, USCB, *Tenth Census of the United States, 1880*. According to *NCN*, January 24, 1880, Samuel Tate was the proprietor of the Grand Central Hotel. It is almost certain that Martha was the Mattie "Hawkins" who was doing general housework for J. R. Sousley in 1880, although no marriage record for Martha Hampton to a Hawkins has been found. Mattie Hawkins is on the same page as Edith Hampton, Celia Hampton Hicks, and Henry Hampton in the 1880 census.
69. *Nebraska City and Otoe County Directory*.
70. Edith Hampton household, 413 Second Corso, family 27, Otoe County, Nebraska City, p. 71 (stamped), USCB, *Twelfth Census of the United States, 1900*; Clementine, age one, listed in Gilbert Hampton household, dwelling 33, family 33, Fremont County, Iowa, Franklin Township, PO Hamburg, p. 448 (stamped), USCB, *Ninth Census of the United States, 1870*.
71. Marriage record of Celia Hampton, age eighteen, born in Atchison County, Missouri, to Charles Hix, June 10, 1875, Nebraska, Marriage Records, 1855–1908; Charles Hicks household, 164 California Street, family 173, Otoe County, Nebraska City, p. 290 (stamped), USCB, *Tenth Census of the United States, 1880*; "C. Hicks v. C. Hicks," *NCN*, 12 April 1884; *NCN*, December 27, 1879.

72. USCB, *Fourteenth, Fifteenth, and Sixteenth Censuses of the United States, 1920, 1930, 1940*; Cecelia Nichols (?–1944), memorial ID 62858717, Greenwood Hills Cemetery, section 6, Find a Grave, https://www.findagrave.com; *Portland Oregonian*, dated April 8, 1944. Cecilia Nichols or Hampton was in Multnomah County, Oregon, Portland, for the 1920–40 censuses. In 1920 she was in daughter Ada and son-in-law Charles Weaver's household, 410 Couch Street, family 90; in 1930 she was listed as Cecelia Hampton, servant, John K. Giltner household, 1448 East 13th Street, family 31; and in 1940 she was renting with her daughter, Ada Weaver, at 947 N. Russell Street, dwelling 270. USCB, *Fourteenth, Fifteenth, and Sixteenth Censuses*.

73. Otoe County Marriages, vol. H:127, *Nebraska, Marriage Records, 1855–1908*; *NCN*, December 26, 1885. The marriage record states Makins was born in Rockingham County, Virginia, son of Elijah Makins and Malinda Shipman. Brainard's death certificate has his mother's maiden name as Malinda Smith instead of Malinda Shipman. Because the marriage certificate information was likely furnished by Brainerd himself, Shipman is the more probable name for his mother.

74. Brainerd Makins household, Choctaw Nation, Indian Territory, Township 4, p. 2–3, USCB, *Twelfth Census of the United States, 1900* (listed as "Albertha," she was the mother of six children, five living); B. C. Makins household, Muskogee County, Oklahoma, Boynton, dwelling 41, family 41, USCB, *Thirteenth Census of the United States, 1910*, microfilm; marriage record of Brainard C. Makins to Mary A. Brown, September 1902, Oklahoma County Marriage Records, 1900–1995. The youngest child in the household was thirteen-year-old Edith Schooler Makins, named for her grandmother.

75. Nebraska Territory, *House Journal, Sixth Session*, 44; Lucinda Bourne Nuckolls to Dear Brother: July 21, 1859; "A Distinguished N——," *NCN*, January 22, 1868.

76. "Old Nebraska Slave Prospers," *Omaha Bee*, February 16, 1907.

77. USCB, 1870 U.S. Census for West Feliciana Parish, Louisiana, First Ward, St. Francisville PO, p. 328 (stamped), dwelling 119, family 158, Eveline Grayson household, Jackson, age fifty. The 1880 census, p. 26 (written), lists no dwelling or family numbers for the Jackson "Greyson" household; Jackson, age forty-five, cannot read or write, and his children are listed as stepchildren (all "mulatto," while Jackson and Eveline are Black). USCB, 1900 U.S. Census, image database, p. 5944 (written), dwelling 39, family 40, Jack Greyson household, states: born January 1835, farmer, age sixty-five, married thirty years, owns home and farm; Jackson Grayson Estate, West Feliciana Parish, Louisiana, Deed Book Z:472.

In 1910 the widowed Eveline was residing with her son Charles Temple. Of Eveline's three children, two were still living. Civil War Pension File, December 15, 1885, Jackson Grayson, application no. 556.572; cert. no. 546.369; Widow's

Pension File, November 24, 1908, Widow, Evilina Grayson, widow's pension application no. 908.583, certificate no. 676.346; service of Jackson Grayson (alias Jack Greyson, Shack Greyson), private USCT Co. C, 79th Louisiana Infantry, and Co. B, 84th Louisiana Infantry, Civil War and Later Pension Files, RG 15: Records of the Department of Veterans Affairs.

78. "Lulu N. Wesner, Descendant of the Nuckolls Clan," *NDNP*, November 22, 1929.

79. Compiled Military Service Records of Volunteer Union Soldiers Who Served the United States Colored Troops 56th–138th USCT Infantry, Fold3.com, and Jackson Grayson pension 546.369 (Pvt. Co. C 79th United States Colored Troops; and Co. B 84th United States Colored Troops) Civil War and Later Pension Files, Department of Veterans Affairs, Record Group 15, NARA. Both Jackson Grayson's and his widow's Civil War pensions provide much information about Jackson's life in Louisiana, while confirming that he appeared in regimental records under the first names of Shack, Jack, and Jackson.

80. Jackson Grayson, Civil War Pension.

81. USCB, *Eighth Census of the United States, 1860, Pacific City, Mills Co, Iowa*, p. 8; "Slavery in Nebraska," *BDHE*, quotes Nuckolls regarding his enslaved people, their origins with his father, and their family relationship. The Ezra Nuckolls account book does not have a birth entry for him, but the book is incomplete.

82. "Slave Auctions Held in City in Early Days," *NCNP*, December 23, 1954 (this account is long and marred by multiple errors); *NCNP*, quoted in "Nebraska Scene" column, *Omaha World Herald*, August 22, 1948. Others mention Shade going at the same time as Celia and Eliza: *NCNP*, July 4, 1954; "Nebraska Had Her Slaves," *NDNP*, November 14, 1929; "Flipping Back the Leaves of History," *NDNP*, July 24, 1932. A 1954 version claimed that both Shack and Shade left Nuckolls before Celia and Eliza did, "spirited away" by John Kagi in 1857 (not 1858). "Kick Column," *NCNP*, January 22, 1954. *NCNP*, August 8, 1956, further confuses Eliza's rescue with Shack and Shade's experience. In fact, numerous articles claim that both Shack and Shade were taken away by abolitionists, none written contemporaneously with the events.

83. *Pittsburgh (PA) Press*, December 8, 1901; A. T. Richardson, *Conservative* 3, no. 10 (1900): 10. This last version adds that Shade was a legislator in Alabama.

84. *NDNP*, November 14, 1929. Family historian Charles R. Nuckolls also asserts that Shade went to South Carolina. C. Nuckolls, *Roses*, 198. The South Carolina account is repeated online with no citations, oddly asserting that Shade, a.k.a. Samuel "Nuckolls," served in the South Carolina legislature, yet died in Colorado and was buried in Turkey Creek Ranch Cemetery in Morrison, Jefferson County, where Columbus Nuckolls was also buried. Samuel "Shade" Nuckolls (1815–?), memorial ID 167836915, Find a Grave, https://www.findagrave.com.

85. *Charleston (SC) Mercury*, February 24, 1868; *(Columbia SC) Daily Phoenix*, May

21, 1868; Work et al., "Some Negro Members"; U.S. Congress, *Report of the Joint Select Committee*, 1158. For more about Samuel Nuckles, see Gail Shaffer Blankenau, "Who Was Samuel Nuckles's Enslaver?," *Discover Family History* (blog), August 11, 2020, https://www.discoverancestry.org/post/who-was-samuel-nuckles-s-enslaver.

86. Ari Shapiro and Maureen Pao, "After Slavery, Searching for Loved Ones in Wanted Ads," NPR, February 22, 2017; Last Seen: Finding Family after Slavery, accessed May 4, 2023, https://informationwanted.org/.

Bibliography

Archives

Adams-Snyder Papers. Abraham Lincoln Presidential Library, Springfield IL.
Atchison County District Court. Rock Port MO.
Atchison County Marriages. Atchison County Clerk, Rock Port MO.
Atchison County Probate Court. Atchison County Clerk, Rock Port MO.
Fremont County District Court Docket 2 (1858–61): Cases 30 & 31. Fremont County Clerk, Sidney IA.
Fremont County Probate Court, Fremont County Clerk, Sidney IA.
Grayson, Jackson. Succession Record, 1908–9. West Feliciana Parish LA, Clerk of Court, St. Francisville LA.
Grayson County VA Order Book, 1844–51. Mary B. Kegley Collection, Kegley Library Vertical Files, Blacks Part 1, Wytheville Community College.
History Nebraska Archives, Lincoln.
    Dougherty, John. Collection.
    Hall-Kinney Collection, 1821–1902.
    Ingraham, William W. Typescript copies of letters to brother Edward (Ned) B. Ingraham, 1847–48. Donated by Virginius H. Chase.
    Morton, J. Sterling. Collection.
    Nebraska Territorial Census Records.
    Nebraska Territorial Courts, 1855–61.
    Nuckolls Family Papers.
    Otoe County Records.
    Pearman, John Wallace. Collection.
    Seacrest Nebraska Settlement Collection.
    Ware, Ellen Kinney. Reminiscences.
Louisa County VA. Deed books. Library of Virginia, Richmond. https://www.familysearch.org/search/catalog/281398.
Louisiana Freedmen's Bureau Office Records, 1865–72. https://www.familysearch.org/search/collection/2333781.
Merritt, J. F. Papers. Iowa State Historical Society, Des Moines.

National Archives and Records Administration, Washington DC.
>Case Files of Approved Pension Applications, 1861–1934.
>Case Files of Approved Pension Applications for United States Colored Troops.
>Case Files of Approved Pension Applications of Widows and Other Dependents of Civil War Veterans, 1861–1910.
>Compiled Military Service Records of Confederate Soldiers Who Served in Organizations from the State of Missouri.
>Compiled Military Service Records of Volunteer Union Soldiers Who Served the United States Colored Troops: 56th–138th USCT Infantry, 1864–66.
>Records of the Bureau of the Census, 1790–2007.
>Records of the Department of Veterans Affairs.

New River Notes. Grayson County, Virginia, personal property lists, 1794–1835. https://www.newrivernotes.com/grayson_index.htm.

Nuckolls-Bourne Letters. Private collection of Bourne descendant Brett Conover.

Otoe County District Court. Case files. Nebraska City.

Page County. Docket books (1858–61). Page County Clerk. Clarinda IA.

Siebert, William H. Underground Railroad Collection. Ohio State University Collections, Columbus.

State Historical Society of Iowa, Iowa City.
>Nuckolls & Borchers. Ledger book, 1855–57. Special Collections.
>Parker, Leonard F. Papers.

Tabor Historical Society, Tabor IA.
>Todd, John. Marriages Solemnized by Rev. John Todd.
>———. Meeting minutes.

West Feliciana Clerk of Court. St. Francisville LA.
>Land Records.
>Succession Records.

Works Progress Administration. Slave Narratives, 1936–38. Library of Congress, Washington DC.

Published Works

Abbott, Lynn, and Doug Seroff. *Out of Sight: The Rise of African American Popular Music, 1889–1895.* Jackson: University Press of Mississippi, 2009.

Ackley, Richard Thomas. "Across the Plains in 1858." *Utah Historical Quarterly* 9 (1941): 191–92.

Adelman, Jeremy, and Stephen Aron. "From Borderlands to Borders: Empires, Nation-States, and the Peoples in between in North American History." *American Historical Review* 104, no. 3 (1999): 814–41.

Anderson, Galusha. *The Story of a Border City during the Civil War*. Boston: Little Brown, 1908.

Anderson, Margo J. "Sectional Crisis and Census Reform in the 1850s." In *The American Census: A Social History*, 40–63. 2nd ed. New Haven CT: Yale University Press, 2015.

Andreas, Alfred T. *History of the State of Nebraska: Containing a Full Account of Its Growth [. . .]*. Chicago: Western Historical, 1882. http://www.kancoll.org/books/andreas_ne/hon_tabl.html.

Arnesen, Eric, ed. *Encyclopedia of U.S. Labor and Working-Class History*. New York: Routledge, 2007.

Atchison County Historical Society. *Gone, but Not Forgotten, Directory of the Deceased in Atchison County, Missouri, from Earliest Records through 1990, and Items of History and Interest*. Rock Port MO: Atchison County Historical Society, 1991.

Auchampaugh, Phillip G. "Political Techniques, 1856, or Why the Herald Went for Fremont." *Western Political Quarterly* 1, no. 3 (1938): 243–51.

Babcock, Willoughby M. "Steamboat Travel in 1848." *Minnesota History* 7, no. 1 (March 1926): 54–61.

Bartling, Edward. *John Henry Kagi and the Old Log Cabin Home*. Nebraska City: self-published, 1943.

Behrens, Jo Wetherilt. "Missteps by an Episcopal Priest That Led to Segregation, 1868–1893," *Nebraska History* 102, no. 2 (Summer 2021): 57–71.

Bellamy, Donnie D. "Free Blacks in Antebellum Missouri, 1820–1860." *Missouri Historical Review* 67, no. 2 (January 1973): 198–226.

Bennet, Hiram P. "The First Territorial Legislature of Nebraska: Reminiscences by H. P. Bennet." *Proceedings and Collections of the Nebraska State Historical Society* 2, no. 7 (1898): 88–92.

Berlin, Ira. *Generations of Captivity: A History of African-American Slaves*. Cambridge MA: Belknap Press of Harvard University Press, 2003.

———. *Many Thousands Gone: The First Two Centuries of Slavery in North America*. Cambridge MA: Harvard University Press, 1998.

Bermann, Leola N. "The Negro in Iowa." *Iowa Journal of History and Politics* 46 (1969): 9–14.

Billington, Monroe Lee, and Roger D. Hardaway, eds. *African Americans on the Western Frontier*. Boulder: University Press of Colorado, 1998.

The Biographical Dictionary and Portrait Gallery of Representative Men of Chicago. Chicago: American Biographical Publishing Company, 1893.

Biographical Directory of the American Congress, 1774–1949: The Continental Congress September 5, 1774, to October 21, 1788 and the Congress of the United States from the First to the Eightieth Congress March 4, 1789 to January 3, 1949, Inclusive. Washington DC: U.S. Government Printing Office, 1950.

Bish, James. "The Black Experience in Selected Nebraska Counties, 1854–1920." Master's thesis, University of Nebraska–Omaha, 1989.

Black, Samuel W. *Message of Samuel W. Black, Governor of Nebraska, on the Bill for "An Act to Prohibit Slavery": Delivered in the Council of the Legislative Assembly, January 9*. [Nebraska?, 1860?]. African American Pamphlet Collection, Library of Congress. https://www.loc.gov/item/92838871/.

———. *Veto Messages of Hon. Samuel W. Black, Governor of Nebraska, on the Bills to Prohibit Slavery: Passed at the Sessions of 1860 and 1861*. Omaha: E. D. Webster, 1861.

Blackett, Richard J. M. *The Captive's Quest for Freedom*. Cambridge: Cambridge University Press, 2018.

———. "Resistance to Slavery in Middle Tennessee." *Tennessee Historical Quarterly* 76, no. 4 (Winter 2017): 300–341.

Blake, Gordon J. "Government and Banking in Territorial Nebraska." *Nebraska History* 51 (Winter 1970): 425–35.

Blassingame, John W. "Using the Testimony of Ex-Slaves: Approaches and Problems." *Journal of Southern History* 41, no. 4 (November 1975): 473–92.

Blight, David W. *Passages to Freedom: The Underground Railroad in History and Memory*. New York: HarperCollins, 2006.

———. *A Slave No More: Two Men Who Escaped to Freedom, Including Their Own Narratives of Emancipation*. New York: Houghton Mifflin, 2007.

Blockson, Charles L. *The Underground Railroad: First Person Narratives of Escapes to Freedom in the North*. Washington DC: National Geographic Society, 1984.

Bloom, Robert L. "Kansas and Popular Sovereignty in Pennsylvania Newspapers, 1856–1860." *Pennsylvania History: A Journal of Mid-Atlantic Studies* 14, no. 2 (April 1947): 77–93.

Bonner, James C. *Milledgeville, Georgia's Antebellum Capital*. Athens: University of Georgia Press, 1978.

Bordewich, Fergus M., and Peter Jay Fernandez. *Bound for Canaan: The Underground Railroad and the War for the Soul of America*. New York: Amistad, 2006.

Bowes, John. *Exiles and Pioneers: Eastern Indians in the Trans-Mississippi West*. Cambridge: Cambridge University Press, 2007.

Bradford, Sarah H. *Scenes in the Life of Harriet Tubman*. Auburn AL: W. J. Moses, 1869. https://archive.org/details/scenesinlifeofha00brad/page/n8/mode/2up.

Bradwell, Myra, ed. *Chicago Legal News: A Journal of Legal Intelligence*. Vol. 27, September 1894, to August 24, 1895. Chicago: Chicago Legal News Company, 1895.

Brandt, Nat. *The Town That Started the Civil War*. New York: Bantam Doubleday Dell, 1990.

Brown, John, William Ellery Channing, Lydia Maria Child, Joshua Coffin, William Lloyd Garrison, John Hossack, Daniel O'Connell, Wendell Phillips, and Edward Lillie Pierce. "Nebraska Territory." In *Anti-Slavery Tracts*, ser. 2, no. 15, "The Fugitive Slave Law and Its Victims," 10. New York: American Anti-Slavery Society, 1861.

Brown, Marion Marsh. "The Brownville Story: Portrait of a Phoenix, 1854–1974." *Nebraska History* 55 (1974): 1–141.

Burke, Diane Mutti. *On Slavery's Border: Missouri's Small Slaveholding Households*. Athens: University of Georgia Press, 2010.

Burlingame, Michael. *Abraham Lincoln: A Life*. 2 vols. Baltimore: Johns Hopkins University Press, 2008.

Butler, Anne, and Helen Williams. *Bayou Sara: Used to Be*. Lafayette: University of Louisiana at Lafayette Press, 2017.

Caldwell, Elizabeth. "The Financial Frontier: Slave Mortgaging and the Creation of the Deep South." PhD diss., Brown University, 2012.

Campbell, Stanley W. *The Slave Catchers: Enforcement of the Fugitive Slave Law, 1850–1860*. Raleigh: University of North Carolina Press, 1970.

Casimir-Paz, Lynn A. "Footprints of the Fugitive: Slave Narrative Discourse and the Trace of Autobiography." *Biography* 24, no. 1 (Winter 2001): 215–24.

Caskey, J. Homer. "Truth and Fiction in Eighteenth-Century Newspapers." *Modern Language Notes* 45, no. 7 (November 1930): 438–40.

Combs, H. Jason. "Slavery in the Platte Region." *Nebraska Anthropologist* 117 (1999): 8-=30. http://digitalcommons.unl.edu/nebanthro/117.

The Compendium of History and Biography of Cass County, Iowa. Chicago: Henry Taylor, 1906.

Connelley, William Elsey. *James Henry Lane: The Grim Chieftain of Kansas*. Topeka KS: Crane, 1899.

Connor, James. "The Antislavery Movement in Iowa." *Annals of Iowa* 40 (1970): 450–79.

Cooley, Verna. "Illinois and the Underground Railroad to Canada." *Illinois State Historical Library* 23 (1917): 76–98.

Costa, Tom. "What Can We Learn from a Digital Database of Runaway Slave Advertisements?" *International Social Science Review* 76, nos. 1–2 (2001): 36–43.

Coxe, Simeon O., comp. *The Ancestry of John Nuckolls (1755–1835)*. Self-published, n.d.

Crafts, Hannah. *The Bondwoman's Narrative*. Edited by Henry Louis Gates. New York: Warner Books, 2002.

Crawford, Stephen C. "Quantified Memory: A Study of the WPA and Fisk University Slave Narrative Collections." PhD diss., University of Chicago, 1980.

Crooks, Elizabeth Williams. *Life of Rev. A. Crooks, A.M.* Syracuse NY: D. S. Kinney Wesleyan Methodist, 1875.

Currey, Richard O. *A Geological Visit to the Virginia Copper Region*. Knoxville TN: Beckett, Haws, 1858.

Curtis, George T. *Digest of the Decisions of the Courts of Common Law and Admiralty*. Boston: Little, Brown, 1855.

Davis, Edwin Adams. "Social and Economic Life in West Feliciana Parish, Louisiana, 1830–1850, as Reflected in the Plantation Diary of Bennet H. Barrow." PhD diss., Louisiana State University, Baton Rouge, 1936.

Day, Bess Eileen. *The Mortons of Arbor Lodge: Their Early Years in Nebraska Territory*. Lincoln NE: iUniverse, 2001.

Debats, Donald A. "Hide and Seek: The Historian and Nineteenth-Century Social Accounting." *Social Science History* 15, no. 4 (Winter, 1991): 545–63.

DeForest, John William. *A Volunteer's Adventures: A Union Captain's Record of the Civil War*. New Haven CT: Yale University Press, 1946.

Deyle, Steven. *Carry Me Back: The Domestic Slave Trade in American Life*. New York: Oxford University Press, 2005.

Dictionary and Portrait Gallery of Representative Men of Chicago, Iowa and the World's Columbian Exposition. Chicago: H. C. Cooper, Jr., 1893.

Douglas, Stephen A. *Speech of Hon. S. A. Douglas, of Illinois, in the Senate, January 30, 1854, on the Nebraska Territory*. Washington DC: Sentinel Office, 1854.

Douglass, Frederick. *Narrative of the Life of Frederick Douglass, an American Slave*. Boston: Anti-Slavery Office, 1846. Kindle.

Drake, St. Clair, and Horace R. Cayton. *Black Metropolis: A Study of Negro Life in a Northern City*. New York: Harcourt, Brace and World, 1970.

Drew, Benjamin. *A North-Side View of Slavery: The Refugee or the Narratives of Fugitive Slaves in Canada*. Boston: John P. Jewett, 1856.

———. *The Refugee or the Narratives of Fugitive Slaves in Canada. Related by Themselves, with an Account of History and Condition of the Colored Population of Upper Canada*. Boston: J. P. Jewett, 1856.

Duke, Larry D. "Nebraska Territory." *Journal of the West*, 16, no. 2 (1977): 72–84.

Dunaway, Wilma A. "Slavery and Emancipation in the Mountain South: Sources, Evidence and Methods." Slave Narratives, Virginia Tech Online Archives. https://scholar.lib.vt.edu/faculty_archives/mountain_slavery/.

———. *Slavery in the American Mountain South*. New York: Cambridge University Press, 2003.

Dunbar, Erica Armstrong. *Never Caught: The Washingtons' Relentless Pursuit of Their Runaway Slave, Ona Judge*. New York: Simon and Schuster, 2017.

Edwards, Lewis C. *History of Richardson County, Nebraska*. Indianapolis: R. F. Bowen, 1917.

Ellis, Clifton, and Rebecca Ginsburg. "Introduction: Studying the Landscapes of North American Urban Slavery." In Ellis and Ginsburg, *Slavery in the City*, 3–20.

———, eds. *Slavery in the City: Architecture and Landscape of Urban Slavery in North America*. Charlottesville: University of Virginia Press, 2017.

Epps, Kristen. *Slavery on the Periphery: The Kansas-Missouri Border in the Antebellum and Civil War Eras*. Athens: University of Georgia Press, 2016.

Ernest, John. "The Reconstruction of Whiteness: William Wells Brown's *The Escape; or, A Leap for Freedom*." PMLA 113, no. 5 (October 1998): 1108–21.

Escott, Paul D. *Slavery Remembered: A Record of Twentieth-Century Slave Narratives*. Chapel Hill: University of North Carolina Press, 1979.

Etcheson, Nicole. *Bleeding Kansas: Contested Liberty in the Civil War Era*. Lawrence: University Press of Kansas, 2006.

———. "The Great Principle of Self-Government." *Kansas History: A Journal of the Central Plains*, 27 (2004): 14–29.

———. "Where Popular Sovereignty Worked: Nebraska Territory and the Kansas-Nebraska Act." In *The Nebraska-Kansas Act of 1854*, edited by John R Wunder and Joann M. Ross, 159–82. Lincoln: University of Nebraska Press, 2008.

Etulain, Richard W., ed. *Does the Frontier Experience Make America Exceptional?* Boston: Bedford St. Martin, 1999.

Ewing, Martha K. "Place Names in the Northwest Counties of Missouri." Master's thesis, University of Missouri–Columbia, 1929.

Faulkner, Charles H. "Slavery in Knoxville, Tennessee: In, but Not Entirely of, the South." In Ellis and Ginsburg, *Slavery in the City*, 125–41.

Federal Emergency Management Agency (FEMA). "The Lost River Town: History and Archaeology of Bayou Sarah." Baton Rouge LA: Coastal Environments, 2019.

Federal Writers' Project. *Slave Narratives: A Folk History of Slavery in the United States from Interviews with Former Slaves*. Washington DC, 1941.

Fehrenbacher, Don E. *The Dred Scott Case: Its Significance in American Law and Politics*. New York: Oxford University Press, 1981.

Fields, Bettye-Lou, and Jene Hughes, eds. *Grayson County: A History in Words and Pictures*. Winston-Salem NC: Hunter, Grayson County Historical Society, 1976.

Finkelman, Paul. *Slavery in the Courtroom: An Annotated Bibliography of American Cases*. Union NJ: Lawbook Exchange, 1998.

Flamming, Douglas. *African Americans in the West*. Santa Barbara CA: ABC-CLIO, Culture of the American West, 2009.

Foner, Eric. *Freedom's Lawmakers: A Directory of Black Officeholders during Reconstruction*. New York: Oxford University Press, 1993.

———. *Gateway to Freedom: The Hidden History of the Underground Railroad*. New York: W. W. Norton, 2015.

Forbes, Alice Ferguson. "Fenner Ferguson, First Chief Justice of Nebraska." In *Nebraska Law Bulletin*, 308–16. Lincoln: Nebraska State Bar Association, 1924.

Franklin, John Hope, and Loren Schweninger. *Runaway Slaves: Rebels on the Plantation*. New York: Oxford University Press, 2000.

Frazee, George. "The Iowa Fugitive Slave Case." *Annals of Iowa*, 4 (1899): 118–43.

Freehling, William. *Road to Disunion*. Vol. 2, *Secessionists Triumphant*. New York: Oxford University Press, 2007.

Frost, Karolyn Smardz. *A Fluid Frontier: Slavery, Resistance and the Underground Railroad in the Detroit River Borderland*. Detroit: Wayne State University Press, 2016.

Gara, Larry. "The Underground Railroad: Legend or Reality?" *Proceedings of the American Philosophical Society* 105, no. 3 (1961): 334–39.

Giddings, Joshua R. *Speeches in Congress*. Boston: John P. Jewett, 1853.

Glymph, Thavolia, *Out of the House of Bondage: The Transformation of the Plantation Household*. Cambridge: Cambridge University Press, 2008.

Goodspeed, Weston Arthur, and Daniel D. Healy. *History of Cook County, Illinois: Being a General Survey of Cook County History, Including a Condensed History of Chicago and Special Account of Districts outside the City Limits, from the Earliest Settlement to the Present Time*. 1909. Reprint, La Crosse WI: Brookhaven, 2000.

Grattan, Peachy R. *Reports of Cases in the Supreme Court of Appeals of Virginia*. Richmond: Colin and Nowlan, 1852.

Gudmestad, Robert H. *A Troublesome Commerce: The Transformation of the Interstate Slave Trade*. Baton Rouge: Louisiana State University Press, 2003.

Hagedorn, Ann. *Beyond the River: The Untold Story of the Heroes of the Underground Railroad*. New York: Simon and Schuster, 2004.

Hail, Susan Pearman. "Settlers' First Christmas." In *Nebraska City, 1854–1954*. Nebraska City: Women's Division of the Nebraska City Chamber of Commerce Centennial Committee, 1954.

Hall, Randal L. *Mountains on the Market: Industry, the Environment, and the South*. Lexington: University Press of Kentucky, 2012.

Hallock, Thomas. *From the Fallen Tree: Frontier Narratives, Environmental Politics, and the Roots of a National Pastoral, 1749–1826*. Chapel Hill: University of North Carolina Press, 2003.

Halty, Nina. "From Slaves to Subjects: Forging Freedom in the Canadian Legal System." Master's thesis, Florida Atlantic University, 2017.

Hämäläinen, Pekka, and Samuel Truett. "On Borderlands." *Journal of American History* 98, no. 2 (September 2011): 338–61.

Hamilton, Holman. *Prologue to Conflict: The Crisis and Compromise of 1850*. New York: W. W. Norton, 1966.

Hammond, John Craig. *Slavery, Freedom, and Expansion in the Early American West*. Charlottesville: University of Virginia Press, 2007.

Handy, Gertrude, and Robert W. Handy. *Someday: A Tale of Civil Bend by the River*. [Percival IA]: R. W. Handy, 1973.

Handy, Robert. *Civil Bend: Legend of Reality*. San Jose CA: Authors Choice Press, 2000.

Hartley, William G. "The Nauvoo Exodus and Crossing the Ice Myths." *Journal of Mormon History* 43, no. 1 (January 2017): 30–58.

Harvey, Augustus F. *Sketches of the Early Days of Nebraska City, Nebraska Territory, 1854–1860*. St. Louis: Western Insurance Review Book and Job Printing House, 1871.

Hening, William Waller. "What Persons Are Tithable." In *The Statutes at Large, Being a Collection of All the Laws of Virginia from the First Session of the Legislature, in the Year 1619*, 1:413. New York: R. & W. & G. Bartow, 1823.

Hepburn, Sharon A. Roger. "Following the North Star: Canada as a Haven for Nineteenth-Century American Blacks." *Michigan Historical Review* 25, no. 2 (Fall 1999): 91–126.

Herrold, Stanley. *The Rise of Aggressive Abolitionism: Addresses to the Slaves*. Lexington: University Press of Kentucky, 2004.

Hill, James L. "Migration of Blacks to Iowa 1820–1860." *Journal of Negro History* 66, no. 4 (Winter 1981–82): 289–303.

History of Holt and Atchison Counties, Missouri. St. Joseph MO: National Historic, 1882.

History of Jackson County, Indiana. Chicago: Brand & Fuller, 1886.

History of the Arkansas Valley, Colorado. Chicago: Baskin, 1881.

Holt, Michael F. *The Fate of Their Country: Politicians, Slavery Extension and the Coming of the Civil War*. New York: Hill and Wang, 2005.

Horne, William Iverson. "Negotiating Freedom: Reactions to Emancipation in West Feliciana Parish, Louisiana." Master's thesis, George Washington University, 2013.

Howe, Henry. *Historical Collections of Virginia*. Charleston SC: Babcock, 1846.

Hoyt, William D., Jr. "Thomas Donaldson on the Materials of History—1846: An Early Advocate of Newspapers as Sources." *Mississippi Valley Historical Review* 32, no. 1 (June 1945): 77–88.

Hughes, Amy, and Naomi J. Stubbs, eds. *A Player and a Gentleman: The Diary of Harry Watkins, Nineteenth-Century U.S. American Actor*. Lansing: University of Michigan Press, 2019.

Inscoe, John C. "Race and Racism in Nineteenth-Century Southern Appalachia: Myths, Realities, and Ambiguities." In *Appalachia in the Making: The Mountain South in the Nineteenth Century*, edited by Mary Beth Pudup, Dwight B Billings, and Altina L. Waller, 103–31. Chapel Hill: University of North Carolina Press, 1995.

Jacobs, Harriet A. *Incidents in the Life of a Slave Girl, Written by Herself.* 1861. Reprint, New York: Dover Edition, 2001.

Johnson, Clifton H. "The American Missionary Association, 1846–1861: A Study of Christian Abolitionism." PhD diss., University of North Carolina, 1958.

Johnson, Harrison. *Johnson's History of Nebraska.* Omaha: H. Gibson Herald, 1880.

Jones, Kelly Houston. "'A Rough, Saucy Set of Hands to Manage': Slave Resistance in Arkansas." *Arkansas Historical Quarterly* 71, no. 1 (Spring 2012): 1–21.

Jones-Rogers, Stephanie E. *They Were Her Property: White Women as Slave Owners in the American South.* New Haven CT: Yale University Press, 2019.

Kammer, Sean M. "Public Opinion Is More Than Law: Popular Sovereignty and Vigilantism in the Nebraska Territory." *Great Plains Quarterly* 31, no. 4 (2011): 309–24.

Karp, Matthew. "The People's Revolution of 1856: Antislavery Populism, National Politics, and the Emergence of the Republican Party." *Journal of the Civil War Era* 9, no. 4 (2019): 524–45.

Keckley, Elizabeth. *Behind the Scenes: Thirty Years a Slave and Four Years in the White House.* New York: G. W. Carleton, 1868.

Keele, Luke, William Cubbison, and Ismail White. "Suppressing Black Votes: A Historical Case Study of Voting Restrictions in Louisiana." *American Political Science Review* 116, no. 1 (2021): 694–700.

Kerwin, Lee Klein. *Frontiers of Historical Imagination: Narrating the European Conquest of Native America, 1890–1990.* Berkeley: University of California Press, 1997.

Kolchin, Peter. *American Slavery, 1619–1877.* New York: Hill and Wang, 2003.

Kukis, Margaret. "Master and Slaves at Work in the North Carolina Piedmont: The Nicholas Bryor Massenburg Plantation, 1834–1861." Master's thesis, Rice University, 1993.

Lamar, Howard Roberts. *Dakota Territory, 1861–1889: A Study of Frontier Politics.* New Haven CT: Yale University Press, 1956.

———. *The Far Southwest, 1846–1912: A Territorial History.* Rev. ed. Albuquerque: University of New Mexico Press, 2000.

Landon, Fred. "The Negro Migration to Canada after the Passing of the Fugitive Slave Act." *Journal of Negro History* 5, no. 1 (1920): 22–36.

———. "Social Conditions among the Negroes in Upper Canada before 1865." *Report for the Ontario Historical Society, Papers and Records* 22 (1924): 144–61.

Laporc, Jill. "Historians Who Love Too Much: Reflections on Microhistory and Biography." *Journal of American History* 88, no. 1 (June 2001): 129–44.

Laroche, Cheryl Janifer. "Coerced but Not Subdued: The Gendered Resistance of Women Escaping Slavery." In *Gendered Resistance: Women, Slavery, and the Legacy of Margaret Garner*, edited by Mary E. Frederickson and Delores M. Walters, 49–76. Urbana: University of Illinois Press, 2013.

———. *The Geography of Resistance: Free Black Communities and the Underground Railroad*. Urbana: University of Illinois Press, 2014.

Larson, Kate Clifford. *Bound for the Promised Land*. New York: Random House, 2009.

———. "Racing for Freedom: Harriet Tubman's Underground Railroad Network through New York." *Afro-Americans in New York Life and History* 36, no. 1 (January 2012): 7–33.

Larson, T. A. *History of Wyoming*. 2nd ed. Lincoln: University of Nebraska Press, 1978.

Lehman, Christopher P. *Slavery in the Upper Mississippi Valley, 1787–1865; A History of Human Bondage in Illinois, Iowa, Minnesota and Wisconsin*. Jefferson NC: McFarland, 2011.

Limerick, Patricia Nelson. *The Legacy of Conquest: The Unbroken Past of the American West*. New York: W. W. Norton, 1987.

Lingenfelter, Littleberry. *History of Fremont County, Iowa: Containing a History of the County, Its Cities, Towns, Etc., a Biographical Directory of Many of Its Leading Citizens . . . Etc.* Des Moines: Iowa Historical, 1881.

Lubet, Steven. *Fugitive Justice: Runaways, Rescuers, and Slavery on Trial*. Cambridge MA: Harvard University Press, 2010.

Maizlish, Stephen E. *A Strife of Tongues: The Compromise of 1850 and the Ideological Foundations of the American Civil War*. Charlottesville: University of Virginia Press, 2018.

Majors, Alexander. *Seventy Years on the Frontier: Alexander Majors' Memoirs of a Lifetime on the Border*. Lincoln: University of Nebraska Press, 1989.

Malavasic, Alice Elizabeth. *The F Street Mess: How Southern Senators Rewrote the Kansas-Nebraska Act*. Chapel Hill: University of North Carolina Press, 2017.

McDonald, J. J. *Life in Old Virginia*. Norfolk: Old Virginia, 1907.

McFayden, Kenneth. "Destroyer in Our Midst: Wesleyan Missionary Jarvis C. Bacon's Labors in Grayson County, Virginia, 1845–1852." Master's thesis, Emory & Henry College, 2013.

McMahon, Edward. "Stephen A. Douglas: A Study of the Attempt to Settle the Question of Slavery in the Territories by the Application of Popular Sovereignty, 1850–1860." *Washington Historical Quarterly* 2, no. 3 (1908): 209–32.

Meese, David E. "Origins of the Buchanan-Douglas Feud Reconsidered." *Journal of the Illinois State Historical Society* 67, no. 2 (1974): 154–74.

Merritt, William. *A History of the County of Montgomery from the Earliest Days to 1906*. Red Oak IA: Express, 1906.

Miles, Tiya. *Ties That Bind: The Story of an Afro-Cherokee Family in Slavery and Freedom*. Berkeley: University of California Press, 2005.

Miller, Mark F. *Dear Old Roanoke: A Sesquicentennial Portrait, 1842–1992*. Macon GA: Mercer University Press, 1992.

Mooar, George. *Cummings Memorial: A Genealogical History of the Descendants of Isaac Cummings*. New York: B. F. Cummings, 1903.

Moore, Courtney A. "Free in Thought, Fettered in Action: Enslaved Adolescent Females in the Slave South." PhD diss., University of Florida, 2010.

Moore, Shirley Ann Wilson. *Sweet Freedom's Plains: African Americans on the Overland Trails, 1840–1869*. Norman: University of Oklahoma Press, 2008.

Morgans, James Patrick. *John Todd and the Underground Railroad: Biography of an Iowa Abolitionist*. Jefferson NC: McFarland, 2006.

Morton, J. Sterling, and Albert Watkins. *History of Nebraska: A History of Nebraska from the Earliest Explorations of the Trans-Mississippi Region*. Vol. 3. Lincoln NE: Western, 1913.

——. *Illustrated History of Nebraska: A History of Nebraska from the Earliest Explorations of the Trans-Mississippi Region*. Vols. 1–2. Edited by George L. Miller. Lincoln NE: Jacob North, 1906–7.

Nebraska City and Otoe County Directory, 1881–1882. Nebraska City: Wood and Sroat, 1882.

Nebraska City Directory, 1870. Nebraska City: J. M. Wolfe, 1870. Typescript copy at Morton James Library, Nebraska City.

Nebraska State Historical Society. *Transactions and Reports of the Nebraska State Historical Society*. Vols. 1–3. Lincoln: State Journal, 1885, 1887, 1892.

Nebraska Territory. *Council Journal of the Legislative Assembly of the Territory of Nebraska, Fifth Session*. Thomas Morton and Theodore H. Robertson, 1859.

——. *Council Journal of the Legislative Assembly of the Territory of Nebraska, Sixth Session*. Thomas Morton, 1860.

——. *House Journal of the Legislative Assembly of the Territory of Nebraska, Fifth Session*. Nebraska City: Thomas Morton, 1859.

——. *House Journal of the Legislative Assembly of the Territory of Nebraska, Sixth Session*. Nebraska City: Thomas Morton, 1860.

——. *Journal of the House of Representatives. At the Fourth Session of the General Assembly of the Territory of Nebraska*. Omaha: Edwin S. Chapman, 1858.

——. *Laws, Joint Resolutions, and Memorials Passed at the Second Session of the Legislative Assembly of the Territory of Nebraska*. Omaha City: Hadley D. Johnson, 1856.

Nichols, Roy F. "The Territories: Seedbeds of Democracy." *Nebraska History* 35 (1954): 159–72.

Noble, Glenn. *John Brown and the Jim Lane Trail*. Broken Bow NE: Purcells, 1977.

Norman, William M. *A Portion of My Life: Being a Short and Imperfect History Written While a Prisoner of War on Johnson's Island, 1864*. Winston-Salem NC: J. F. Blair, 1959. Kindle.

Nuckolls, Benjamin Floyd. *Pioneer Settlers of Grayson County, Virginia*. Bristol TN: King, 1914.

Nuckolls, Charles R. *The Roses: The Nuckolls Family, the Lyman Family, and One Hundred Fifty Immigrants Who Helped Shape America*. New York: iUniverse, 2010.

Nuermberger, Ruth K., ed. "Letters from Pioneer Nebraska by Edward Randolph Harden: Territorial Judge, 1854–1856." *Nebraska History* 27 (1946): 18–46.

Nye, Russell B. *Fettered Freedom: Civil Liberties and the Slavery Controversy, 1830–1860*. East Lansing: Michigan State University Press, 1963.

Oakes, James. "The Political Significance of Slave Resistance." *History Workshop* 22, Special American Issue (Autumn 1986): 89–107.

Oertel, Kristin Tegtmeier. *Bleeding Borders: Race, Gender and Violence in Pre–Civil War Kansas*. Baton Rouge: Louisiana State University Press, 2009.

Olson, James C. *J. Sterling Morton*. Lincoln, University of Nebraska Press, 1942.

Olson, James C., Ronald C. Naugle, and John J. Montag. *History of Nebraska*. 4th ed. Lincoln: University of Nebraska Press, 2015.

Pasley, Jeffrey L., and John Craig Hammond. *A Fire Bell in the Past: The Missouri Crisis at 200*. Vol. 1, *Western Slavery, National Impasse*. Columbia: University of Missouri Press, 2021.

Paterson, David E. "Slavery, Slaves, and Cash in a Georgia Village, 1825–1865." *Journal of Southern History* 75, no. 4 (November 2009): 879–930.

Perley, Oman Ray. *The Repeal of the Missouri Compromise: Its Origin and Authorship*. Cleveland OH: Arthur H. Clark, 1909. https://archive.org/details/repealofmissouri00raypuoft/page/n8/mode/2up.

Peterson, Henry K. "The First Decision Rendered by the Supreme Court of Iowa." *Annals of Iowa* 34, no. 4 (1958): 304–7.

Phillips, Ulrich Bonnell. *American Negro Slavery: A Survey of the Supply, Employment and Control of Negro Labor as Determined by the Plantation Regime*. New York: D. Appleton, 1918. https://archive.org/details/americannegrosla00phil/page/n8/mode/2up.

Poeschl, Peg. "Housing Nebraska's Governors: 1854–1980." *Nebraska History* 61 (1980): 259–79.

Portrait and Biographical Album of Otoe and Cass Counties, Nebraska. Chicago: Chapman Bros., 1889.

Potter, David M. *The Impending Crisis: America before the Civil War, 1848–1861*. Completed and edited by Don E. Fehrenbacher. 1977. Reprint, New York: HarperCollins, 2011.

Potter, James E. "Fact and Folklore in the Story of John Brown's Cave and the Underground Railroad in Nebraska." *Nebraska History* 83 (2002): 73–88.

———. *Standing Firmly by the Flag: Nebraska Territory and the Civil War, 1861–1867*. Lincoln: University of Nebraska Press, 2012.

Potts, James Byron. "Nebraska Territory, 1854–1867: A Study of Frontier Politics." PhD diss., University of Nebraska, 1973.

———. "North of 'Bleeding Kansas': The 1850s Political Crisis in Nebraska Territory." *Nebraska History* 73 (1992): 110–18.

Price, David H. "Sectionalism in Nebraska: When Kansas Considered Annexing Southern Nebraska, 1856–1860." *Nebraska History* 53 (1970): 387–409.

Pudup, Mary Beth, Dwight B. Billings, and Altina L. Waller, eds. *Appalachia in the Making: The Mountain South in the Nineteenth Century*. Chapel Hill: University of North Carolina Press, 1995.

Rawley, James A. *Race and Politics: Bleeding Kansas and the Coming of the Civil War*. Philadelphia: Lippincott, 1969.

Reed, Christopher Robert. "African American Life in Antebellum Chicago, 1833–1860." *Journal of the Illinois State Historical Society* 94 (Winter 2001–2): 356–82.

———. "The Early African American Settlement of Chicago, 1833–1830." *Journal of the Illinois State Historical Society* (1998): 108, no. 304 (Fall/Winter 2015): 211–65.

Reese, Renford. "Canada: The Promised Land for U.S. Slaves." *Western Journal of Black Studies* 35 (2011): 208–16.

Regosin, Elizabeth Ann, and Donald Robert Shaffer. *Voices of Emancipation: Understanding Slavery, the Civil War, and Reconstruction through the U.S. Pension Bureau Files*. New York: New York University Press, 2008.

Reid, Richard. "The 1870 United States Census and Black Underenumeration: A Test Case from North Carolina." *Histoire Sociale / Social History* 28 (1995): 487–99.

Richardson, James D., ed. *A Compilation of the Messages and Papers of the Presidents*. Vol. 5, part 4, *James Buchanan, March 4, 1857, to March 4, 1861*. Washington DC, 1899. https://www.gutenberg.org/ebooks/11021.

Riddell, William Renwick. "Slave in Upper Canada." *Journal of Criminal Law and Criminology* 14, no. 2 (May 1923–February 1924): 249–78.

Rives, John C., ed. *Appendix to the Congressional Globe, Containing Speeches, Important State Papers, Laws, etc., of the Third Session, Thirty-Fourth Congress*. Washington DC: Congressional Globe, 1857.

Robinson, Gwendolyn, and John W. Robinson. *Seek the Truth: A Story of Chatham's Black Community*. Chatham ON: self-published, 1989.

Rohrbough, Malcolm J. *Trans-Appalachian Frontier: People, Societies, and Institutions, 1775–1850*. Bloomington: Indiana University Press, 2008.

Rothman, Adam. *Slave Country*. Cambridge MA: Harvard University Press, 2009.

Rubenstein, D. S. "A History of the County Court in Virginia." Honors thesis, University of Richmond, 1937.

Salafia, Matthew. *Slavery's Borderland: Freedom and Bondage along the Ohio River*. Philadelphia: University of Pennsylvania Press, 2013.

Saler, Bethel. *Settler's Empire: Colonialism and State Formation in America's Old Northwest*. Philadelphia: University of Pennsylvania Press, 2019.

Sanders, Eulanda A. "African American Slave Appearance: Cultural Analysis of Slave Women's Narratives." PhD diss., University of Nebraska–Lincoln, 1997.

Sanford, Mollie Dorsey. *Mollie: The Journal of Mollie Dorsey Sanford in Nebraska and Colorado Territories*. 1959. Reprint, Lincoln: University of Nebraska Press, 2003.

Schneiders, Robert Kelley. *Unruly River: Two Centuries of Change along the Missouri*. Lawrence: University Press of Kansas, 1999.

Schwartz, Marie Jenkins. *Born in Bondage: Growing Up Enslaved in the Antebellum South*. Cambridge MA: Harvard University Press, 2000.

Shambaugh, Benjamin F., ed. *The Messages and Proclamations of the Governors of Iowa*. Iowa City: Iowa State Historical Society, 1903.

Shapiro, Herbert. "The Ku Klux Klan during Reconstruction: The South Carolina Episode." *Journal of Negro History* 49, no. 1 (January 1964): 34–55.

Shearer, Benjamin F., ed. *The Uniting States: The Story of Statehood for the Fifty United States*. Vol. 2, *Louisiana to Ohio*. Westport CT: Greenwood, 2004.

Sheldon, Addison E. *History and Stories of Nebraska*. Chicago: University Publishing Company, 1914.

———. *Nebraska: The Land and the People*. Chicago: Lewis, 1931.

———, ed. *Nebraska Blue Book*. Lincoln: Nebraska Legislative Bureau, 1915.

Shephard, E. Lee. "This Being Court Day: Courthouses and Community Life in Rural Virginia." *Virginia Magazine of History and Biography* 103, no. 4 (October 1995): 459–70.

Sheppard, Robert Dickinson, and Harvey B. Hurd. *History of Northwestern University and Evanston*. Chicago: Munsell, 1906.

Siebert, Wilbur H. "Light on the Underground Railroad." *American Historical Review* 1, no. 3 (1896): 455–63.

———. *The Underground Railroad from Slavery to Freedom: A Comprehensive History*. New York: Macmillan, 1898.

———. "Underground Railroad in Michigan." *Detroit Historical Monthly* 1, no. 1 (1923): 14–15.

Silliman, Lee. "'Up This Great River': Daniel Weston's Missouri Steamboat Diary." *Montana Magazine of Western History* 30, no. 3 (Summer 1980): 32–41.

Silverman, Jason Howard. "Unwelcome Guests: American Fugitive Slaves in Canada, 1830–1860." PhD diss., University of Kentucky, 1981.

———. *Unwelcome Guests: Canada West's Response to American Fugitive Slaves, 1800–1865*. Millwood NY: Associated Faculty, 1985.

Simpson, Donald George. *Under the North Star: Black Communities in Upper Canada*. Trenton NJ: Africa World, 2005.

Smedley, Robert. *History of the Underground Railroad in Chester and the Neighboring Counties of Pennsylvania*. Lancaster PA: Office of the Journal, 1883. https://archive.org/details/DKC0089.

Snodgrass, Mary Ellen. *The Underground Railroad: An Encyclopedia of People, Places, and Operations*. New York: Routledge, 2015.

Soike, Lowell. *Busy in the Cause: Iowa, the Free-State Struggle in the West, and the Prelude to the Civil War*. Lincoln: University of Nebraska Press, 2014.

———. "Iowa's Anti-Slavery Movement." *Iowa Heritage Illustrated* 90, no. 2 (Summer 2009): 44–49.

———. *Necessary Courage: Iowa's Underground Railway in the Struggle against Slavery*. Iowa City: University of Iowa Press, 2013.

Speer, John. *Life of Gen. James H. Lane: "The Liberator of Kansas."* 2nd ed. Garden City KS: John Speer, 1897.

Spindel, Donna J. "Assessing Memory: Twentieth-Century Slave Narratives Reconsidered." *Journal of Interdisciplinary History* 27, no. 2 (1996): 247–61.

Stampp, Kenneth. *The Peculiar Institution: Slavery in the Ante-Bellum South*. New York: Vintage Books, 1956.

Stapel, Henry Frederick. *Biographical History of Atchison County, Missouri*. Rock Port MO: Atchison County Mail, 1905.

"Steaming up the Missouri." *Cosmopolitan Art Journal* 2, no. 1 (December 1857): 18–21.

Steckel, Richard H. "The Quality of Census Data for Historical Inquiry: A Research Agenda." *Social Science History* 15, no. 4 (1991): 579–99.

Still, William. *Still's Underground Rail Road Records*. 2nd ed. Philadelphia: William Still, 1886.

———. *The Underground Rail Road*. Philadelphia: Porter & Coates, 1872.

St. Louis Directory, 1859. St. Louis: R. V. Kennedy, 1859. http://repository.wustl.edu/concern/texts/wp988n581.

Stone, Robert Benjamin. "The Legislative Struggle for Civil Rights in Iowa, 1947–1965." Master's thesis, Iowa State University, Ames, 1990.

Stowe, Harriet Beecher. *A Key to Uncle Tom's Cabin*. Boston: John P. Jewett, 1853.

———. *Uncle Tom's Cabin, or, Life among the Lowly*. 1851. Reprint, New York: Houghton, Mifflin, 1896.

Stuart, Addison A. *Iowa Colonels and Regiments: Being a History of Iowa Regiments in the War of the Rebellion*. Des Moines: Mills, 1865.

Tademy, Lalita. *Cane River*. New York: Warner Books, 2001.

Tadman, Michael. "The Demographic Cost of Sugar: Debates on Slave Societies and Natural Increase in the Americas." *American Historical Review* 105 (2000): 1534–75.

———. *Speculators and Slaves: Masters, Traders, and Slaves in the Old South*. Madison: University of Wisconsin Press, 1989.

Taylor, Quintard. *In Search of the Racial Frontier: African Americans in the American West, 1528–1990*. New York: W. W. Norton, 1999.

Taylor, Quintard, and Shirley Ann Wilson Moore. *African American Women Confront the West, 1600–2000*. Norman: University of Oklahoma Press, 2008.

Tenth Annual Council of the Protestant Episcopal Church, Diocese of Nebraska. Omaha: Omaha Book Printer, 1877.

Thatcher, Oliver Joseph. *The Library of Original Sources, 1833–1865*. New York: Chicago University Research Extension, 1907.

Thavenet, Dennis. "The Territorial Governorship: Nebraska Territory as Example." *Nebraska History* 51 (1970): 386–409.

Thomas, William G. *A Question of Freedom: The Families Who Challenged Slavery from the Nation's Founding to the Civil War*. New Haven CT: Yale University Press, 2020.

Thompson, V. Elaine. *Clinton, Louisiana: Society, Politics, and Race Relations in a Nineteenth-Century Southern Small Town*. Lafayette: University of Louisiana Press, 2003.

Tipton, Thomas Weston. *Forty Years of Nebraska: At Home and in Congress*. Lincoln NE: State Journal, 1902.

Todd, John. *Early Settlement and Growth of Western Iowa, or Reminiscences*. Des Moines: Historical Department of Iowa, 1906.

Tolbert, Lisa. "Murder in Franklin: The Mysteries of Small-Town Slavery." *Tennessee Historical Quarterly* 67, no. 4 (Winter 1998): 204–17.

Trexler, Harrison Anthony. "Slavery in Missouri, 1804–1865." PhD diss., Johns Hopkins University, Baltimore, 1914.

Troup, Mrs. Alexander C. [Elsie DeCou]. *Once upon a Time in Nebraska*. 2nd ed. Omaha: Colonial Dames, 1916.

True, Ransom. "The Louisa Economy in the Years 1765–1812." *Louisa County Historical Magazine* 7, no. 1 (1975): 21–23.

Turnmire, Rebekah Elaine. "'Worthy to Be Classed': Slavery and Its Legacy in Grayson County, Virginia." Honors thesis, College of William and Mary, 2013. https://scholarworks.wm.edu/honorstheses/643.

Twain, Mark. *Life on the Mississippi*. New York: Harper and Brothers, 1917. www.archive.org.

Urniss, Jack. "Devolved Democracy: Federalism and the Party Politics of the Late Antebellum North." *Journal of the Civil War Era* 9, no. 4 (2019): 546–68.

U.S. Census Bureau (USCB). *Decennial Census of the United States*. Nos. 5–16. Washington DC: National Archives and Records Administration, 1830–1940.

U.S. Congress. *A Century of Lawmaking for a New Nation: U.S. Congressional Documents and Debates, 1774–1875*. Statutes at Large. Library of Congress, Washington DC.

———. *Report of the Joint Select Committee to Inquire into the Condition of Affairs in the Late Insurrectionary States, Made to the Two Houses of Congress February 19, 1872*. Washington DC: U.S. Government Printing Office, 1872.

Watkins, Albert, ed. *Publications of the Nebraska State Historical Society*. Vol. 20. Lincoln: Nebraska State Historical Society, 1922.

Wayne, Michael. "The Black Population of Canada West on the Eve of the Civil War." *Social History* 28 (1995): 465–85.

Webb, Barbara L. "Plantation Performance of the 1890s." *Theatre Journal* 56, no. 1 (March 2004): 63–82.

Wharton, Vernon Lane. *The Negro in Mississippi 1865–1890*. New York: Harper & Row, 1947.

White, Deborah Gray. *Ar'n't I a Woman? Female Slaves in the Plantation South*. Rev. ed. New York: W. W. Norton, 1999.

Wiecek, William M. "Slavery and Abolition before the United States Supreme Court, 1820–1860." *Journal of American History* 65, no. 1 (June 1978): 34–59.

Williams, George W. *History of the Negro Race in America from 1619 to 1880: Negroes as Slave, as Soldiers, and as Citizens*. New York: G. P. Putnam's Sons, 1883.

Williams, Helena Roberta. "Old Wyoming." *Nebraska History* 27, no. 2 (April–June 1936): 78–90.

Williams, Keith Alphonso. "Taking Flight: Fugitive Slaves and the Literary Imagination." PhD diss., Cornell University, 2001.

Winks, Robin. *The Blacks in Canada: A History*. 2nd ed. Montréal: McGill-Queen's University Press, 2014.

Wishart, David J. *Unspeakable Sadness: The Dispossession of the Nebraska Indians*. 1994. Reprint, Lincoln: University of Nebraska Press, 1997.

Wood, Anthony William. "The Erosion of the Racial Frontier: Settler Colonialism and the History of Black Montana, 1880–1930." Master's thesis, Montana State University, April 2018.

Work, Monroe N., Thomas A. Staples, H. A. Wallace, Kelly Miller, Whitefield McKinlay, Samuel E. Lacy, R. L. Smith, and H. R. McIlwaine. "Some Negro Members of Reconstruction Convention and Legislatures and of Congress," *Journal of Negro History* 5, no. 1 (January 1920): 63–119.

Worsham, Gibson. "A Survey of Historic Architecture in Grayson County, Virginia Including the Towns of Independence and Fries." Richmond: Historic 1908 Courthouse Foundation, 2001–2.

Wunder, John R., and Joann M. Ross, eds. *The Nebraska-Kansas Act of 1854*. Lincoln: University of Nebraska Press, 2008.

Younger, Richard D. "Southern Grand Juries and Slavery." *Journal of Negro History* 40, no. 2 (1955): 166–78.

Zorn, Roman J. "An Arkansas Fugitive Incident and Its International Repercussions." *Arkansas Historical Quarterly* 16, no. 2 (Summer 1957): 139–40.

Index

Italicized page numbers refer to illustrations.

Acton, Asa M., 144
agriculture, in Atchison County MO, 38
Aimy (enslaved), 15–16, 183n24
Aird, Hugh, 167
Anderson, Galusha, 129
Anderson, Garland, 25–26, 27–28
Anderson, George, 139
Anderson, John W., 162
Anthony, Horace, 106
antislavery Christians, 20
Appalachian slavery. *See* mountain slavery
Armstrong, John, 82
Atchison County MO, 32, 36, 37, 38, 78, 87–88
Avery, Egbert (Edgar), 115–16

Bacon, Jarvis C., 19, 20–23, 25
Ballard (enslaved), 76
Baltimore Sun, 132
Barnett, Dick Lewis, 150
Bartlett, Alfred, 23–24, 25–26
Bartlett, Samuel, 23–24, 25–26
Baughman, Christopher C., 31
Baxter, James, 102
Beck, N. B., 127, 129–30, 131
Beebe, Mary, 133
Beecher Stowe, Harriet, 106
Bellevue Gazette, 80
Bennet, Hiram P., 47, 53, 54, 55, 81, 109

Bennet, William, 109
Berlin, Ira, 7, 104
Biddeford Maine and Eastern Journal, 52
Bish, James, 2
Bittle, David, 31
Bixby, Amos and Augusta, 102
Black, Samuel W., 121–22, 145–46
Blackett, Richard J. M., 3
Blackman, Harvey C., 123–24
Black Republicans, 3, 89, 119, 143, 144
Blanchard, Ira, 93, 95–96, 99, 115, 116, 128, 129–30, 202n10
Bleeding Kansas, 3, 108
Borchers, Henry Augustus "Gus," 36–37, 176
Borchers, Rosamond Nuckolls, 36–37, 176, 187n13
Botts, Barney, 165
Boulware, John, 49, 81
Bourne, Harvey Gordon, 41–42, 86, 110, 176, 188n32
Bourne, Rosamond, 15
Bourne, William, 15, 176
Bourne Curran, Mary, 156
Bourne Dickinson, Molly, 176
Bourne Hail, Rosa, 176
Bourne Nuckolls, Frances, 42, 67, 176, 188n32
Bourne Nuckolls, Lucinda: control of, 66–67; death of, 157; description of,

Bourne Nuckolls, Lucinda (*cont.*) 32–33; family of, 36, 41, 176, 188n32; home of, 59–61, *61*; letters of, 83–84, 110, 155–57, 168; moving of, 33, 153, 154, 156–57; photo of, *35*; quote of, 68, 88; sewing society of, 67–68; social life of, 67–69; viewpoint of, 93

Bradford, Alexander, 186–87n5

Bradford, Allen A., 32, 47, 53, 99–100, 115

Bradley, James, 85

Brooke, Ed, 129–30

Brown, Albert G., 132

Brown, James E., 21, 22–23, 27–28

Brown, John, 4, 114, 146, 152

Buchanan, James, 79, 80, 122, 137

Buckingham, Peregrine, 22

Burbanks, J. A., 125

Burke, Diane Mutti, 8, 9, 67, 84

Burke, Sarah Woods, 16

Burlington Daily Hawk-Eye, 72, 103

Burlington Weekly Hawk-Eye, 103

Burt, Armistead, 50–51

Burt, Francis, 50–51, 190n12

Butler, Alfred, 163, 164

Butler, Andrew, 123

Butler, Maria, 163, 164

Calvin (enslaved), 56

Canada, 146, 150–51, 152, 153

Cass, Lewis, 42

Charles Raleigh "Rolly" (enslaved), 56, 87, 135, 170

Charlotte (enslaved), 75

Cheyenne Leader, 154–55

Cheyenne WY, Stephen Nuckolls in, 154

Chicago Daily Tribune, 139–40

Chicago Free Press, 72

Chicago IL, 126, 132–40

Chicago Tribune, 138, 139, 143–44, 146

children, in slavery, 18. *See also specific children*

Christian abolitionists, 20

church, slave attendance of, 39

Civil Bend IA, 92–93, 95–98, 100, 101, 202n7

Civil War, end of, 146

Clark (enslaved and freed by John Cornutt), 27

Clay, Henry, 4, 43, 45

Clayton (enslaved), 56, 87, 170

Clements, John, 23–24, 25–26, 27

Clifford, Nathan, 140

Clinton County IA, 102, 104–5

Colfax, Schuyler, 161

Coltrane, Ira, 80

Compromise of 1850, 43

Corneau, Stephen, 132

Cornutt, John, 22, 25, 27

Council Bluffs Non-Pareil, 128

Cowles, Charles H., 47, 48

Cox, David, 23

Craig, James, 128

Craig, Seth H., 128, 131

Crooks, Adam, 19, 20, 25

Crosby, Thomas, 160

Crowdes, Emily Graves, 40

Cuming, Thomas, 112

Cummings, Origen, 116, 205n33

Curran, Mary Bourne, 156

Curtis, Benjamin, 140

Daily, Samuel G., 112–14, 118

Danites, in Democrat party, 138

Davis, J. R., 89

Dawson, Jacob, 91–92

DesLondes, Edward A., 118

Detroit MI, 151

DeWolf, Calvin, 135, 139

Dick (enslaved), 100

Dickinson, Martin, 176
Dickinson, Molly Bourne, 176
Dickinson, William, 181n7
Doane, George W., 118, 119
Dorsey Sanford, Mollie, 65, 85
Douglas, Stephen A., 6, 45, 51–52
Douglas Democrats, 138
Douglass, Frederick, 69, 150
Downs, Hiram P., 49, 55
Dred Scott decision, 107–8, 122, 139, 140
Drummond, Thomas, 139–40
Dumesnil, Theodule, 169
Dunaway, Wilma, 8
Dundy, E. S., 143

economy, downturn of, 81
Edwards, Lewis C., 130
Eliza (enslaved) (Frances Overton), 102–3
Eliza Caroline (enslaved), 56
Ely, Thomas, 78
Epps, Kristen, 8, 9
escapees. *See* freedom seekers
Etcheson, Nicole, 145
executions, 26–27, 89, 185–86n56

Fairfield Ledger, 70, 71
Fehrenbacher, Don E., 107–8
Ferguson, Fenner, 54
Fillmore, Millard, 79
Fleming, William, 117
Flenoy, Celia Toucey, 151
Fort Kearny, 2, 49
Fort Randall, 2
Francis (enslaved and freed by John Cornutt), 27
Franklin, John Hope, 90, 160
Frazee, George, 100
freedom seekers: advantages of, 92; article regarding, 95; in Canada, 151; due process regarding, 43–44; hanging of, 26–27, 89, 185–86n56; in Nebraska City NE, 124–25; population of, 179n7; statistics regarding, 3. *See also specific persons*
Frémont, John C., 79–80
Fremont Herald, 101–2
Fugitive Slave Law of 1793, 43
Fugitive Slave Law of 1850, 43, 99, 100, 115, 151
fugitive slaves. *See* freedom seekers
Fulton, Andrew Steele, 22
Fulton, Samuel, 25–26
Furnas, Robert W., 113

Garland, Charles, 12, 14, *18*, 181n7
Garland Nuckolls, Mary, 11, 12–13, 176
Garner, Eliza, 127
Garner, Henry, 111, 127–29
Garner, Maria, 127, 128–29
Garner family, 96–97, 100. *See also specific members*
Garner v. Nuckolls, 111
Gaston, Alexander, 115–16
Gaston, George, 115, 116, 128
Gaston Platt, Elvira, 95
Gay, Sydney Howard, 85
geography, four corners, 4, *5*
geography, magic of, 3–7, 52, 143, 149–50
George (enslaved and freed by John Cornutt), 27
Giddings, Joshua R., 44
Gilman, John, 156
Gordon-Reed, Annette, 1
Granny Beck (enslaved), 15
Grant, Ulysses S., 161
Graves, Sarah Frances Shaw, 39–40
Graves Crowdes, Emily, 40
Grayson, Celia: background of, 6, 8, 11; daily life of, 17, 37, 38, 40, 64; as

Index   251

Grayson, Celia: (*cont.*)
  enticed, 104; escape of, 1, 91–93, 99, *105*, 106; family of, 15, 56, 167–68, 174–75; freedom of movement of, 66; home of, 59–61, *61*; moving of, 31, 33, 62; resistance of, 84; search for, 93, 95–96, 97–98, 102–3, 136–37; significance and symbolism of, 10, 121; value of, 116–17
Grayson, Edith, 57
Grayson, Eliza: background of, 6, 8, 11; in Canada, 146, 150–51, 153; capture of, 133–34; case regarding, 132–40; as celebrity, 138; daily life of, 17, 37, 38, 40, 64; description of, 2; as enticed, 104; escape of, 1, 91–93, 99, *105*, 106, 135; family of, 15, 56, 167–68, 174–75; freedom of movement of, 66; home of, 59–61, *61*; as Lottie Grayson, 126; moving of, 31, 33, 62; resistance of, 84; search for, 93, 95–96, 97–98, 102–3, 132–40, 136–37; significance and symbolism of, 10, 121, 137; value of, 116–17; work of, 133; writings regarding, 143–44, 146
Grayson, Shack (Jackson/Jack), 33, 63–64, 66, 95, 168–69
Grayson, Shade, 56, 57, 58, 66, 77, 87, 136, 169–70
Grayson County VA: Celia and Eliza in, 8; courthouse in, 184n39; execution in, 26–27; exercise of power in, 40–41; Nuckolls family in, 13–14; photo of, *12*; religious life in, 19–23; slave catching in, 23–29; slavery in, 15, 16–17; slavery viewpoint in, 19; Vigilance Committee, 26, 27–28
Greer, Shadrack, 25–26
Grimes, James, 51

Hackler, Conrad, 16–17
Hadden, John, 47
Hail (Hale) Nuckolls, Lucinda, 11, 14, 54, 86
Hail, Curran, 24, 109, 198n67
Hail, Fielden L., 42, 75, 76
Hail, Frances, 76
Hail, G. W., 110
Hail, Martin, 75–76
Hail, Rosa Bourne, 176
Hail, Stephen, 176
Hail, Susan Pearman, 198n67
Hail, William B., 24, 25–26, 27, 42, 81, 109, 141–42, 176, 196n41
Hail Mitchell, Sophia, 74, 76
Hale, Lewis, *17*
Hale, Stephen, 21, 22
Hamburg IA, 37
Hampton, Belle Tarwater, 165
Hampton, Edith Schooler, 158–63, 222n52
Hampton, Georgia Robinson, 164
Hampton, Gilbert, 149, 160–61, 162, 221–22n43
Hampton, Harding, *159*, 160–61, 163–66, 169
Hampton, Henry G., 167
Hampton, Jane, 161, 167
Hampton, Martha (Mattie), 167
Hampton, Mary Albertha (Birdie), 167–68
Hampton Hicks, Celia, 167
Harden, Edward Randolph, 54, 55, 68, 76–77
Harris, Holland H., 139
Harry (enslaved), 75
Hart, Alexander, 165
Harwood, Nahum, 64–65
Haskell, John G., 9–10
Hawke, Robert, 83

Hayden, Lewis, 78
Henley, William, 130
Henry (enslaved by Ezra Nuckolls), 56, 87
Henry (enslaved by Reeves Cox), 23, 24, 25, 26
Henry (enslaved by William Mann), 78
Henson, Josiah, 152
Hercules (enslaved), 140–42
Hicks, Celia Hampton, 167
Hicks, Charles (Charlie), 167
Hill, Benedict, 102
Hill, Edgar, 116
Hill, Edwin, 116
Hitchcock, George, 115–16
Holly, Charles F., 47, 48, 113, 118, 141
Horton, H. B., 116
Hosmer, Rufe, 72
Howard, Jim, 39–40
Hoyne, Philip, 133
Hunter, John, 102
Hurd, Jacob, 127–28, 129–30, 131

Iowa: debate in, 47, 51; as free state, 4; fugitive slave case in, 100; lawsuits in, 110; map of, *94, 105*; Underground Railroad in, 204n21; unrest in, 130–31; violence in, 109. *See also specific locations*
Iowa Gazette, 103–4
Izard, Mark W., 55, 79

Jack (enslaved), 23, 24, 25–26
Jacobs, Harriet, 69
Jane (enslaved), 56, 87, 170
Jenks, Chancellor L., 133–35, 139
Jennings, Jeremiah, 74, 75
John Brown's Cave, 5
Johnson, Clifton, 20
Johnson, John, 162

Jones-Rogers, Stephanie E., 14
Joy, Hiram, 133, 134

Kagi, John, 79
Kansas, 3, 113
Kansas-Nebraska Act, 3, 6, 50, 51, 52–53, 112, 123
Kearny County NE, 2
Kelley, William, 89
Kentucky, slavery in, 9–10
Kinney, Ellen, 65
Kinney, John F., 83, 200n24
Knickerbocker, Wesley H., 115–16

Ladd, Benjamin, 100, 116
Lambert, Jack, 25
Lambert, William, 32
Lane, James Henry, 4, 146
Lane, William, 116
Langley, E., 139
Larimore, J. C., 98–99
Lecompton Constitution, 113
Lehman, Christopher, 6
Lewis (enslaved), 23, 24–26
Lewis IA, 102
Lincoln, Abraham, 132, 143
Linden MO, 32, 36, 186n5
Lisbes, Henry, 139
Long, Mary, 110
Louisa County VA, 12–13
Louisiana Purchase, 44–45, 122, 123, 145
Lynch, Bernard, 129

Maizlish, Stephen, 42
Majors, Alexander, 69, 83, 84, 118, 124–25
Makins, Brainard, 165, 167–68
Malinda (enslaved), 56
Mann, William, 78, 198n69
Mariah (enslaved), 78

Index 253

marriage, slave as gift for, 14–15
Martha (enslaved), 140–42
Martin, Abner, 78
Mary (enslaved), 87, 88, 135, 170
Mason, Oliver P., 55, 99–100, 115, 123, 162
May, Charles, 2
McBride, Jesse, 25
McCamant, Samuel, 80, 176
McComas, Rufus F., 164
McDougall, John, 106
Mercer, Benjamin, 139
Merritt, Julius F., 97, 116
Merritt, William W., 97
Methodists, in Grayson County VA, 19–23
migration, *30*
Miller, George L., 118, 119
Miller, Joseph, 115
Mills, Oliver, 102
Missouri: debate in, 47; *Dred Scott* case in, 107–8; Kansas-Nebraska Act and, 51; map of, *94*; slave marriage law in, 160; slavery in, 9–10; viewpoints regarding, 123. *See also specific locations*
Missouri Compromise, 44–45, 122
Missouri Democrat, 130, 131
Missouri River, 84, 92, 106, 202n6
Mitchell, Sophia Hail, 74, 76
Moore, Hannah, 16–17
Morton, J. Sterling, 3, 63, 70, 71–73, 81, 82, 113, 155, 169–70
Morton, Thomas, 63–64
mountain slavery, 8, 29. *See also* slavery
Mueller, Gus, 164
Myers, William, 89

National Era, 111–12
Nebraska: appeal of, 41–42; capital debate in, 53–54; climate of, 86; debate regarding, 51–52; governance structure of, 53; map of, *5, 48, 94*; popular sovereignty in, 146; population of, 53; settlement of, 7, 41–42, 47, 50; slavery debate in, 7, 79, 89, 107, 111–13, 117, 118–26, 144–45; slavery legacy in, 158–63; slavery prohibition in, 121, 145; slavery statistics of, 2; as society with slaves, 7–10, 57; statehood debate in, 123–24; unrest in, 130–31; veto in, 122; violence in, 109; voluntary servitude in, 119–20. *See also specific locations*
Nebraska Advertiser, 143, 145
Nebraska bill, 42, 44, 45
Nebraska City Daily News Press, 146
Nebraska City NE: Black population in, 2; celebrations in, 61, 166; demographics of, 60, 165–66; description of, 59, 61–62, 65–66, 83; fire at, 200n16; four corners geography of, 4, *5*; freedom seekers' escape from, 124–25; freed slaves in, 161; growth of, 6, 62, 83; illustration of, *viii*, *60*; indictment in, 109; John Brown's Cave in, 4–5; newspaper office in, *63*, 63–64; Nuckolls House in, 82, 200n16; origin of, 50; photo of, *63*; population of, 165–66; post-slavery conditions of, 161; schools in, 161; slavery in, 5–6, 64–70; slave sale in, 70–74, 140–42; on the Underground Railroad, 85–86; writings regarding, 125
Nebraska City News: announcement in, 93, 95; origin of, 63–64; quote in, 52, 70, 73, 89–90, 99, 101, 109, 119, 122, 125, 126, 138, 142–43, 161, 162; viewpoint of, 118
Nebraska Palladium, 53

254 Index

New York Dispatch, 129
New York Times, 70–71
Norman, William M., 38, 56
North Platters, 81, 112, 124
Northwest Ordinance, 42, 44
Nuckles, Samuel, 170
Nuckolls, Alice, 41
Nuckolls, Benjamin Floyd, 11
Nuckolls, Bruce, 158
Nuckolls, Clark, 76
Nuckolls, Columbus "Lum," 56–57, 81–82, 136, 169, 176
Nuckolls, Eli, 76
Nuckolls, Ezra: background of, 11–12; concerns of, 74; cultural capital of, 29; death of, 86; description of, 137; estate of, 87, 191n37; family of, 14, 86, 176; freedom seekers' trial and, 25–26; Jarvis Bacon and, 21; moving of, 56; property of, 56; quote of, 56, 74; slaves of, 13–15, 75, 87, 149, 158, 174; as smallholding class, 9; viewpoint of, 23, 74; will of, 86–87, 88; work of, 15
Nuckolls, Frances Bourne, 42, 67, 176, 188n32
Nuckolls, Heath: business of, 57; family of, 176; inheritance of, 88; lawsuit against, 110; moving of, 42; property of, 163–64; quote of, 77, 86; slaves of, 50, 88, 192n41
Nuckolls, Houston: background of, 130; as delegate, 113; election of, 114; family of, 176; moving of, 42; property of, 57; quote of, 130; representation by, 123; slaves of, 87, 88, 135; viewpoint of, 131
Nuckolls, James, 13
Nuckolls, John, 11, 12–13, 176
Nuckolls, Lafayette, 54, 136, 176

Nuckolls, Lucinda Bourne. *See* Bourne Nuckolls, Lucinda
Nuckolls, Lucinda Hail (Hale), 11, 14, 54, 86
Nuckolls, Mary Garland, 11, 12–13, 176
Nuckolls, Mastin, 76
Nuckolls, Peter Paul (Paul), 153, 157–58
Nuckolls, Richmond, 86
Nuckolls, Robert, *18*
Nuckolls, Stephen Friel: arrest of, 98; background of, 31; business of, 36, 40, 56, 81–82, 83, 154, 157; campaign of, 154; case of, 115–17; criticism of, 154–55; death of, 157; as delegate, 113; description of, 33, 66, 122–23; election of, 114, 155; escaped slaves and, 93, 95–96; estate of, 157–58; family of, 32–33, 36, 41, 176; Francis Burt and, 50–51; Fugitive Slave Law and, 115; grief of, 86; home of, 59–61, *61*; honor to, 155; indictment of, 109–10; influence of, 53, 54, 82–83, 86, 137; J. Sterling Morton and, 81; lawsuits of/against, 110–11, 115–17, 210n37, 212n2; marriage of, 32–33; moving of, 6, 33, 50, 153, 154, 156–57; photo of, *34*; popularity of, 157; property of, 40, 49, 163–64; quote of, 114; reputation of, 69; reward from, 136; searching by, 1–2, 93, 95–98, 102–3, 108–9, 132–40, 136–37; slave sale and, 70–74; slaves of, 50, 57, 135, 173, 187n6; as smallholding class, 9; social life of, 67–68, 153–54; status and influence of, 8–9; suffrage viewpoint of, 156; testimony of, 130; trial of, 99–100; viewpoint of, 10; work of, 31–32; writings regarding, 103–4
Nuckolls, Virginia Ann, 41

Nuckolls, William (Billy), 41, 157–58
Nuckolls Borchers, Rosamond, 36–37, 176, 187n13
Nuckolls House (Nebraska City), 82, 200n16
Nuckolls Schooler, Polly, 42, 57, 158, 176

Oberlin College, 93
Old Mose (enslaved), 74–75, 197nn54–55
Oliver, Robert W., 164
Omaha City NE, 112
Omaha Daily Bee, 168
Omaha Nebraskian, 54, 114
Omaha Republican, 125
Organic Act, 123
Osawatomie KS, 114
Otoe County, 2, 140–47

Pacific City Herald, 191–92n37, 206n47
Pacific City IA, 104, 136, 169, 192n37, 206n47, 215n40
Paddock, Algernon, 165
Page County Herald, 110–11, 131
Patterson, John S., 71
Pearman, J. W., 60
Pennsylvania Freeman, 28
personal liberty laws, 43
Pierce, Franklin, 54, 55, 79
Pierce, Marcus, 115–16
Platt, Elvira Gaston, 95
Platt, Lester W., 116
Platte Valley Bank, 81
Plessy v. Ferguson, 165
popular sovereignty, 6, 48–49, 80, 112, 118–26, 146, 199n7
Potter, David M., 79–80
Potter, James, 5
Pottie, George, 13
Preemption Act of 1841, 49, 190n6

Price, John, 137
Prigg v. Pennsylvania, 43
property rights, debate regarding, 47–48
punishment, in slavery, 16–17, 18, 39–40

Rankin, Benjamin P., 117
Rebecca (enslaved and freed by John Cornutt), 22, 27
Rebecca (enslaved by Ezra Nuckolls), 56, 87, 135
Reed, Thomas, 116
Reeves, John, 23
Reeves, Mills S., 123
Reynolds, Milton W., 119–20, 125, 142–43
Richard (enslaved), 87, 88, 135, 170
Richardson, William A., 113
Riden, Martin, 54, 62
Robinson, Andrew, 74, 75
Robinson Hampton, Georgia, 164
Rulo Guide, 125
Rutherford, Thomas, 100

Salem People's Press, 28
Salt Lake City UT, 156–57
Sam (enslaved), 76–77
Sanford, Mollie Dorsey, 65, 85
Sarah Ann (enslaved), 78
Schooler, Polly Nuckolls, 42, 57, 158, 176
Schooler, Wrice D., 42, 50, 57, 176
Schooler Hampton, Edith, 158–63, 222n52
Schwartz, Marie Jenkins, 18
Schweninger, Loren, 90, 160
Scott, Dred, 107–8, 122, 139
search party, 96–97
secession, 113–14, 143
Shadd, Mary Ann, 152
Shaw Graves, Sarah Frances, 39–40

Sheldon, Addison E., 111
Simon (enslaved), 23, 24, 25–26
slavery: apologists of, 38; children in, 18; debate regarding, 6–7; expansion of, 37–38, 47; geography and, 3–4, 149–50; hiring out in, 74–78; labor in, 7–8, 18–19, 64; mobility of, 57–58; mountain, 8; name changes following, 150; in Nebraska City NE, 5–6; Nebraska statistics regarding, 2; prohibition of, 121, 145; punishment in, 16–17, 18, 39–40; regional interpretation of, 42–44, 112, 138–39; sales in, 70–74, 78, 87–88, 140–47; slave pens in, 129; slave societies in, 7–10; smallholding and, 9; small town, 66–69; statistics regarding, 3; urban, 9
smallholding, 9, 69
Smith, Cora, 166
Smith, Daniel, 165
Smith, Edward, 21
Smith, Robert Lee, 104–5
South Platters, 53, 81, 112, 113–14, 124
Springfield IL, 132
Springfield Illinois Journal, 52
Squatter Sovereign, 71
states, territories vs., 138–39
Staunton Spectator, 28
steamboats, *30*, 31, 33–36, 84, 85
Stewart, Arafura, 166
Still, William, 85
St. Joseph Convention, 47–49
St. Joseph Gazette, 96
St. Louis MO, 129
suffrage, 156
Supreme Court, 144
Sweet, James, 111
Syracuse Journal, 165

Tabor IA, 96, 99, 101
Taney, Roger B., 108
Tarwater Hampton, Belle, 165
Tate (enslaved and freed by John Cornutt), 27
Taylor, William H., 118–19, 120–21, 123, 168
territorial officials, 80–81
territories, states vs., 138–39
Thomas, Tim, 162
Thompson, Corbin, 129
Thompson, William, 103
Thomsen, Mortimer Q. (Q. K. Doesticks), 84–85
Tilden, Jones, 157
Tolbert, Lisa, 66
Toucey Flenoy, Celia, 151
Tower of Freedom (Windsor, Canada), 151
Tubman, Harriet, 92, 149, 150
Twain, Mark, 85

Uncle Tom's Cabin (Stowe), 106
Underground Railroad, 4, 85–86, 93, 95–96, 133, 151, 204n21
urban enslavement, 9

Van Deusen, G. G., 50
Vigilance Committee (Grayson County), 26, 27–28
Virginia Institute (Roanoke College), 31, 186n2

Waggoner, Sarah, 39
Warren, Joseph, 72
Watkins, Harry, 80
Waverly Republican, 107
Webster, Daniel, 4, 139
Wesleyans, in Grayson County VA, 19–20

Wesner, Lulu, 169
White, J. N., 134
Wilcox, Cyrus, 24, 25–26
Wildey, Joel, 127, 128, 129–30, 131
Williams, Isaiah H., 139
Williams, Reuben, 97, 98–99, 100, 110–11, 115–16, 210n37
Williams, T., 89
Williams Hampton, Angeline, 163
Williamson, John, 1, 91, 97, 116, 127–28
Wilmot, David, 42

Windsor, Canada, 151–52
Winney (enslaved), 76, 198n62
Woodruff, Charles, 130
Woods, David, 16
Woods Burke, Sarah, 16
Wright, Susan, 110
Wyoming NE (Wyoming Station), 91–92

Young, Fielden, 25–26